Before this book came out, good information
Joseph Hurley has done a terrific job of mak
on these plans. It's well researched and authoritative, yet easy to read. Best of
all, there's a thorough analysis of features in every existing plan. You'll learn
what these features are, and find the plan that's right for you. This is a must
read for anyone who is thinking of using one of these plans—or considering
an alternative, such as a custodial account or Coverdell education savings
account. It has my highest recommendation.

Kaye A. Thomas, Esq.
Fairmark Press Tax Guide for Investors
Fairmark.com

Fortunately, this book is exactly what the title states: a comprehensive and
clearly written guide to saving for college.

The CPA Journal

The leading book on 529s.

Jeff Brown, Financial Writer

The definitive guide.

Warren Boroson, Financial Writer

Finally, a book explaining college savings programs in a way we can all
understand.

Deena B. Katz
Partner, Evensky & Katz Wealth Management,
internationally recognized financial advisor and author
of six books on financial planning

There is just no option when it comes to figuring out college savings plans:
Get your hands on this book.

David Kinchen
Huntington News

Your book is great—I bought two copies, one for my attorney.

Lynn Davis, California

I acquired your book, and I think you have done a fantastic job in dealing with the subject in depth and clarity. It is one of the finest handbooks of its type I have ever seen.

Bruce Berger, Writer

Unsolicited Comments Found on the Web:

The best book ever written about saving for college! This book unlocks the secrets of saving for college like the 401k plan did for saving for retirement. A real must for all families to understand.

A fantastic summary of 529 plans. This book should be read by anyone planning to send a child to college.

Terrific guide to a new way to save for college. Highly recommended. It's well-written, comprehensive, and objective, and it gave me enough information to make an informed decision.

THE
BEST WAY
TO SAVE FOR
COLLEGE

A COMPLETE GUIDE TO 529 PLANS

THE
BEST WAY
TO SAVE FOR
COLLEGE

A COMPLETE GUIDE TO 529 PLANS

2013–14 EDITION

Joseph F. Hurley, CPA

Saving for College, LLC
Pittsford, NY

Published in the United States by:
Saving for College, LLC.
1151 Pittsford-Victor Rd, Ste 103
Pittsford, NY 14534
TELEPHONE: (800) 400–9113
INTERNET: www.savingforcollege.com
E-MAIL: Support@savingforcollege.com

Library of Congress
ISSN 1932-6440 (print)
ISSN 2160-4320 (online)

Additional copies of this book may be ordered directly from the publisher.

Interior design and typesetting by Desktop Miracles, Inc.

Publisher's Cataloging-in-Publication
(Provided by Quality Books, Inc.)

Hurley, Joseph F.
    The best way to save for college : a complete guide to 529 plans / Joseph F. Hurley. — 2013-14 ed.
    p. cm.
    Includes index.
    ISSN: 1932-6440
    ISBN 978-0-9815491-9-4

    1. Prepaid tuition plans—United States. 2. Education, Higher—United States—Finance. 3. College costs—United States—States. I. Title.
LB2340.94.H868 2013   378.3'8'0973

                             QBI13–600035

Disclaimer

The author has endeavored to research and write this book with the greatest accuracy possible and with the necessary factual depth to serve as a general guide. However, the reader should understand that there may be both typographical and substantive mistakes within the text of this book. Consequently, this book must be employed as a general guide and not as the rendering of legal, accounting, tax, investment, or other professional services. The reader should, when required, seek the proper professional services in these areas.

The views and opinions expressed herein are those of the author and do not necessarily represent the views and opinions of any company or professional organization of which the author is an employee or member.

The intent of this book is the education and entertainment of the reader. The author and publisher will not be liable or responsible if the content of this book causes, or allegedly causes, directly or indirectly, any losses or damages to any person, organization, or entity.

If any purchaser of this book does not want to be obligated by the disclaimer above, you may request your money back in full except for international shipping and handling costs.

All comments received will be considered in future revisions of this book.

Table of Contents

Section One

529 Plans Explained

Section Two

State by State Comparisons

About the Author

Joseph F. Hurley, CPA

Joe Hurley, a certified public accountant for over 25 years, is generally regarded as one of the top Section 529 experts in the country. His interest in the topic began in 1997 when his home state of New York enacted a law authorizing the formation of a "qualified state tuition program," now known as a 529 plan. Over the next year and a half, Joe wrote several articles and conducted the research for the first edition of this book.

In early 1999, Joe decided to devote his career to helping people understand 529 plans and other college-savings options. He appeared at hearings before the IRS and Treasury in Washington D.C. to provide comments on the proposed regulations issued under Internal Revenue Code Section 529, started a publishing company, and put together a website at www.savingforcollege.com. He became a frequent speaker at conferences around the country and authored several articles for professional journals.

In addition to a professional interest, Joe and his wife Virginia had a personal interest in planning for college costs—they faced the prospect of financing future college degrees for their two children. Over time, they established accounts in over 30 different 529 plans (the large number justified only by the purpose of research).

Aside from offering web content, publications, and other information services, the author and the publisher are independent with respect to the states and program managers that operate 529 plans. The views and opinions expressed in this book are not conditioned on, or influenced by, the approval of any state official or other employee associated with these programs.

The author does not render personal investment advice. Requests for other consulting and speaking services, and comments about this book, can be directed to Joseph Hurley, Saving for College, LLC, 1151 Pittsford-Victor Rd, Suite 103, Pittsford, New York 14534. You may also contact him via e-mail at joe@savingforcollege.com.

Visit www.savingforcollege.com

Here's Why

Our web site at www.savingforcollege.com is the perfect companion to this book. Here is what you will find when you visit:

- Up-to-date descriptions of all 529 plans with links to their official websites.
- A 529 plan comparison tool, college savings calculator, and other useful tools.
- Federal, industry, and state news affecting 529 plans.
- Our exclusive "5-Cap Ratings" of all 529 plans.
- An active message board for those with questions, and for those with answers.
- Subscriber-only section containing quarterly investment performance rankings for all 529 savings plans, a portfolio expense look-up tool, underlying fund allocations, state tax calculators, and other resources for investment professionals.

Preface

When I wrote and published the first edition of this book in 1999, our daughter Megan was in the eighth grade, and our son Chris was still in elementary school. College seemed a long way down the road, but we knew it really wasn't, and my wife Ginny and I had already taken it upon ourselves to start saving for college in earnest.

As one might anticipate from the title of this book, most of our college funds were placed into 529 plans. In fact, we started opening accounts with various 529 plans in 1997, attracted by their tax advantages and ease of enrollment.

As the markets advanced or retreated over the years, so did our 529 accounts. We attempted to maintain an appropriate balance between stocks and fixed-income investments, and we witnessed first-hand the advantages of the automatic asset allocation approach offered through the "age-based" options in many 529 plans. Once the college bills started rolling in, we began tapping those accounts and taking full advantage of the federal and state tax exclusions for the substantial earnings that had built up.

Did I mention that our family of four had over fifty 529 accounts spread among as many as 34 different states? I do not recommend that you do the same, however, or you will become as overwhelmed with statements, notices, and emails from the programs as we have been. We've participated in so many different programs only because it has helped my research. And the low minimums in many 529 plans made it possible to spread a modest amount over multiple accounts.

I am thankful for all of the friends and associates who have provided invaluable assistance and support in the 14 years since the first copy of this book rolled off the presses in Rochester, New York, especially the fine people who have worked alongside me: "long-timers" Jared Fine, Marie Osypian, Chris Stack, and Elaine Moody; my daughter Megan Hurley who is now our 529 research director and son Chris Hurley who works elsewhere but provides assistance when called; and our new company's CEO, Marcos Cordero. I also wish to thank all the dedicated and enthusiastic individuals working for the states and their vendors who have been so cooperative with our many requests and intrusions, as well as the many investors and advisors around the country who express their support for our mission.

Most importantly, I thank my best friend and wife, Ginny, who has been a source of unwavering support, a valued advisor, and a wonderful mother to our two children.

To Megan and Chris.
I am proud of your accomplishments in school
and wish the best for you in life.

Special thanks and love to
Ginny, my wife,
without whom none of
this would be possible.

Introduction

Religion, morality, and knowledge, being necessary to good government and the happiness of mankind, schools and the means of education shall forever be encouraged.

NORTHWEST ORDINANCE, enacted by Congress July 13, 1787

For many young people in our society, a college degree is the key that unlocks the door to opportunity. The evidence comes from studies showing a wide disparity between the incomes of those who graduate from college and those who do not,[1] from the actions of our elected officials as they place college accessibility high on the nation's political agenda, and even from our own college experiences; many of us have seen our lives enriched and improved by the formal recognition of our academic achievements.

But college is expensive, and will become even more so in the future. This means that parents face a formidable challenge in paying for the higher education expenses of their children. Although a considerable amount of assistance is available to ease this burden, in the form of government support, student-aid programs, private scholarships, and perhaps some help from grandparents or other relatives, most parents cannot eliminate the

---

1. In 2010, the median annual earnings of full-time workers, ages 25–34, with at least a bachelor's degree was 50% higher than of those with only a high school diploma or equivalent. U.S. Department of Education, National Center for Education Statistics. (2012). *The Condition of Education 2012*, NCES 2012-045, Washington, DC: U.S. Government Printing Office.

need to prepare for the cost of sending their children to college. It becomes a matter of saving.

This book is all about a remarkable savings program available to American families facing future college costs. Its formal name is the qualified tuition program, sometimes abbreviated as QTP, but more often referred to as a "Section 529 plan" or just plain "529 plan." Originally developed by the states, and given special status under federal tax law, it is a savings program you should know about. If you are looking for an effective way to save for your children, your grandchildren, or even yourself, a 529 plan may be a large part of the solution.

Section 529 refers to the specific provision in the Internal Revenue Code, our federal tax law, which describes this particular type of college savings vehicle and lays down some rules that the programs must abide by in order to assure their participants of its tax-beneficial treatment. Forty-nine states, and the District of Columbia, now operate a 529 plan. Some states have more than one. Many of these programs are open to residents of any state, and most of them offer the same benefits no matter if your child attends school in-state or out. In addition, the Private College 529 Plan was launched in 2003 as the first—and so far the only—institutional prepaid tuition plan eligible for Section 529 treatment under an expansion of the law authorized by Congress in 2001. The Private College 529 Plan offers a prepayment program, without state involvement, on behalf of over 270 participating private colleges across the country.

The plethora of 529 plans creates a great deal of choice in your selection of a college savings program, and perhaps more than a little confusion. In addition, you will want to compare competing college-savings vehicles— including Coverdell education savings accounts, U.S. savings bonds, and mutual funds. By reading this book, you will be better prepared to make the right decisions for yourself and for your family.

How much does college cost?

According to the College Board, the price of one year at the average four-year private college for 2012–13, including published tuition and fees, room and board, and other expenses was over $43,000, and for the resident student at the average four-year public college or university the price exceeded $22,000.[2] During the past ten years, the annual rate of increase has averaged over five percent.

This trend is not new. Since 1980, college prices have been rising at a rate of two to three times the increase in the Consumer Price Index. If the pattern continues, the future sticker price of a four-year private-college degree for today's newborn will be in excess of $500,000, and for the student at a four-year public institution more than $250,000. Even more troubling is the fact that median family income has not been keeping pace with rising college costs.

Various policy groups and Congressional committees have become increasingly vocal in calling for colleges to control costs and make higher education more affordable for families. A provision contained in 2008 legislation to reauthorize the Higher Education Act (HEA) creates a tuition "watch list" identifying colleges with the largest percentage increases in tuition. The HEA also now requires that every postsecondary institution that participates in Title IV federal student aid programs provide an online "net price calculator" that estimates the net price of attendance (cost of attendance less grants and scholarships) for students and prospective students based on their individual circumstances.

Several wealthy universities, including Harvard and Stanford, have implemented changes in their financial-aid packages for families with incomes below certain levels. For example, the student with family income between $65,000 and $150,000 who attends Harvard in 2012–13 will pay an amount not exceeding 10 percent of family income.

However, most Americans should not expect to see significant relief from the tuition spiral anytime soon. Several factors—including increasing costs relating to technology needs, campus improvements, and faculty salaries—suggest that college cost increases may continue to outpace the general inflation indices at least for the next several years.

---

2. The College Board, *Trends in College Pricing 2012* (Washington, D.C., 2012). The College Board is a nonprofit association serving students, schools and colleges. These figures are for students who are living away from home while attending college.

For those who lack sufficient financial resources to simply pay the college bills when they arrive, the traditional means of outside assistance—federal, state, and institution-based financial-aid programs—will still be available. Indeed, the money available for student aid has picked up considerably in recent years after a long decline through the 1980s and early 1990s. During the ten years between 2001 and 2011, the federal government's investment in student aid through grants, loans and work-study increased by more than 134 percent in current dollars, to $155.5 billion.[3] However, statistical averages fail to reflect the widening income disparity between high and low earners, and the growing problem of "unmet need" among lower-income students.

How are families coping with these costs?

There is no shortage of surveys showing how families view and respond to the challenges of saving and paying for college. The bottom line is that many Americans do not feel adequately prepared.

- Eighty-eight percent of parents feel it is important that their children be able to attend college if they wanted to (College Savings Foundation, 2012), and the majority believe that having a college degree now is more important than it used to be (Sallie Mae and Ipsos Public Affairs, 2013).
- Although on average parents expect to cover 57 percent of their children's college costs, the typical family is on track to cover just 30 percent (Fidelity Investments, 2012), and only 38 percent are somewhat or extremely confident they will be able to meet the costs of their children's college education (Sallie Mae and Ipsos Public Affairs, 2013).
- In 2012, only 48 percent of families with the goal of saving for college had actually started saving towards that goal, down from 56 percent fifteen years earlier (Princeton Survey Research Associates International, 2012).

---

3. The College Board, *Trends in Student Aid 2012* (Washington, D.C. 2012).

Where is higher education on the nation's list of priorities?

Clearly, higher education is regarded in the halls of Congress and state capitols as a priority worthy of public subsidy. The nature of the subsidy has shifted, however, away from direct support of institutions in favor of tax incentives for individuals. Tax breaks now help the individual who is paying for college, and the one who is saving for college. More money is being invested in tax-advantaged college savings plans than ever before. In fact, over eleven million 529-plan accounts are now being managed, and total assets in all 529 plans stood at over $190 billion at the end of 2012. With significant sums building up in their college-savings accounts, many families will be looking for the best college education that money can buy.

The turnaround in education-friendly tax legislation since the mid–1990s has been remarkable. Before 1996, only a few tax breaks were aimed at helping individuals pay for their own or their children's college expenses. They included the exclusion of interest on the redemption of certain U.S savings bonds used to pay for college costs; the employer-provided educational assistance plan, whereby an employee could receive up to $5,250 to pay for undergraduate costs as a tax-free benefit; and income exclusions for certain qualified scholarships received by an individual and, in narrow circumstances, for student loan forgiveness.

IRS Publication 970, Tax Benefits for Education, now describes 12 separate tax incentives targeted to families paying for postsecondary education. In a span of just two years—1996 and 1997—Congress approved 529 plans, the Education IRA (now the Coverdell education savings account), two separate but related tuition credits (the Hope credit and the Lifetime Learning credit), and a waiver of the 10 percent penalty on premature distributions from an IRA to pay college expenses. In 2001, employer-provided educational assistance plans were expanded to include graduate school costs, and new tax deductions were approved for the payment of college tuition and for the payment of interest on college-related debts. And then in 2009, the American Opportunity tax credit was created, replacing the Hope credit and providing an even richer incentive for college attendance.

Traditional means of saving for college

Families who could afford to set aside savings for education purposes before the advent of tax-advantaged 529 plans and Coverdell education savings accounts still had several options. They could establish investment accounts for children and grandchildren, either in the parents' or grandparents' names; in the child's name in an UGMA or UTMA account; or in special education trusts drafted by attorneys and trust companies. Zero coupon municipal bonds, stock mutual funds, and insurance products offered some degree of tax relief and were often the investments of choice within these accounts.

But in the face of the new tax-advantaged savings vehicles, the traditional approaches to college saving have rapidly lost popularity. Although favorable tax rates on long-term capital gains and qualified dividends can effectively reduce the tax burden in traditional accounts, those rates jumped at the beginning of 2013 for high-income taxpayers and may rise further under any future "tax reform." Furthermore, the opportunity to shift investment income to a child's tax bracket is much more limited now that the "kiddie tax" applies to many children as old as 23 years (see chapter 11).

How confusing are all these incentives?

Unfortunately, they can be very confusing. There are now so many alternatives available that you are likely to have a difficult time selecting the ones that are most appropriate in your circumstances. And some of these options are mutually exclusive; your use of one program may restrict or eliminate the use of another. During Congressional hearings held in July 2012, the U.S. Government Accountability Office testified that 14 percent of eligible filers in 2009, representing over 1.5 million tax returns, failed to maximize the federal tax benefits available for payment of postsecondary education costs. The good news is that Congress now recognizes the unprecedented level of complexity in the maize of education tax benefits and before long is likely to consolidate and simplify those benefits.[4]

---

4. Hearings before the U.S. Senate Committee on Finance (July 25, 2012).

Why focus on 529 plans?

Section 529 plans provide some powerful and unique tax advantages not available with other college-savings options. What other tax-advantaged program allows everyone to participate, without regard to age or income level? What other program allows the accumulation of over $300,000 in a tax-sheltered account for one child's future college costs? What other mechanism allows someone with a large estate to immediately reduce that estate by $70,000 per child (or grandchild) without triggering gift tax, and without giving up control of the assets?

The answer is that no other tax-advantaged program provides the combination of benefits 529 plans offer. They are unique and powerful creations that come in as many different variations as there are states and institutions to sponsor them. They are intended to serve one purpose—providing a way for families of any income level to save for future college costs in the most effective way possible. But they also have investment, tax, retirement, and estate-planning implications that reach far beyond this one purpose.

This book will help you make the most effective use of the savings opportunities presented by 529 plans. It explains the many strategies to consider and choices to make before deciding to enroll in a 529 plan, and, once enrolled, the changes you can make along the way. This book also compares 529 plans to the other alternatives available to a family in saving for college, so that the best options can be selected from the array of choices.

Glossary

A number of terms used in this book deserve some explanation. An effort has been made to use the most common terminology, although not necessarily the language found in tax law, and to be as consistent as possible in the use of the terms. You will find, however, that the various state programs and other descriptive resources are not uniform in this regard.

529 plan—a qualified tuition program described in Section 529 of the Internal Revenue Code. This may also be referred to as a **Section 529 Plan** or **QTP**.

Account owner—the person with ownership and control of the 529 account, usually but not necessarily the **contributor to the account** or **purchaser of the contract**. Many 529 plans refer to the account owner as the **participant**.

Basis—the sum of all cash contributed or paid into the account, plus the basis portion of qualifying rollovers to the account, less the basis portion of distributions previously made from the account. The basis is also called the **principal of the account** or the **investment in the account**.

Designated beneficiary—the individual for whom the account or contract is established. All 529 plans require a designated beneficiary be named for each contract or account, except for accounts established by state or local governments or 501(c)(3) charitable organizations for scholarship purposes.

Distribution—an amount of cash withdrawn from a 529 account, or the value of educational benefits provided by a 529 plan. Most 529 savings programs use the term **withdrawal**. Distributions not in excess of the designated beneficiary's qualified higher education expenses are called **qualified distributions** or **qualified withdrawals**. Distributions in excess of the designated beneficiary's qualified higher education expenses are called **nonqualified distributions, nonqualified withdrawals,** or **refunds**.

Earnings—the total account value less the basis. Distributions from a 529 plan consist of pro-rated amounts of earnings and basis.

Prepaid program—a type of 529 plan (another type, the savings program, is described below) that promises to pay the beneficiary's future college tuition and other specified costs in return for your purchase of the program's prepaid educational arrangement or contract. Prepaid programs that sell tuition by the semester or year are referred to in this book as **contract-type prepaid programs**. Some prepaid programs offer units, with the value of each unit pegged to a fixed percentage (often 1%) of one year's tuition. These programs are referred to in this book as **unit-type prepaid programs**.

Private prepaid program—A 529 plan operated by an eligible educational institution, not by a state. The only existing private prepaid program is the Private College 529 Plan.

Qualified higher education expenses (QHEE) —the postsecondary education expenses incurred by a designated beneficiary that are counted in determining the tax treatment of distributions from a 529 plan. Section 529 describes the types of higher education expenses that qualify, generally tuition, fees, books, supplies, equipment, additional expenses of special needs beneficiaries, and a limited amount of room and board.

Rollover—a transfer of funds between 529 plans that is not treated as a distribution because it satisfies certain conditions under Section 529.

Savings program—a type of 529 plan (another type, the prepaid program, is described above) in which a **contribution to an account is invested in** a portfolio of mutual funds or other types of underlying investments. Most 529 savings programs offer a menu of portfolios, or **investment options,** from which to select. The value of the account is determined by the performance of the underlying investments. Some states will refer to their 529 savings program as an **investment program** to underscore the fact that accounts can lose value.

ONE

History of 529 Plans

The states—not the federal government—deserve the credit for inventing 529 plans. Section 529 was not even part of the Internal Revenue Code at the time Michigan Governor James J. Blanchard, in his January 1986 State-of-the-State Address, proposed the creation of a new state-run prepaid tuition program "designed to help parents guarantee to their children the opportunity of a Michigan college education." With tuition costs spiraling, such a program would address the increasing anxiety in many thousands of Michigan households. The result of this proposal was the Michigan Education Trust (MET), a newly-created fund to which the state's residents could pay a stipulated amount in exchange for the trust's promise to pay future tuition for a named beneficiary at any Michigan public college or university. The essential benefit was the opportunity to prepay future tuition so as not to be affected by future tuition increases.

The Michigan proposal generated interest in other states, with Wyoming and Florida the first to launch prepaid tuition programs of similar design. Michigan delayed its own launch so that a ruling could be requested from the Internal Revenue Service regarding the tax aspects of the arrangement. The IRS responded to Michigan with both good news and bad news.[1] The good news was that the purchaser of the "prepaid tuition contract" would not be taxed on the accruing value of the contract until the year in which funds were distributed or refunded. The bad news was that the trust established by the state of Michigan to receive prepayments and operate the program would be subject to income tax on earnings from the invested funds. According to the IRS, the trust did not qualify as a tax-exempt state instrumentality.

Lacking IRS' full blessing, MET went ahead anyway and in 1988 began entering into prepaid tuition contracts with Michigan's residents. Fifty-five thousand individuals signed up for the program. MET paid federal income tax on its investment earnings, and in 1990 filed suit for refund from the IRS. The case was first decided in favor of the IRS, but on appeal in 1994, the Sixth Circuit Court of Appeals reversed the district court judge's decision and found in Michigan's favor.[2]

The irony of the Michigan experience is that MET was forced in 1990 to stop issuing new contracts, due not so much to the burden of paying income taxes, but because it had been selling the prepaid tuition contracts at prices later determined to be too low. When originally establishing contract pricing, program administrators had relied on overly optimistic projections of the rate of return on invested funds in relation to the trust's obligation to pay for rising tuition prices. Simply put, the trust was headed towards insolvency. (The program later resumed with more appropriate pricing and remains today as one of the largest and most successful prepaid programs.)

Not long after its 1994 defeat in the Sixth Circuit, the IRS began considering other ways to keep participants in prepaid tuition programs from gaining a tax advantage, one of which was to tax beneficiaries each year on the increasing value of their prepayment contracts. Concerned that such treatment would be a disincentive for savings, Congress passed new legislation authorizing qualified State tuition programs ("QSTPs") as part of the Small Business Job Protection Act of 1996. Section 529 was added to the

---

1. IRS Letter Ruling 8825027

2. Michigan v. United States, 40 F.3rd 817 (6th Cir. 1994), rev'g 802 F. Supp. 120 (W.D. Mich 1992)

Internal Revenue Code by the Act, conferring tax exemption to qualifying state programs, and deferring tax on participants' undistributed earnings.

Although the enactment of Section 529 attracted little notice at the time, it no doubt helped to advance the Clinton administration's highly-publicized agenda to create significant new tax incentives for higher education, an effort that culminated a year later with the Taxpayer Relief Act of 1997 (TRA). The TRA introduced the Hope and Lifetime Learning credits, a tax deduction for interest on student loans, and penalty-free IRA withdrawals for higher education. Substantial changes were also made to Code Section 529 by the TRA, adding room and board to the list of qualifying expenses and providing special estate and gift tax treatment for participants in a 529 plan.

The TRA also gave rise to a new tax-advantaged savings vehicle for college named the Education IRA. Unlike Section 529, which provided that earnings were taxable even when withdrawn for qualified higher education expenses (albeit at the student's tax rate), the Education IRA offered federal tax exemption for the earnings when withdrawn for the same purpose. While this was seen as a significant advantage, the Education IRA was hobbled by age and income restrictions, and by a $500 annual per-beneficiary contribution limit.

With the ink barely dry on the 1997 TRA, the Republican-controlled Congress began pressing to make tax-free Education IRA distributions available to families sending their children to private and parochial grade schools. A bill was drafted to add elementary and secondary school expenses as approved expenses. With much less fanfare, another provision was added to the bill to make Section 529 distributions tax-free, not just tax-deferred, when used for college. Although the bill passed Congress, President Bill Clinton vetoed it, likening the expanded Education IRA to private school vouchers. A similar effort in 1999 failed for the same reason.

The stage was set for President George W. Bush when he took office in January 2001. New tax bills were crafted in both the Senate and the House of Representatives containing the previously-vetoed changes. With strong bipartisan support, the Economic Growth and Tax Relief Reconciliation Act (EGTRRA) of 2001 was signed into law on June 7, 2001. The expansion of the Education IRA exemption to include qualifying expenses for kindergarten through 12th grade, along with an increase in the annual contribution limit from $500 to $2,000, were hailed as major accomplishments. (Soon after EGTRRA's enactment, the Education IRA was renamed the Coverdell education savings account, giving recognition to Senator Paul Coverdell as champion of the K–12 provision.)

The favorable changes made by EGTRRA to Section 529 received relatively little notice at the time, but have turned out to have much more impact on families' college savings. Not only did qualified distributions from 529 plans gain tax-free status for federal purposes—and for state tax purposes in those states that piggyback on the federal tax treatment—but other major improvements came along as well. The requirement that states collect a penalty on nonqualified distributions was replaced by a 10 percent tax penalty to be paid with the federal tax return; same-beneficiary rollovers between 529 plans were now permissible, albeit restricted to one rollover per beneficiary in any 12-month period; and educational institutions were given permission to establish their own 529 prepaid tuition programs without any state involvement, thus requiring that the formal name for these programs change from qualified State tuition programs (QSTP) to qualified tuition programs (QTP).

Due to federal budget constraints, EGTRRA was made subject to a general sunset clause, such that every tax provision within the new law would expire on December 31, 2010. In effect, the improvements to Section 529, to the Education IRA, and to many other parts of the tax law were merely temporary. If any of the changes were to last beyond 2010, it would be up to Congress and the president to extend them through subsequent legislation.

With improved federal tax treatment, and in spite of the 2010 sunset, new 529 plans began springing up across the country, creating a wave of enthusiasm among the professional financial community and capturing the interest of the press. An institution-sponsored 529 plan representing over 200 private colleges, the Independent 529 Plan (later renamed Private College 529 Plan), was launched. Articles and feature stories extolling the benefits of 529 plans were appearing at an increasing pace in the national and regional media. And substantial dollars were finding their way into 529 plans: the $9 billion invested at the beginning of 2001 jumped to nearly $27 billion by the end of 2002.

In January 2003, the momentum was temporarily disrupted by the Bush administration's proposal to establish new Lifetime Savings Accounts (LSAs), which would permit individuals of any age and income level to contribute up to $7,500 annually to an investment account, and take withdrawals at any time and for any purpose free from federal income tax. The flexibility and simplicity of the LSA promised to attract a substantial number of college savers, along with their investment dollars. Failing to gain any traction in Congress, the LSA proposal withered, and assets in 529 plans grew by another $18 billion in 2003, to over $45 billion.

As the level of assets and number of accounts grew, so did the anxiety over the looming expiration of the 529 tax exclusion at the end of 2010. The media and many financial advisors became cautious when discussing or writing about 529 plans, and the pace of contributions began to slow. The Pension Protection Act of 2006 (PPA) ultimately saved the day for 529 plans and their millions of participants. In the final hours before its passage, Congressional leaders agreed to insert a provision in the PPA that would make permanent all of EGTRRA's changes to Section 529, including tax-free treatment for qualified distributions. President Bush signed the law in August 2006. With the cloud of uncertainty lifted, contributions once again began pouring in to 529 plans, and by the end of 2007, assets in all 529 plans totaled nearly $130 billion.

But as the economy and financial markets headed south in 2008, so did assets in 529 plans, finishing the year at only $105 billion. Concerns over "losses" in college savings accounts, and being "locked in" to undesired investment options, captured headlines in the financial press. The IRS reacted by issuing a notice to 529 plans (Notice 2009-01) that increased the number of permitted investment changes in a 529 account from one per year to two per year. The increased flexibility was temporary, however, and applied to 2009 only.

In 2009, another improvement was made to 529 plans that turned out to be temporary. The American Recovery and Reinvestment Tax Act of 2009 added computer technology costs to the list of qualified higher education expenses, mirroring a provision already enjoyed by Coverdell education savings accounts related to K-12 expenses. The change applied only to the 2009 and 2010 tax years, and was not extended by subsequent legislation.

Computer technology costs after 2010 are eligible for tax-favored 529 treatment only if explicitly required for enrollment or attendance at a college or university.

As the economy slowly gained strength after 2009, 529 plans began growing again. Assets in all 529 plans rose to $190.7 billion by December 31, 2012, a 15.7 percent increase from the $164.9 billion a year earlier. In addition, the total number of accounts increased by 3.7 percent during 2012 to 11.1 million accounts. Approximately 12 percent of accounts took a distribution in 2012, presumably to pay college costs.[3]

Changes to the structure and marketing of 529 plans over the years have contributed to their growth. Often at the behest of the investment firms hired to operate their 529 plans, many states early on opened up marketing and distribution outside state borders to a national audience. Today we see a large number of these widely-available programs being distributed under selling agreements with broker-dealers. By partnering with the professional investment community, the states are able to offer 529 plans with the look and feel of mutual funds. Registered brokers and investment advisors can directly assist families in understanding 529 plans and selecting appropriate investments, whereas state program administrators are generally prohibited from providing investment advice.

Investment offerings available through 529 savings programs have also evolved over the years. The earliest programs offered a single fixed-income investment. In the late 1990s, several states introduced an "age-based" investment strategy providing a blend of equity and fixed-income investments. The allocation would shift to a more conservative mix as the beneficiary approached college age. The age-based option was seen as particularly useful in light of Section 529's prohibition on investment direction, which prevented participants from changing investments on their own.

Next was the introduction of "static" or "fixed-allocation" investment options as alternatives to the age-based approach, creating a menu of investment offerings for the program participant. These options appealed to investors who desired more control over their asset allocation. Unfortunately, the prohibition on investment direction meant that a program

---

3. College Savings Plans Network at www.collegesavings.org, March 13, 2013.

participant in the early years could not later change his mind and opt for a different investment option within his 529 account.

Most investors were not truly locked in. A "rollover" made it possible to move funds to a different 529 account in the plan, or to another state's 529 plan, and end up with different investments. Originally, however, a rollover was tax-free only if the beneficiary designation was changed to a member of the original beneficiary's family. The 2001 EGTRRA made things significantly easier, permitting a same-beneficiary rollover between programs once in any 12-month period. The IRS, sensing the prohibition against participant investment direction contained in Section 529 had become a paper tiger in the wake of EGTRRA, subsequently announced in September 2001 (Notice 2001–55) that a program could permit investors to change their investment selection once every calendar year, or whenever a beneficiary change took place. No longer was it necessary to transfer 529 funds to another 529 plan in order to effect a change in investments.

Whereas in their early years 529 plans were largely viewed as somewhat quirky and of limited usefulness, by 2002 they had broken out into the mainstream. Their tax advantages, investment offerings and near-universal accessibility now made them attractive to the majority of families in a position to save for college. The states have ceded much of their direct involvement in running the programs to the large financial institutions that are more experienced and effective in marketing and managing an investment product. And they have allowed their programs to be marketed across state lines to a national audience, injecting a competitive element that occasionally tests the collegial atmosphere in which states' elected officials and agency heads have worked together to develop and promote the concept of 529 plans.

Why do the states decide to operate 529 plans?

Besides Wyoming, which dismantled its program in 2006, every state offers at least one 529 savings or prepaid tuition program. (Even before Congress fully sanctioned 529 plans in 1996, nine states had been operating prepaid tuition programs for their residents.) The states' commitment to 529 plans doesn't end with merely offering a program. Thirty-four of the 41 states with a personal income tax, along with the District of Columbia, offer their residents a state income tax deduction or credit for some or all of their contributions to the home-state 529 plan (and in five of these states, to an out-of-state plan as well). And many times we see states embellishing their 529 plans with matching contribution programs, laws protecting account assets from the claims of creditors, scholarship contests, and other incentives.

But why do the states make this commitment? Expenditures for staff and other state resources in establishing and maintaining a 529 plan can be significant and state tax subsidies can be costly. Few states expect to see any net revenue from program fees charged to participant accounts.

The primary reason for the states' interest in 529 plans is the conviction that education is an essential function of state government, and that establishing tax-advantaged savings programs targeted for education allows more individuals to obtain a college degree without taking on a crushing debt load. This argument is met with some degree of skepticism, however, since the amount of direct support provided by many states to their public systems of higher education has not kept pace with costs, forcing state schools to increase their tuition to even higher levels.

Some cynics also believe that the primary motivation for states to commit money in establishing and maintaining 529 plans is political. The programs allow elected officials to look good to the voters. Education is a powerful campaign issue. The governor and state treasurer who champion legislation making it easier for people to afford a college education will take credit for being "pro-family." Some of the impetus and support for the expanding 529 market comes from the National Association of State Treasurers, which has formed an affiliate, the College Savings Plans Network (CSPN), as a means to coordinate resources among its members and share ideas concerning state-sponsored programs. Composed of state officials and program administrators, CSPN meets at least annually to discuss issues and communicate ideas and new developments.

Most of the older 529 plans were developed by the states as prepaid programs, while the majority of newer 529 plans are savings programs (see chapter 5 for a comparison of the two program types). Many prepaid programs are restricted to state residents and cover only undergraduate tuition and fees. Savings programs are generally more flexible in their application to all the qualifying costs of higher education, and are more familiar to American families accustomed to IRAs and 401(k) plans. Savings programs are also easier to administer and less costly to the state, particularly when an outside financial-services company is willing to offer turnkey management under attractive financial arrangements with the state.

How are 529 plans regulated?

As a state-issued security, an interest in a 529 plan is not subject to the same level of federal oversight as most other types of securities and is exempt from registration with the Securities and Exchange Commission (SEC). However, the SEC can still bring suit against a state or its 529 administrative agency when alleging fraud.

The Municipal Securities Rulemaking Board (MSRB), a self-regulatory agency created by Congress and subject to SEC administrative oversight, has broad regulatory authority over the sale of 529 plans by "dealers" and has been active in issuing new investor-protection rules. The Financial Industry Regulatory Agency (FINRA) enforces the MSRB's rules, along with its own.

As the college-savings industry has grown, these federal regulators have increased their scrutiny of 529 plans and the sales practices surrounding them. Much of the attention has been focused on the sale of out-of-state 529 plans by brokers to residents of states offering tax deductions and other benefits for participation in the home-state 529 plan. In 2006, the MSRB finalized a set of disclosure requirements and suitability standards for brokers selling out-of-state 529 plans, which became effective in August of that year.[4] FINRA's enforcement efforts have been aimed at ensuring that its member broker-dealers install appropriate policy and supervisory procedures in connection with sale of 529 plans by registered representatives, and several member firms have faced fines for insufficient supervisory procedures and other infractions.

---

4. MSRB Notice 2006–23 (August 7, 2006)

But because federal authority extends only to 529 plans distributed through dealers, several of the direct-sold 529 savings programs, along with prepaid tuition programs, have only their own states to answer to. The states are intent on preserving their right to self-regulate 529 plans, and depend in large part on the College Savings Plans Network (CSPN) to define and coordinate self-regulatory efforts. (In practice, the direct-sold 529 plans generally attempt to conform to the same standards required by the MSRB of dealer-distributed 529 plans.)

In 2004, public criticism of 529 plans increased after several programs were singled out for charging high expenses or providing insufficient disclosure to investors. Subcommittees of both the U.S. House of Representatives and the Senate held hearings to explore these issues and to question the ability of the states to self-regulate 529 plans. In response, CSPN accelerated its efforts on behalf of the states to formulate disclosure guidelines for 529 savings plans. The initial guidelines were approved in mid–2004 and adopted by nearly all states. The guidelines have since been revised several times and adopted by all the states, and they have proven to be very beneficial to investors.

Why have states been allowed to restrict their incentives to the in-state 529 plan?

The federal tax advantages with 529 plans are the same regardless of which particular 529 plan you decide to use. But states are free to offer extra incentives to college savers, and to restrict those incentives to their own 529 plans. For example, every state with a matching contribution program will invest the match dollars in its own 529 plan. Also, 30 out of the 35 states—if you include the District of Columbia—offering a tax deduction or credit for contributions deny the benefit for any contributions made to an out-of-state 529 plan.

But five states have adopted "tax parity." They offer their taxpayers the same state tax benefit for investing in an out-of-state 529 plan that they earn for investing in the home-state 529 plan. The tax-parity states, in order of legislative approval, are Maine, Kansas, Pennsylvania, Arizona, and Missouri. Parity legislation has been and will continue to be considered in several other states. For several reasons, however, many state legislatures, treasurers, and governors oppose the notion of tax parity. They may wish to retain a competitive advantage for the home state 529 plan; they may oppose the notion of using state tax dollars to subsidize other states' 529 plans over which have no control; or they simply find tax parity to be too costly when approving state budgets.

A case that came before the Supreme Court in 2007 threatened the states' right to restrict their 529 benefits to the states' own 529 plans. In *Kentucky Department of Revenue v. Davis*, the plaintiffs challenged the right of Kentucky to exempt interest income on Kentucky bonds while imposing Kentucky tax on interest from out-of-state municipal bonds, arguing that such tax discrimination was unconstitutional. The Supreme Court ultimately ruled in Kentucky's favor.[5] Had the Davises prevailed, there would have followed a rash of similar lawsuits against any state that restricts its tax benefits to the in-state 529 plan.

What's in store for the future?

The future for 529 plans is exceptionally bright. Favorable federal legislation in the areas of tax, financial aid, and asset protection; ongoing program improvements and lowering of expenses; generous state incentives; positive media coverage; and the ever-increasing cost of sending a child to college all point to the increasing popularity of 529 plans and a surge of new contributions.

Perhaps the biggest challenge to the continuing growth of 529 plans comes from competing tax-advantaged vehicles—particularly IRAs and defined-contribution retirement plans—that can soak up a family's available savings. The Coverdell education savings account may also become more popular now that all of the improvements made to it in 2001 have been made permanent under the American Taxpayer Relief Act of 2012.

A future president and the U.S. Treasury Department may even resurrect proposals for the Lifetime Savings Account. But even if the LSA were to make it through Congress, the chances of its being watered down in the

---

5. *Department of Revenue of Kentucky et al. v. Davis et ux*, 553 U.S. ___ (2008)

process are high. And while any new federal tax-advantaged savings vehicle could significantly impair the growth of 529 plans, the impact would not be fatal. Section 529 plans will continue under any circumstances to offer several key benefits—e.g. state tax breaks, tuition prepayment options, and high contribution limits—that LSAs could never match.

We will continue to witness the evolution of the 529 plans. Many states will continue to press for further improvements in their programs, although some may ultimately decide that they can no longer compete in the college-savings marketplace on their own and will seek to join forces with other states by combining plans, or will shutter their plans and refer participants to other states' plans, as Wyoming and Tennessee have done in the past. Several of the larger investment firms, and perhaps a few smaller ones as well, will be committing substantial resources to gain or maintain a foothold in the burgeoning 529 industry, while others that are currently involved may decide to drop out. (Wells Fargo—the former program manager for Wisconsin's 529 plans—decided to exit the 529 management business in 2012).

The U.S. Treasury Department and the IRS will be working on a new set of proposed tax regulations to replace the proposed regulations issued in 1998. The forthcoming set of regulations will respond to a Congressional directive, included as part of the Pension Protection Act of 2006, calling for Treasury to develop rules to prevent the "abuse" of 529 plans by taxpayers. On January 18, 2008, the IRS released an Advance Notice of Proposed Rulemaking (ANPR) describing a general anti-abuse rule and other new rules it expects to include in new proposed regulations.[6] Although the proposed general anti-abuse provision would be applied retroactively, most other new rules would be applied prospectively. Based on the several sets of comments submitted to the IRS in response to the ANPR, coming from the American Bar Association and other interested parties, it appears likely that the new set of proposed regulations may differ significantly from proposals described in the ANPR.

---

6. Advance Notice of Proposed Rulemaking, 73 Fed. Reg. 3441 (Jan.18, 2008)

The 2008 Advance Notice of Proposed Rulemaking from the IRS contains several new rules, and modifications to existing rules, that could be made part of upcoming regulations, including the following:

♦ A general anti-abuse rule under which the IRS may deny the favorable transfer tax treatment of Section 529 when 529 accounts are established or used for purposes of avoiding or evading gift, estate, or generation-skipping transfer taxes or for other purposes inconsistent with Section 529. See chapter 12.

♦ A change in the gift-tax treatment when the designated beneficiary is changed to a lower-generation family member to make the account owner, not the old beneficiary, liable for any gift tax. See chapter 8.

♦ A restriction against non-individuals being named as account owners. However, the contributor could still be a non-individual. See chapters 3 and 6.

♦ A new requirement that an account owner who takes a non-qualified distribution report as income not only the earnings portion, but also the return of principal to the extent it represents prior contributions into the account from donors other than the account owner. See chapter 3.

♦ Special rules and restrictions applicable to beneficiary changes on accounts established for the contributor's own benefit or for the benefit of a minor under the Uniform Gifts to Minors Act (UGMA) or Uniform Transfers to Minors Act (UTMA). See chapters 6 and 11.

♦ A set of rules describing the circumstances under which the value of a 529 account is included in the estate of a deceased beneficiary. See chapter 8.

♦ A requirement that expenses be paid in the same year as the distribution or by March 31 of the year following the distribution in order to be counted as qualified higher education expenses. See chapters 3 and 12.

♦ Confirmation that a loss sustained in the liquidation of a 529 account may be claimed as a miscellaneous itemized deduction. See chapters 3 and 12.

TWO

Why You Should Consider a 529 Plan

As everyone knows, children "grow up too fast." Yet, too few parents make a serious attempt to figure out how much it will cost to send their children to college, or consider available options in planning for those costs. Perhaps you expect your child to receive a full athletic or other merit scholarship to a major university. Is your seventh-grader already up to six-foot-four and able to hit four out of five from beyond the three-point line? Was she the national champ in her age group for the 200-meter butterfly? Has he been the headline performer at Carnegie Hall? If so, congratulations! College costs should not be a problem for you, assuming your child's injury-free dedication to the sport or other activity continues through high school. If not, welcome to the group of us who cannot count on a full scholarship and need to face the prospect of coming up with the resources to fund our child's education.

That prospect can be overwhelming. Let's face it, just meeting every-day expenses is challenging enough, never mind trying to save significant dollars on top of that. It is difficult to conceptualize the amount that the experts are telling us a private college will cost in 2026 when today's newborn will be enrolling. Over $500,000? Why even bother to try?

Some of us believe there will always be other ways to pay for college if personal savings are not sufficient. Thanks to our educational institutions and government, a safety net currently does exist, in the form of federal, state, and institution-based financial-aid programs. But even with the programs now available—including loans, grants, and work-study—many qualified students and their families face financial pressures that impact their desire and ability to attend college.

And then there's the question of priorities: college savings versus retirement savings. The common advice is to satisfy your retirement needs before attempting to save for college. After all, no bank will offer you a loan for your retirement. But generalized advice is not always the best advice. Certainly, you will want to take advantage of a match offered by your employer into your 401(k) plan. But beyond that, no one should fault you for your decision to build a college savings account with money that might otherwise be saved for retirement. In a 2007 online poll conducted by Savingforcollege.com, 80 percent of respondents said they would postpone their retirement by two years if by doing so their child could attend the college of his or her choice without taking on more debt.

Before 529 plans came along, some parents were unwilling to establish dedicated college savings accounts even when they had the resources to do so. Putting assets in a Uniform Gifts to Minors Act (UGMA) or Uniform Transfers to Minors Act (UTMA) account was often recommended as a way to shelter college savings from income taxes, but many parents were reluctant to accept the risk that the child will decide to fund an "alternative" lifestyle that does not include college. Alternatively, they could place the assets in trust with provisions that prevent unauthorized use of the funds, but the establishment of the trust may involve significant time and money, and then it requires annual maintenance. This left home equity, bank savings accounts, and taxable mutual funds as the primary vehicles for college savings.

But now, 529 plans offer an attractive alternative, with their many features and tax incentives to overcome families' reluctance to save for college. In fact, they are likely to be your best option for college savings if you

have school-age children or grandchildren and are looking to invest significant amounts of money (tens or even hundreds of thousands of dollars).
If your savings goals are more modest, the 529 plan remains competitive
with Coverdell education savings accounts (chapter 9) and other college
savings strategies designed for investors with more limited resources. No
matter what your family's circumstances—large or small, low-income or
high-income, decided on a particular college or undecided, transient or
settled—there are 529 plans available to accommodate your college saving
desires in simple, flexible, and tax-efficient ways. In fact, 529 plans offer
advantages even to those without school-age children or grandchildren.
Who's to say that the older individual will not want to return to school at
some point in the future? We see more "nontraditional" students enrolling in postsecondary schools every year, for graduate work, for a change
of career, or just for enjoyment and self-improvement. A 529 plan can
be a great way to save for this possibility, even if the idea is eventually
abandoned.

What's so great about 529 plans?

Here are the advantages, in a nutshell:

Federal income tax advantages

- ♦ Earnings build up in your account on a tax-deferred basis.
- ♦ Distributions from your account that are used for qualifying college
  costs are tax-free.

Estate and gift tax benefits

- ♦ Your contributions to a 529 account are treated as completed,
  present-interest gifts to the beneficiary for purposes of the federal
  gift tax and generation-skipping transfer tax. The money comes out
  of your taxable estate, and the gifts qualify for the $14,000 gift-tax
  annual exclusion.

♦ A special election allows your contributions to be treated as if they were made over a five-year period for gift and generation-skipping transfer tax purposes. This means that $70,000 can be contributed to a 529 plan account gift-tax free (assuming you make no other gifts during that five-year period).

Availability and flexibility

♦ Unlike so many other tax breaks, a 529 plan imposes no income limitations. A high-income individual can take advantage of a 529 plan when other alternatives (such as a Coverdell education savings account) are not available.

♦ In most 529 plans, over $300,000 can be contributed to an account for a single beneficiary. At $2,000 per year, a Coverdell education savings account just doesn't measure up.

♦ Despite the treatment of your contributions as completed gifts, you still retain ownership and control of the account. This creates powerful and unique advantages. You, not the beneficiary, decide when to take distributions and for what purpose. You can change the beneficiary of the account; you can even revoke the assets. Any concern that you may have about losing control of your investments is greatly diminished.

Investment benefits

♦ 529 plans offer a variety of options, providing the opportunity to select an approach that matches your own investment objectives. Some programs offer a way for your savings to keep up with increases in tuition costs; others offer a menu of investments from which to select, ranging from low-risk, fixed-income funds to higher-risk stock funds; while still others will automatically allocate your account among stocks, bonds and money market investments based on the age of your beneficiary or the number of years to expected matriculation. Many programs have no residency requirements, making the range of savings options available to all.

- You can obtain professional investment management at a reasonable cost. Fees and expenses will vary considerably among 529 plans, and they should always be a factor in your decision to invest. But for most families the tax benefits of a 529 plan outweigh the extra expense, and the sponsoring states are intent on keeping the costs as low as possible, particularly for their own residents. Some programs utilizing mutual funds are able to acquire the lowest-cost "institutional" shares, thereby reducing the overall expense to you.

- Many programs accommodate automatic payment plans through payroll deduction or electronic funds transfer from your bank account, making education budgeting simple and providing the discipline that some parents need.

State tax benefits

- Nearly all states follow federal income tax treatment in excluding the earnings in your 529 account from state and local income taxes, and many offer a deduction or tax credit for all or part of your contributions into their programs.

- A few states also provide other financial benefits to program participants, such as scholarships, matching contributions, or favorable treatment in determining eligibility for state-funded financial aid.

Asset protection

- In some states, the law provides specific protections from creditors' claims.

- Under changes made to the federal bankruptcy law in 2005, qualifying assets in 529 plans and Coverdell education savings accounts are protected in bankruptcy.[1]

---

1. Under the Bankruptcy Abuse Prevention and Consumer Protection Act of 2005, up to $5,000 in contributions made to a 529 plan between 365 days and 720 days prior to the filing of the bankruptcy petition, and an amount of contributions up to program limits for contributions more than 720 days prior, are excluded from the account owner's or contributor's bankruptcy estate. The account beneficiary must be the debtor's child, stepchild, grandchild, or step-grandchild.

If these programs are so great, why doesn't everyone know about them and use them?

The answer is that everyone *should* be aware of 529 plans, and in fact the word has been spreading. Surveys show that with each passing year more Americans gain familiarity with 529 plans. Over eleven million accounts now exist—an impressive number when you consider that approximately 2 million students will be graduating from high school in 2013 and enrolling in college the same year.[2]

Growth in 529 assets has also been impressive. At the beginning of 2002 there was approximately $14 billion in all 529 plans. This figure had increased to over $190 billion by the end of 2012. It is reasonable to expect continued rapid growth over the next few years.

What accounts for the popularity of 529 plans?

We can point to several factors:

- **Wide availability and full public acceptance of 529 plans.** Although several states have a tuition savings program dating back to the late 1980s, it was not until 1996 that Section 529 was added to the Internal Revenue Code, and the majority of programs now in operation are new since 1997. Except for Wyoming, every state has at least one 529 plan, many states have two, and a few have three or more. Educational institutions now have the authority to develop and offer their own 529 prepaid programs.

- **An outpouring of media interest** in 529 plans, particularly in the wake of the tax law changes in 2001 that granted a federal income-tax exemption for qualified distributions. Many personal finance periodicals, including *MONEY* and *Kiplinger's Personal Finance Magazine*, regularly mention 529 plans. Many of the country's top financial writers now recognize the advantages of 529 plans and recommend them through their books, websites, public appearances, and newspaper columns.

---

2. The Chronicle of Higher Education estimates there will be 2,912,480 new public high school graduates in 2013, and the U.S. Census Bureau finds that approximately 68.1 percent of high schoolers immediately enroll in college following graduation.

◆ **Increased awareness of 529 plans among the professional investment and insurance community.** Before 2001, most brokers, investment advisors, and financial planners had little reason to promote 529 plans over other more traditional investment products because none of the state programs paid a commission. That has all changed now. Every segment of the professional planning community—hourly fee-based, asset fee-based, commission-based, or some combination—has a way to introduce 529 plans into its clients' portfolios and be compensated for their advice and guidance. In fact, advisor-sold 529 plans represent approximately one-half of all 529 assets, reflecting the large number of investors who rely on financial professionals in making investment decisions.[3] For those individuals who wish to conduct their own research and make their own investment decisions while incurring lower fees and expenses, "direct-sold" 529 plans will be the preferred option.

◆ **Workplace enrollment.** Many employers are receptive to the idea of facilitating employee use of 529 plans by offering group enrollment and payroll deduction. As an after-tax voluntary deduction program, a workplace 529 program has no payroll tax implications, no discrimination testing, and few, if any, eligibility requirements. Hence, this additional "benefit" can be made available to employees at low or no cost to the company. Special considerations come into play, however, in deciding which particular 529 plan or group of plans to offer under a group-enrollment format. Since the dollars being contributed are coming from the employee, it is incumbent upon the employer to consider whether the 529 plans selected are the ones that offer the best benefits to their particular employees.

◆ **Private company affiliations.** An increasing number of private companies view higher education as a national priority and have recognized 529 plans as a way to help families that are facing the challenge of paying for college costs. Several of the customer loyalty programs have affiliated with 529 plans. By using particular credit cards or buying specific products, you earn "rewards" that can be automatically deposited into your 529 accounts. Upromise and Fidelity cur-

---

3. Financial Research Corporation at www.frcnet.com.

rently operate the largest rewards programs under formal agreements with 529 plans. And now we have several college "crowdfunding" sites available to families, such as GradSave.com, that make it easy to involve friends and family in 529 account-building.

But don't 529 plans require that I send my child to an in-state public school?

This is one of the most common misconceptions about 529 plans. In fact, every state's 529 plan permits your account to be used at colleges and universities anywhere in the United States (and in many foreign countries as well). Some 529 plans provide better benefits for in-state schools, but none lock you into a specific institution or state public education system.

I've heard about the 529 plan in my state and it doesn't really excite me. That leaves me out, right?

Not at all. You should consider other states' programs. Many of the best 529 plans are operated by states that impose no residency restrictions. They are open to all.

I have already set up a 529 account in my state. So I guess I'm all set.

Guess again. Have you selected the program with the best benefits? If not, you may be better off rolling over your account to a different state's 529 plan. If a rollover is not a viable option (because of certain restrictions under federal law or the fees imposed by some 529 plans), you can leave your current account where it is and open a second account (or third account, etc.) with another state that offers a more attractive program.

My financial advisor tells me I am better off using his recommended mutual funds to save for college costs. Is he right?

Your advisor could be right, but it really depends on your particular circumstances and investment objectives. The better question is: How much does your financial advisor know about 529 plans? Until recent years, few were knowledgeable, and many felt threatened by the concept of a 529 plan, viewing it as a competitive product that provided little or no compensation. That situation has largely changed now that many states have approved commission-based 529 plans for distribution through broker-dealers. Financial professionals across the country, including commission-based advisors as well as fee-only planners, have begun embracing 529 plans as a potential solution for clients, and are finding ways to effectively incorporate them into long-term financial plans. Knowledge level remains the key, however. If you rely on a broker or financial planner in making investment decisions, be sure the advisor is up to speed on the technical and comparative aspects of 529 plans.

My child is a senior in high school. Isn't it too late for me to start using a 529 plan?

Not necessarily. Assess your potential for tax savings by looking at your most recently filed income tax return. Did you pay any tax on interest, dividends, or capital gains distributions? If you did, a 529 plan represents an opportunity to convert taxable investment income into tax-free investment income. Even if the account has a life of only a few years—remember that it will usually take two to five years or even longer to earn a degree—you will be saving taxes. In fact, many parents facing college bills in the near future want to have their money in safe, interest-paying investments. This is the where the tax protection of a 529 plan provides the greatest advantage.

It gets even better if you live in a state that offers a state income tax deduction for contributions to a 529 plan. Instead of paying college bills out-of-pocket, you can reap the benefit of a state income tax deduction by first making a contribution to the 529 plan, and then using your account to pay the bills. Bottom line: college expenses become a write-off for state income tax purposes.

Section 529 plans sound too good to be true. Won't the IRS or Congress shut them down?

Not likely. Millions of American families are now investing in 529 plans and there is every indication that our elected officials in Washington want to see them become more popular, not less. This point was underscored at a June 2004 hearing held by the House Financial Services Subcommittee on Capital Markets. "The success of 529 tuition savings plans is good news," declared Rep. Michael G. Oxley in his opening statement. Since then, the federal government has passed several laws favoring 529 plans, including the Pension Protection Act of 2006 that made permanent the 529 tax exemption.

There must be some disadvantages to 529 plans. What are they?

No single investment, including a 529 plan, is the perfect option for every investor. The advantages and disadvantages of 529 plans are discussed throughout this book. The fact that most 529 plans charge a fee to participants, as mentioned earlier in this chapter, is certainly one of the most obvious considerations. Here are some other significant disadvantages.

- Section 529 plans are confusing. It is not easy to feel comfortable with all the special rules and different options with 529 plans. There are plenty of places where you can learn about IRAs, savings bonds, and the like, and the rules for these programs are fairly uniform: one sponsor's IRA is not going to be much different from another. The same is not true for 529 plans. Rather than one basic model, there are several to choose from, and each 529 plan has unique features that make comparisons between different programs tricky. Many financial and legal advisors have not yet learned enough about the programs to effectively counsel their clients in this area. You can find quite a few helpful articles in the financial press, and the materials available from the programs themselves provide a great deal of useful information. In addition, the Securities and Exchange Commission and certain industry groups such as the Financial Industry Regulatory Authority (FINRA), Municipal Securities Rulemaking Board (MSRB), and the Securities Industry and Financial Markets Association (SIFMA) have put together explanatory booklets for the investing public. But apart from this book and the information on our companion website at www.savingforcollege.com, there is currently little comprehensive literature available from independent sources.

♦ The lower tax rates on capital gains and dividends do not apply to gains in your 529 account. Of course, if things work out right your earnings will be entirely tax-free, but if any part of a withdrawal turns out to be a nonqualified distribution, the earnings portion is taxable at ordinary income rates. There will also be a 10 percent penalty on earnings, unless you can apply one of the exceptions (see chapter 3).

♦ If your account loses value, you cannot simply sell the investment and claim a capital loss. You may be able to claim a miscellaneous itemized deduction in the year you completely liquidate a 529 account, but many taxpayers will find little or no tax benefit in doing this because miscellaneous itemized deductions reduce taxable income only to the extent the total exceeds 2 percent of your adjusted gross income.

♦ Investment selection in a 529 savings program is limited—although less so than in the past—and your ability to change investments is subject to restrictions. The ultimate responsibility for the investment and administration of your account rests with the state agency acting as trustee under the program trust. The state makes the rules, and the state can change the rules, provided the program continues to satisfy certain federal requirements. To date, most program changes have been beneficial to the participant but that may not always be the case.

♦ You may decide to invest with a particular 529 plan based in part on the program's selection of a particular mutual fund company or financial services firm as program manager, only to find that the program manager is replaced in a later year with a different investment firm. The contracts between the states and their outside program managers have terms lasting anywhere from two to 30 years, and at the end of the contract term a state can decide to bring in someone new. If that happens, it is likely that your account will have new investments and different expenses.

- The fact that you retain ownership and control over the account may work against you in certain situations. For instance, an account owner applying for Medicaid may find that the state Medicaid agency requires the 529 account first be used to pay for medical and long-term care expenses before Medicaid payments can begin. Or perhaps your 529 account is not eligible for special protections under state law or the federal bankruptcy law and a creditor attempts to reach your account for unpaid debts. These are risks you should discuss with your attorney.

- Your 529 account, and any distributions from it, can have an impact on the student's eligibility for need-based financial aid. However, depending on the relationship of the account owner and beneficiary, and the specific aid program in question, you may find the 529 plan treated much more favorably than alternative investment vehicles. This particular issue is covered in detail in chapter 4 and throughout the other chapters in this book.

I'm not sure I like the idea of the state holding my money. What's to prevent the state from appropriating the program funds for other purposes?

In most states, your contributions and account earnings are maintained in a separate legal trust that cannot be reached by the state for other purposes. If you have concerns about this, you should not hesitate to contact the program administrator in the state operating the program and obtain specific assurances.

My employer has recently started promoting a payroll deduction plan for college savings. Is this something I should consider?

Contributing to a 529 plan through payroll deduction can be a simple and relatively painless way to budget for college savings. Your employer may be interested in helping you learn more about the benefits of saving with a 529 plan and may even offer assistance in the enrollment process. Often the support and education is provided directly by a 529 program manager, or a financial advisor representing a 529 plan, under special arrangement with the employer. You will usually have the opportunity to attend special educational sessions, study program materials, and get your questions answered.

You should not assume that your employer's 529 plan is the best one for you. You will always have the option to establish an account on your own. Some employers will give you more choice by including two or more 529 plans on the payroll deduction platform. Employers will generally disclaim any responsibility for determining your suitability for the investment.

Contributions to a 529 plan through payroll deduction are made on an after-tax basis. Unlike a 401(k), your contributions are not subtracted from your taxable earnings, and they generally do not involve any payroll taxes or discrimination testing on the part of the employer.

I understand that 501(c)(3) exempt organizations can open accounts in 529 plans, but why would they want to?

Under the law, a charitable organization, or state or local government agency or instrumentality, opening a 529 account as part of a scholarship program is not required to name a beneficiary to the account, making it possible to establish the account now and select the scholarship recipients later on. Even with this flexibility, most scholarship-granting organizations will see little reason to use a 529 plan. They do not reap any benefit from the tax exemption under Section 529—charitable organizations do not pay tax on investment income anyway—and most have already established internal policies controlling the investment of their scholarship funds. However, organizations that do not currently have a scholarship program might be interested in starting one. The 529 plan makes available professional investment management and account administration at low cost. Many states and their program managers will be eager to facilitate the objectives of the scholarship program, including the processing of scholarship withdrawals to the institutions attended by scholarship recipients. There might also be valuable cross-promotional opportunities between the charitable account holder and the state.

THREE

Section 529 Mechanics

This chapter describes the provisions of Section 529, including the tax benefits for the participant, the tax rules for distributions, and the various qualification requirements. It is a fairly technical chapter that includes information needed by the professional advisor who will be working closely with clients considering these investments.

Unfortunately, the amount of guidance coming from the Treasury Department and IRS has not been sufficient to address all the questions that can arise. Regulations are important because they interpret and supplement the tax law. The literal reading of the law must be coordinated with the practical demands placed on taxpayers.

The Treasury Department faces some particularly difficult issues in developing regulations under Section 529 due to the unique character of these programs. Proposed regulations were issued in August 1998, and were helpful at the time, but they became largely obsolete as a result of the Economic Growth and Tax Relief Reconciliation Act of 2001. More recently, the Pension Protection Act of 2006 gave Treasury increased authority to plug loopholes and prevent taxpayer abuse of Section 529 through regulations. On January 18, 2008, the IRS issued Announcement 2008–17, Advance Notice of Proposed Rulemaking (ANPR) describing several of the rules expected to appear in a new set of proposed regulations. (Chapter 1 describes the ANPR in more detail.) Nothing further has come from the IRS since then, and the public will have an opportunity to comment before any future set of regulations becomes final.

Meanwhile, we can look to other IRS documents for some help in applying Section 529. Notices, rulings, publications, and the tax forms along with their instructions provide direction but not a lot of detail. The best place for taxpayers to find official IRS guidance is Publication 970, Tax Benefits for Higher Education, available at www.irs.gov.

What is a 529 plan and who can participate?

A 529 plan is a program designed to help families prepare for the cost of postsecondary education that meets certain requirements contained in Section 529 of the Internal Revenue Code for a "qualified tuition program" or "QTP." Section 529 serves two basic purposes.

First, it prevents the IRS from challenging the tax-exempt status of the state-owned trust holding 529 assets. Without statutory protection, the trust could potentially be subject to income tax on its undistributed investment income.[1]

Second, Section 529 describes the federal income and transfer tax treatment of program participants. In some ways, the rules prescribed by Section 529 as they relate to participants directly contradict the "normal" rules under other provisions of the tax law.

Only two groups can offer a 529 plan. The first includes any state or state agency or instrumentality. The second includes any eligible educational institution. An institutional or "private" program could not be qualified under Section 529 prior to the 2001 EGTRRA changes, and in order to qualify now it must meet additional requirements and provide certain protections as discussed below.

---

1. Trust earnings will not be considered "debt-financed income" for purposes of the tax on unrelated business income if the only liability of the program is to its participants.

A state-sponsored 529 plan is one that permits a person to either (1) purchase tuition credits or certificates on behalf of a designated beneficiary which entitle the beneficiary to the waiver or payment of his or her qualified higher education expenses, or (2) make contributions to an account which is established for the purpose of meeting the qualified higher education expenses of the designated beneficiary.

The first type of program described in the preceding paragraph is commonly referred to as a prepaid program, while the second type is commonly referred to as a college savings program or college investment program. A savings program can be viewed as a kind of state-sponsored mutual fund—a participant's contributions to the program are invested and the value of the participant's account is determined by the investment performance of the underlying securities. It is not uncommon for the media to describe 529 plans as only referring to the savings programs.

In prepaid programs, the participant's "return" is not linked directly to investment securities. Some prepaid programs operate like futures contracts, where the participant purchases a contract that obligates the program to deliver a certain bundle of tuition or other benefits in the future, while others act like index funds, where the participant purchases redeemable units or credits whose value is pegged to average in-state public tuition or to some other tuition inflation index. In some significant ways, these unit-type prepaid programs have more in common with the savings programs than they have in common with the contract-type prepaid programs, and a couple of states have even relabeled their unit-type programs, replacing the word "prepaid" with the term "guaranteed savings."

An eligible educational institution that desires its own 529 plan is limited to offering a program that falls only into the first category, i.e. a prepaid program. In addition, it must hold its program assets in a "qualified trust," which is one that meets certain standards normally applicable to individual retirement accounts. The only such program currently in existence is the Private College 529 Plan.

When you establish an account in a 529 plan, you are required to name one living individual as designated beneficiary of the account. Typically, this is your child or grandchild, but it is not necessary that the beneficiary be related to you in any way. Multiple beneficiaries require multiple accounts. Most 529 plans permit you to name yourself as beneficiary of the account you establish.

Accounts established by a state or local government (or agency or instrumentality thereof) or by a 501(c)(3) exempt organization as part of a scholarship program are not required to name a designated beneficiary. Beneficiaries can be selected at the time of distribution, and one account can be used to assist multiple students in paying for college costs.

Almost anyone can participate in a 529 plan. There are no income or age limitations placed on either the account owner, the contributor (if different), or the designated beneficiary. There is no requirement that the participant reside in the sponsoring state or that the beneficiary attend a school located in that state. The 529 plan can establish its own restrictions, however, and so it is important to distinguish the flexibility permitted under federal law from the rules of the particular program you are considering.

What other requirements must a 529 plan meet?

All 529 plans must meet the following requirements in order to qualify under Section 529.[2]

1) The program can only accept contributions in cash, including check, money order, and credit card. Many 529 plans also permit electronic funds transfer from a bank or investment account. Contributions may not be made with investment securities or other types of property. To transfer other investments into a 529 plan you will need to liquidate those investments, possibly triggering taxable income or capital gains. Under certain conditions, you may be able to transfer funds from an existing Coverdell education

---

2. A state-sponsored 529 plan is not required to apply for a ruling or determination from the IRS as to its qualified status, although several states have requested, and some have received, such a ruling. An institution-sponsored program, however, is required to apply for and receive a determination from the IRS that it meets the requirements for qualification as a prepaid program under Section 529. At the time this book was published, only one institution-sponsored program, the Private College 529 Plan, had received such a determination from the IRS.

savings account or qualified U.S. savings bonds without triggering tax. These rules are explained more fully in later chapters.

2) The program must provide a separate accounting for each designated beneficiary. Separate accounting does not mean separate investing, and contributions are typically commingled in the program trust for investment purposes.

3) The program may not permit you or your designated beneficiary to direct the investment of your account. The tax law is specific: investment direction must be left to the sponsoring state. Although this paternalistic provision appears to be very limiting, a savings program will in practice provide substantial investment choice and flexibility to the account owner. Nearly all programs now offer a menu of investment options. A contribution can be directed to one of these options, or in some 529 plans can be spread among the options (a small number of plans require that separate accounts be established if you want to invest in more than one investment option). You can request that your account be reallocated among the program's available investment options whenever you change the designated beneficiary, but if you maintain the same beneficiary you are limited to one such request in any calendar year.[3]

4) The program may not allow accounts to be pledged by the account owner or designated beneficiary as security for a loan.

5) The program must provide adequate safeguards to prevent contributions on behalf of a designated beneficiary in excess of those necessary to provide for the qualified higher education expenses of the beneficiary. All 529 savings programs place a specific dollar limit on contributions, generally expressed as an account balance

---

3. Under IRS Notice 2001–55, 2001–39 IRB (Sept. 24, 2001), a 529 plan that "allows participants to select only from among broad-based investment strategies designed exclusively by the program" may permit an account owner to change investment strategies once per calendar year. Although it is not entirely clear yet what the IRS means by "broad-based investment strategy," the accepted practice among 529 savings plans is to permit reallocation among all available options, with most options consisting of one or more mutual funds, separately-managed accounts, exchange traded funds (ETF), or federally-insured banking products. Notice 2001–55 also fails to state whether related accounts in the same or different 529 plans must be aggregated in applying the once-per-calendar-year limitation.

limit. An account balance limit means that a contribution will not be accepted by the program manager if the account value at the time of the intended contribution is above a specified level, although the account is not prevented from growing beyond that limit based on investment performance.

The IRS' 1998 proposed regulations provided a maximum-contribution safe harbor to programs that limit contributions on behalf of a designated beneficiary to an amount determined by actuarial estimates necessary to pay tuition, required fees, and room and board expenses of the designated beneficiary for five years of undergraduate enrollment at the highest-cost institution allowed by the program. Most programs have abandoned the safe harbor and include graduate school costs and other qualified expenses in the computation of their contribution limits, presumably with assurances from the IRS or legal counsel that they will not jeopardize qualification under Section 529. (In a private letter ruling issued to New York's 529 savings program, the IRS approved a limit based on four years of undergraduate expenses and three years of graduate school expenses.) You will find many 529 plans with contribution account-balance limits in excess of $300,000 with a few approaching $400,000.

The limitation on contributions is imposed by the 529 plan on a per-beneficiary basis. If there is more than one donor to the account, or if there is more than one account in the program for a particular beneficiary, the accounts must be combined for purposes of determining total contributions. The IRS' proposed regulations did not, however, prohibit a designated beneficiary from maintaining accounts in different states and contributing a combined amount that exceeds the individual state limits. Congress presumably did not intend that the "stacking" of accounts be used as a way to circumvent the safeguards imposed by any one program, so it would be reasonable to anticipate that final regulations will impose additional requirements. Some states require a representation from the donor that accounts in multiple programs are not being used as a way to make contributions beyond the level that can be reasonably supported as appropriate for the beneficiary's future higher education needs.

I see some mutual fund companies advertising their own 529 plans. Can any investment firm offer a 529 plan?

No. The reason you see advertisements for 529 plans from mutual fund companies, broker-dealers, and banks is that many of the state-sponsored 529 plans have outsourced program management and marketing to these firms. Tax law requires that the state or institution "establish and maintain" the program but does not prohibit the sponsor from hiring a vendor to assume investment management and administrative duties. These vendors have a direct interest in the success of the programs, as their fees are typically based on the level of assets under management in the program. Under the 1998 proposed regulations, in order to meet its duty, a state must set all the terms and conditions of the program and be actively involved on an ongoing basis in the administration of the program, including supervising all decisions relating to the investment of assets contributed to the program.

What are the federal income tax rules for 529 plan participants?

Your contributions to a 529 plan are not deductible in computing your federal income tax. Your initial tax savings come from the deferral of income—earnings in your account remain tax-free until they are distributed. Distributed earnings may or may not be subject to tax, depending on whether the designated beneficiary incurs sufficient qualified higher education expenses (QHEE), as adjusted (AQHEE), during the year. QHEE and AQHEE are defined on page 52.

If you withdraw funds from your 529 account, or have payments made by the program to the beneficiary's school, the program administrator is responsible for sending Form 1099-Q to you or to your beneficiary after year-end reporting the gross distributions and breaking out the total between earnings and basis (return of principal). Distributions are always allocated pro-rata between earnings and basis. You will need the gross distributions and earnings figures when completing Form 1040, the federal income tax return. Basis always comes out federally tax-free.

If the account beneficiary has incurred AQHEE during the year that in total are equal to, or greater than, the total distributions from all 529 accounts as reported on Forms 1099-Q, the distributions are excluded from income and not reported on Form 1040. If, however, total AQHEE are less than total distributions, only a portion of the distributed earnings is excluded from income, and the remainder has to be reported as ordinary income. The calculation follows this formula:

$$\frac{\text{Gross Distributions} - \text{AQHEE}}{\text{Gross Distributions}} \times \text{Earnings} = \text{Ordinary Income}$$

If withdrawals are made from a Coverdell education savings account for the same beneficiary during the year, QHEE must first be allocated between the 529 distributions and the Coverdell withdrawals. This is because withdrawals from a Coverdell ESA follow the same general taxation rules as distributions from a 529 plan. IRS Publication 970 suggests a pro rata allocation of expenses, but the IRS apparently will permit any other reasonable method. Coverdell ESAs are discussed in chapter 9.

A question that does not appear to be fully resolved is whether your payments for QHEE must match up with the distributions from your 529 account in the same taxable year. The timing of the transaction will not be a concern when the program makes qualifying payments directly to the school, but it can become an issue if you pay the college bills yourself. For example, let's assume you withdraw funds from your 529 account in December 2013 but wait until January 2014 to pay the tuition bill. A Form 1099-Q will be issued for 2013, but the tuition presumably counts as a 2014 expense, and you could end up paying tax and penalty because of the mismatch. This can also happen in the other direction. Let's assume you pay the tuition in late December and request a distribution from the 529 plan to reimburse yourself for the payment. If the distribution is processed in January of the following year, you potentially face a tax problem.

In Announcement 2008–17, the IRS announced that new regulations are expected to include a provision permitting qualified higher education expenses paid during the first three months of the year to be treated as the previous year's expenses. While this would eliminate the problem in the first scenario described above, it would not help with the second scenario (the reimbursement mismatch). Until further guidance is issued by the IRS, you should assume that QHEE and distributions will be accounted for on a cash basis and that 529 account distributions and the payment of qualified expenses must occur within the same calendar year.

Earnings subject to tax because they are part of a nonqualified distribution are also subject to a 10 percent federal additional tax. This tax, which represents the penalty for using a 529 account for purposes other than higher education expenses, is computed on Form 5329 as part of the Form 1040.

Note the following exceptions to the 10 percent federal additional tax:

* The distribution is made because the beneficiary is disabled—i.e., unable to engage in any substantial gainful activity because of a physical or mental condition and the condition is of indefinite duration or is expected to result in death.
* The distribution is made on account of tax-free scholarships or allowances received by the beneficiary, to the extent the distribution does not exceed the amount of scholarship or allowance.
* The distribution is made due to beneficiary's attendance at a U.S. military academy, to the extent the distribution does not exceed the costs of advanced education (as defined in Title 10 of the U.S. Code) at the academy.
* The distribution is paid to the beneficiary (or to the beneficiary's estate) on or after the death of the beneficiary.
* The distribution is included in income only because total qualified higher education expenses had to be reduced by tuition and related expenses used in computing the American Opportunity credit or Lifetime Learning credit.

How does the 529 plan administrator calculate the earnings portion of a distribution?

In producing Form 1099-Q, the 529 plan administrator first calculates the basis portion of the distribution and then subtracts that figure from the total distribution, leaving the earnings portion.[4] In a 529 savings program, the basis portion is calculated using the following equation:

$$\frac{\text{Basis}}{\text{Value of account}} \times \text{Distribution} = \text{Basis portion}$$

Basis generally refers to the total contributions into the account less prior distributions of basis. The value of the account is determined on the day of distribution.

The calculation is slightly different in a prepaid program. The total amount of the distribution is the current value of the tuition and other education benefits your beneficiary receives during the year. The basis portion is calculated from the number of tuition credits used or redeemed during the year as a percentage of total credits purchased. For example, if you originally purchased eight semesters of tuition and you use the program to pay for two semesters in a year, the basis portion of the distribution is two-eighths or 25% of the amount you paid for the prepayment contract.

For purposes of these calculations, all 529 accounts within the same state with the same account owner and designated beneficiary must be treated as one account. Accounts in a prepaid program do not have to be aggregated with accounts in the same state's savings program.

Aggregation is performed by the 529 program administrator, and is not a responsibility of the taxpayer, which means that the administrator will need to track your account's basis over time in order to satisfy the distribution reporting requirements. Rollover contributions from another 529 plan, and tax-free transfers from Coverdell education savings accounts and qualifying U.S. savings bonds, pose a special challenge to program administrators because these transfers include untaxed earnings. (These types of transfers are discussed in further detail below and in later chapters.) The basis of contributions associated with these transfers must be adjusted for their untaxed earnings. IRS Notice 2001–81 prescribes the procedures a 529 plan must now employ to ensure that this information is properly recorded.[5]

---

4. Section 529 applies the provisions of Section 72 to the extent the distribution is not excludable under any other section of the Code (e.g. Section 117 scholarship exclusion).

5. Notice 2001–81, 2001–52 IRB (Dec. 26, 2001).

The government's decision to make program administrators responsible for determining the basis and earnings portions of a distribution lifts some of the paperwork burden from your shoulders. You do not have to maintain your own tax basis records.

Where do I show the beneficiary's qualified higher education expenses to the IRS?

You are not required to list or report the AQHEE on Form 1040 or any other income tax form. You must maintain records and be prepared to present those records in the event your return is audited by the IRS. If the distributions from a 529 plan are entirely excluded—AQHEE equal or exceed total distributions from Forms 1099-Q—no amounts need appear on Form 1040. If earnings must be reported—AQHEE are less than total distributions—they are to be included in "other income" on Line 21 of Form 1040.

Who reports any taxable earnings, the account owner or the beneficiary?

Form 1099-Q will be issued in the name and social security number of the recipient of the distribution (in tax parlance, the "distributee"). In most 529 savings programs, that can be either the beneficiary or the account owner. The recipient is responsible for the proper reporting of the distribution, and for any resulting tax (including the 10 percent additional tax). The account owner selects the recipient when filling out the program's withdrawal request form. Distributions paid directly from the 529 plan to the school are treated as paid to the beneficiary for reporting purposes.

Under the statutory language of Section 529, it appears that the designated beneficiary need only incur sufficient AQHEE for the distribution to be tax-free, no matter who receives the Form 1099-Q. If the parent, as account owner, receives the distribution (along with the Form 1099-Q), it should be excluded from the parent's income just as it would have been excluded from the beneficiary's income had the beneficiary received the distribution. However, because the Form 1099-Q contains a box that will indicate when the recipient is not the designated beneficiary, the account owner may have to deal with "matching" notices from the IRS and justify to the IRS the use of those funds to pay the designated beneficiary's college expenses. Future tax regulations should provide more clarity around this issue.

When the distribution is not a qualified distribution, you may have an opportunity to reduce taxes if the distribution is made payable to a low-bracket beneficiary.

> *Example:* Mr. Brown establishes an account with a 529 plan for his daughter Kelly and makes a one-time contribution of $10,000. Five years later, once Kelly has started college and the account has grown to $15,000, Mr. Brown requests a $9,000 distribution from the account made payable to Kelly. Kelly will receive a Form 1099-Q after the end of the year showing $9,000 in total distributions with $6,000 as the basis portion and $3,000 as the earnings portion. The basis portion is two-thirds of total distributions, as determined by the ratio of the account's basis at the time of distribution ($10,000) to total account value ($15,000). If Kelly can show that she incurred at least $9,000 of adjusted qualified higher education expenses during the year, the entire distribution is federally tax-free. If Kelly can only show $5,000 of AQHEE, then 5/9ths of the $3,000 earnings portion will be tax-free and 4/9ths, or $1,333, will be subject to tax on Kelly's federal income tax return as ordinary income. She will also incur a 10 percent additional tax ($133).

What happens if the school issues a refund?

It is fairly common for payments of tuition or other qualified higher education expenses to be refunded in whole or in part by the educational institution. After paying the school bill, the student may drop credits, or drop out of school altogether. The IRS has not yet issued regulations or other guidance to 529 plan participants regarding the tax treatment of refunds that consist of qualified higher education expenses. You will need to rely on the advice of your tax professional. It may be deemed reasonable to apply the rules set forth in the tax regulations regarding the refund of expenses that were used to claim one of the education tax credits.[6] Using that set of rules, you would reduce the beneficiary's QHEE for Section 529 purposes by any refunds of QHEE received during the same calendar year, or during the following year but prior to the date the tax return is filed. If the refund occurs in the following year after the tax return is filed, or in any subsequent year, the tax liability would have to be increased for the refund year by the tax and 10 percent penalty that would have been incurred if QHEE had been reduced in the year of the 529 distribution.

What about state taxes?

State tax laws are not uniform, but here, generally speaking, is the way it should work for most:

♦ Opening a 529 account in a state other than your own does not subject you or your beneficiary to that state's income tax.

♦ If a distribution qualifies for exclusion from federal taxable income, then it should also qualify for exclusion from your own state's taxable income. Currently, only one state—Alabama—will tax a qualified distribution, and only when that distribution comes from a non-Alabama 529 plan. Qualified distributions from an Alabama 529 plan remain exempt from that state's income tax. (The Alabama legislature has considered—but not yet passed—changes to its laws to remove this particular distinction.)

♦ If a distribution is federally taxable, then it will probably also be taxable on your state income tax return. You may also have to "recapture" any state tax deductions or credits claimed in previous years. Be careful here: some states will treat a federally tax-free rollover as a taxable distribution; and some states will exclude the income on a nonqualified distribution if the distribution is attributable to the beneficiary's death, disability, or receipt of a scholarship.

---

6. See Treas. Reg. 1.125A–5(f).

♦ Most states will follow federal rules regarding the amount and timing of reportable income, and in determining who reports it (account owner or beneficiary).

What are adjusted qualified higher education expenses?

Adjusted qualified higher education expenses (AQHEE) are qualified higher education expenses (QHEE) reduced by expenses used to claim an education tax credit. See the section below concerning the American Opportunity and Lifetime Learning credits for a description of this adjustment.

QHEE means tuition, fees, books, supplies, and equipment required for enrollment or attendance on a full-time or part-time basis at an eligible educational institution, plus, in the case of a "special needs beneficiary," any "special needs services."[7] In addition, QHEE includes room and board expense (both on-campus and off-campus) for students enrolled in eligible college programs on at least a half-time basis.[8] The student's qualifying expenses must be reduced by any tax-free scholarships or payments, and by educational assistance allowances provided under certain federal programs.

QHEE under current law does not include the cost of transportation or personal expenses, even though they may be considered part of the

---

7. The definition of a "special needs beneficiary" has not yet been provided in Treasury Department regulations. The Conference Agreement to Act Sec. 401 of the 2001 EGTRRA references individuals who because of a physical, mental, or emotional condition (including learning disability) require additional time to complete their education.

8. The amount paid for room and board as QHEE cannot exceed (i) the allowance applicable to the beneficiary for room and board included in the "cost of attendance", as defined in section 472 of the Higher Education Act as in effect on June 7, 2001, as determined by the eligible educational institution for that period, or (ii) if greater, the actual invoice amount the beneficiary residing in housing owned or operated by the eligible educational institution is charged for room and board costs for that period. The room and board costs must be incurred during an academic period during which the student is enrolled or accepted for enrollment in a degree, certificate or other program (including a program of study abroad approved for credit by the eligible educational institution) that leads to a recognized educational credential awarded by an eligible educational institution. A student will be considered to be enrolled at least half-time if the student is enrolled for at least half the full-time academic workload for the course of study the student is pursuing as determined under the standards of the institution where the student is enrolled. The institution's standard for a full-time workload must equal or exceed a standard established by the Department of Education under the Higher Education Act.

"cost of attendance" for federal financial aid purposes. Repayment of student loans also does not qualify.

Eligible educational institutions are defined by reference to Section 481 of the Higher Education Act of 1965 and include any accredited postsecondary educational institutions offering credit toward a bachelor's degree, an associate's degree, a graduate or professional degree, or another recognized postsecondary credential. Certain proprietary institutions and postsecondary vocational institutions also are eligible institutions. The institution must be eligible to participate in Title IV U.S. federal financial aid programs. To determine if a particular institution has been assigned a federal school code by the Department of Education, and presumably eligible under Section 529 as meeting these requirements, you may enter the name of an institution at the Department of Education's website at http://fafsa.ed.gov/FAFSA/app/schoolSearch. Many foreign universities are included on the list. Some states have requested that the IRS provide an official listing of eligible educational institutions, but so far none has been published.

When I tried looking up a particular school on the school code list I was not able to find it. Does that mean I cannot use my 529 plan for that school?

First, check to be sure you have correctly spelled the school's legal name on the look-up page. You can also request from that page a list of schools within a particular state or country, or click on "foreign" for a list of all international schools. If you still cannot locate a particular institution, contact the school, explain that you are trying to determine if the school is eligible under Section 529, and request that the school provide you with its federal school code. Although not every postsecondary institution is eligible, nearly all accredited institutions are.

Can I claim the American Opportunity or Lifetime Learning credit in the same year that I withdraw from my 529 account to pay for college?

Yes, the American Opportunity or Lifetime Learning credit (see box below) can be claimed regardless of whether the funds used to pay credit-eligible tuition and related expenses come from a 529 account. However, in order to prevent "double-dipping," Section 529 requires that QHEE be reduced by any expenses used to determine the American Opportunity or Lifetime Learning credit. Unless you pay out-of-pocket an amount at least equal to the amount of tuition and related expenses used in determining the American Opportunity or Lifetime Learning credit, some portion of your 529 distribution will no longer be qualified and will become subject to income tax. The 10 percent penalty tax will not apply in these circumstances.

> *Example:* Eric, a second-year college student, has his own 529 account. He withdraws $24,000 from the account during 2013 to pay for all of his QHEE, including $8,000 in tuition. The entire $24,000 distribution would be tax-free, except that Eric claims the maximum $2,500 American Opportunity credit against $4,000 of his tuition. He must reduce his $24,000 QHEE by $4,000, leaving $20,000. This means that $4,000 (or one-fifth) of his 529 distribution is no longer qualified. If we assume the earnings portion of the distribution is $5,000, then one-fifth of $5,000, or $1,000, is taxable to Eric as ordinary income. If Eric's marginal federal tax bracket is 15%, he incurs $150 in federal tax. The 10 percent penalty tax is waived when the income is caused by this type of adjustment.

You may elect to waive the American Opportunity and Lifetime Learning credit if you decide that its negative impact on 529 distributions is greater than the amount of credit. This will occur in only a very small number of cases because the benefit of the credit will nearly always outweigh the tax on that portion of your 529 distributions.

Note that similar coordination rules apply to withdrawals from a Coverdell education savings account. Furthermore, if withdrawals are taken from both a Coverdell ESA and a 529 account in the same year for the same beneficiary, the QHEE must be divided between them to determine the amount of tax exclusion on the withdrawals from each type of account. See chapter 9 for more information.

How about the above-the-line deduction for qualified tuition and related expenses? Can I claim the deduction for expenses I pay using funds from my 529 account?

If you are eligible to claim the above-the-line deduction for up to $4,000 of qualified tuition and related expenses, the use of your 529 account may affect the amount of deduction you can claim. The earnings portion of a 529 distribution used to pay qualified tuition and related expenses will reduce the deductible amount. The IRS has not yet described how to allocate your 529 distributions between "qualified tuition and related expenses," which reduce the amount eligible for deduction, and other qualified higher education expenses such as books and room and board that are eligible for Section 529 purposes but not for the tuition deduction.

The Credits and Deduction for Tuition Payments

The American Opportunity credit and the Lifetime Learning credit are available to taxpayers with incomes below a certain level who incur qualified tuition and related expenses. The Lifetime Learning credit is nonrefundable, so the amount you claim cannot be greater than your tax liability excluding the credits. However, as much as 40 percent of the American Opportunity credit is refundable to certain eligible taxpayers. You may elect to claim the credits by attaching Form 8863 to your original or an amended federal income tax return. The 2001 tax law created an above-the-line deduction for the same category of expenses. The "tuition and fees" deduction was scheduled to expire at the end of 2012 but has been extended through 2013 under the 2012 American Taxpayer Relief Act. The deduction may not be claimed in any year you elect to claim the American Opportunity or Lifetime Learning credit. The rules surrounding the American Opportunity and Lifetime Learning credits were already complex; the competing deduction makes tax planning and return preparation even more difficult.

American Opportunity credit

The American Opportunity credit is equal to 100 percent of up to $2,000 of qualified tuition and related expenses paid by a taxpayer during the taxable year for the qualified educational expenses of a student during any academic period beginning in each taxable year, plus 25 percent of such expenses over $2,000. The maximum credit is $2,500 per year per student. The American Opportunity credit may be claimed up to four times. The student cannot have completed four years of postsecondary education before the start of the taxable year, and must be at least a half-time student.

For purposes of this credit, the term "qualified tuition and related expenses" means tuition and fees required for the enrollment or attendance of the taxpayer, the taxpayer's spouse, or any dependent of the taxpayer, at an eligible educational institution. Qualified expenses are reduced by tax-free scholarships and allowances.

The American Opportunity credit is phased out for taxpayers with modified adjusted gross incomes (MAGI) between $80,000 and $90,000 (single) or between $160,000 and $180,000 (married filing joint).

Lifetime Learning credit

The Lifetime Learning credit is equal to 20 percent of up to $10,000 of the qualified tuition and related expenses paid by the taxpayer during the taxable year for education furnished during any academic period beginning in the taxable year. The maximum credit is $2,000 per year per taxpayer (not per student). Tuition and related expenses for any course of instruction taken at an eligible educational institution to acquire or improve job skills of the individual are qualified. There is no limit to the number of years in which the Lifetime Learning credit can be claimed.

The Lifetime Learning credit is phased out for taxpayers with modified adjusted gross incomes (MAGI) between $53,000 and $63,000 (single) or between $107,000 and $127,000 (married filing joint). These phase-out ranges are for 2013 and they adjust every year for inflation.

A taxpayer cannot claim an American Opportunity credit and a Lifetime Learning credit for the same student in one year. Also, any expenses used in determining the American Opportunity or Lifetime Learning credit will reduce total qualified higher education expenses used in calculating the tax exclusion for distributions from a 529 plan or Coverdell education savings account. Proper coordination and planning will maximize the benefits of these credits and exclusions over the course of a family's college years.

If you claim your child as a dependent, only you may claim the American Opportunity credit or the Lifetime Learning credit with respect to your child's qualifying educational expenses. Your child may claim the credit if you do not claim the child as a dependent on your tax return. (An otherwise dependent child cannot claim a personal exemption, however, no matter what the parent decides to do about claiming the dependency exemption.)

Your ability to decide whether to claim your child as a dependent provides significant latitude. If your income is above the limits, and your child's income falls below the limits, the child may derive a tax benefit from the credits when you cannot. You will lose the benefit of the dependency exemption, but some high-income parents are unable to derive full benefit from the dependency exemption anyway, due to the income phase-out of the exemption. In that case, you would make the easy decision to forego claiming your child as a dependent, and thereby allow the child to apply the education credit against his or her tax liability.

The above-the-line tuition and fees deduction

An eligible taxpayer may claim an above-the-line deduction under Section 222 of the Internal Revenue Code for a limited amount of qualified tuition and related expenses. These are the same expenses that qualify for the American Opportunity and Lifetime Learning credits. However, the benefits are mutually exclusive: you may not claim the deduction for yourself or your dependent student in any year in which you or that student claim the American Opportunity or Lifetime Learning credit.

To be eligible for the deduction, you must not be a married individual filing separately or the dependent of another individual and your MAGI must be below a certain level. If your MAGI is $65,000 or less ($130,000 or less on a joint return), you may deduct up to $4,000 in qualified tuition and related expenses. If your MAGI exceeds $65,000/$130,000 but does not exceed $80,000 ($160,000 on a joint return), you may deduct up to $2,000 in qualified tuition and related expenses based on a phase-down formula. You must reduce your total qualified tuition and related expenses by the excluded earnings from 529 plan distributions, Coverdell ESA withdrawals, and qualified U.S. savings bond redemptions, which are used to pay for such expenses.

The tuition and fees deduction is slated to expire at the end of 2013.

What are the federal gift and estate tax rules under Section 529?

Section 529 prescribes that the contribution to a 529 plan account is a completed gift for estate and gift tax purposes. The gift is from the individual contributor to the designated beneficiary (assuming the contributor and beneficiary are not the same person). This rule applies despite the fact the account owner retains ownership rights that would otherwise cause the assets to remain in his or her estate. A further advantage is that the funding of the account is treated as the gift of a "present interest" qualifying for the $14,000 gift tax annual exclusion. Finally, Section 529 provides that the contributor may under certain circumstances elect to treat the gift as occurring ratably over a five-year period, so that the $14,000 exclusion can be leveraged to as much as $70,000 in a year. Chapter 8 describes these rules in more detail.

Can I change the beneficiary of my 529 account?

Section 529 allows the account owner to replace the current designated beneficiary with a new beneficiary who is a "member of the family" (see box below). All 529 plans accommodate a change in beneficiary without imposing a penalty, although some may have age or residency restrictions, and some may charge a fee. There are no federal income tax consequences of a beneficiary change; however, there can be gift tax consequences when the new beneficiary is at least one generation below the old beneficiary, as discussed in chapter 8.

Can I transfer my account from one state's 529 plan to another state's 529 plan?

Yes, a qualifying rollover is not treated as a distribution for federal income tax. A transfer of assets from one state's plan to another for the same beneficiary is a qualifying rollover, but this type of rollover can be done only once every 12 months. There is no limit on the frequency of rollovers where the beneficiary is replaced with a qualifying member of the family. A rollover can be transacted either through a direct "trustee-to-trustee" transfer (program permitting), or by a withdrawal of funds followed by the contribution of equivalent funds within 60 days to a different 529 plan. Be sure to find out how the 529 plan you are investigating handles rollover requests, as there may be restrictions imposed by the program. Many prepaid programs will treat such a request as a cancellation of the contract.

Member of the Family

"Member of the family" means an individual who has one of the following relationships to the current beneficiary:

- A son or daughter (natural or legally adopted), or a descendant of either;
- A stepson or stepdaughter;
- A brother or sister (by whole or halfblood), or stepbrother or stepsister;
- The father or mother, or an ancestor of either;
- A stepfather or stepmother;
- A niece or nephew;
- An aunt or uncle;
- A son-in-law, daughter-in-law, father-in-law, mother-in-law, brother-in-law, or sister-in-law;
- The spouse of the designated beneficiary (who must have the same principal place of abode) or the spouse of any of the relatives listed above (who must have the same principal place of abode);
- A first cousin.

Can a corporation or trust be the owner of a 529 account?

Yes, Section 529 refers to a "person," defined under Section 7701 of the Code as an individual, a trust, estate, partnership, association, company or corporation. Many 529 plans permit legal entities to establish accounts, although some do not. There will be special tax considerations whenever a non-individual taxpayer is account owner, and some of the issues surrounding entity ownership have not been fully explored or tested. For corporations, the compensation rules (Section 83) must be considered, and perhaps also the anti-tax shelter provisions. For certain trusts, the effect of 529 plan distributions on "distributable net income" has to be considered. Your attorney and accountant should be consulted in these matters.

Can I transfer the ownership of my account to someone else?

Nothing within Section 529 prohibits or regulates a transfer of account ownership. It is up to the individual 529 plan to provide rules concerning transfer of account ownership. Some programs will accommodate a request to transfer account ownership while others expressly prohibit such transfers prior to the owner's death or legal incapacity. The mere transfer of ownership appears to have no federal income, gift, or estate tax consequences. However, a new account owner will generally have all rights associated with original ownership including the power to revoke the account.

What happens to my account if I die?

The death of the account owner does not cause a 529 account to terminate. Instead, all rights of ownership and control over the account are passed to a successor account owner. The identity of the successor owner depends on the rules of the program and state law. Nearly all 529 plans now permit you to name a successor owner on the account application or upon later submission to the program administrator. The program rules may specify the account owner in other situations, i.e. you fail to name a successor account owner, or the person you name as successor declines the appointment or predeceases you. For example, the 529 plan may specify that, in the absence of a named successor, the beneficiary of the 529 account will become account owner unless the beneficiary is a minor, in which case the beneficiary's living parent or guardian will become account owner. In any situation where there is no clear successor under the terms of your account or the rules of the program, ownership will pass according to your will or your state's laws of intestacy. If you live in a state with a community property law, consult with your attorney regarding the treatment of your 529 account.

FOUR

Financial Aid Considerations

e now turn our attention to one of parents' most significant concerns: the impact of a 529 account on a student's financial-aid eligibility. The news is positive, as the use of 529 plans to save for college under current rules causes little, if any, impact to a student's eligibility for need-based federal student aid. Non-federal awards may utilize different formulas that do not provide the same advantage to 529 plans. The aid process is explained below.

The authorization for federal financial aid comes from Title IV of the Higher Education Act of 1965, as amended (HEA). Financial-aid packages consist of any combination of grants, work-study, and loans. A student's financial need is determined by the institution as the difference between that particular institution's cost of attendance (COA)[1] and the student's expected family contribution (EFC). The EFC represents the amount the family is expected to contribute towards a student's college costs based on its financial situation.

---

1. COA includes tuition, fees, room and board, books, supplies, transportation, and personal expenses. Some institutions will choose not to include transportation and personal expenses in the COA figure.

The EFC is calculated using data submitted to the Department of Education on a form called the Free Application for Federal Student Aid (FAFSA). The FAFSA is filed by high school seniors after January 1 in their final year of high school. In subsequent college years, the student files an abbreviated Renewal FAFSA.

The EFC includes 50 percent of the student's income, net of an income protection allowance of $6,130 for the 2013–14 award year and allowances for federal, state, and social security taxes. It also includes 20 percent of the student's reportable assets.

For dependent students, the EFC also includes between 22% and 47% of the parents' income and between 2.64% and 5.64% of the parents' assets. The parents' income is reduced for this purpose by tax allowances and a maximum $3,900 employment expense allowance. The formula also provides "protection allowances," one for parental income based on the household census (e.g., for 2013–14 the income protection allowance when there are two parents and one student in the household is $21,290) and one for assets based on whether there is one parent or two and on the age of the older parent (e.g., the asset protection allowance for two parents with the oldest being 45 as of December 31, 2013 is $36,200).

The parental contribution to EFC is pro-rated to each member of the family attending college in the upcoming year. This pro-ration can have a dramatic effect and many families that would not qualify for financial aid with one student in college may qualify when they have two or more family members in college at the same time.

In completing the FAFSA, the applicant reports income for the base year, which is the calendar year prior to the start of the school year (e.g. 2012 is the base year for students enrolling in fall 2013). Income includes the adjusted gross income from the student's and parents' Forms 1040 along with certain other items representing "untaxed income and benefits." Assets are reported on the FAFSA at their values on the day the FAFSA is filed. Anyone attempting to position income and assets for improved aid eligibility should keep the timing rules in mind.

Special treatment is provided to low-income families where the student and parents were eligible to file Form 1040A or 1040EZ for the base year, or where they were not required to file any income tax return. The

EFC is automatically zero if the parents earned $24,000 or less. The "simplified needs" formula, which excludes assets but not income, applies if the parents earned more than $24,000 but less than $50,000.

Alternative needs formulas are used for independent students without dependents and for independent students with dependents. A student is automatically considered independent if he or she is at least 23 years old, a veteran of the armed forces, a master's or doctoral candidate, married, or declared independent by a court, or if he or she has legal dependents other than a spouse. Parent assets and income are not considered in the need analysis for these students. The Department of Education maintains an extensive library of publications and other materials relating to federal financial aid on the Web at www.ed.gov.

Does all need-based aid come from the federal government?

No, most states also maintain need-based grant programs. Many of these programs use the federal methodology in determining the student's need while others use state-developed criteria. In some states, the determination of student eligibility for state-funded programs does not count balances in the home-state 529 plan. This can be an incentive to use your state's own 529 plan.

Many institutions, primarily private colleges, provide substantial amounts of gift aid out of their own endowments and other funds. A large number of these colleges utilize an alternative approach in determining need known as the "institutional methodology," developed by the College Board and administered by its affiliate, College Scholarship Service (CSS). To apply for grants at colleges that use the institutional methodology, a student must complete an application called the PROFILE. The PROFILE is similar to the FAFSA in that it follows the same general approach and is used to compute the applicant's expected family contribution. But there are also many differences between the forms, some of which are significant. For example, the PROFILE application requires information about equity in the home and family farm, which are exempt assets under the federal methodology. It will also provide information to the financial aid administrator about any retirement accounts owned by the student. The rest of this chapter focuses primarily on the federal methodology, not the institutional methodology; as you read through it, keep in mind that the treatment of 529 plans can differ. If your child will be applying for financial aid at a college using the institutional methodology, you should contact the college's financial aid office to determine its policies surrounding 529 plans.

Does the federal methodology distinguish between Section 529 prepaid tuition programs and savings programs?

No, although it used to. Before 2006, prepaid tuition plans caused a dollar-for-dollar reduction in need-based awards, but beginning with the 2006–07 award year, all 529 plans are treated the same in the determination of the student's EFC. As opposed to a 529 savings account, the value of a participant's interest in a prepaid tuition plan is not tied to the value of a portfolio of investments. Instead, the FAFSA requires that tuition credits or certificates purchased in a prepaid tuition plan be reported at their refund value.

How are 529 plans treated in the federal aid formula?

A 529 account owned by a dependent student's parent is reported on the FAFSA as a parent asset and assessed in determining the EFC at the parent's rate, which can be no higher than 5.64 percent, depending on income. If the account is valued at $10,000 on the day the FAFSA is filed, the maximum impact on aid eligibility is $564.

However, a 529 account owned directly by the dependent student, or owned indirectly through an UTMA/UGMA, is NOT reported as a student asset. Rather it is included with parent assets. This is good news as the assessment rate on student assets—at 20 percent—is significantly higher.

This favorable treatment for student-owned 529 accounts—also applicable to Coverdell education savings accounts—came about under a change in federal law intended to encourage college savings by minimizing the negative impact on financial-aid eligibility. Prior to 2006, a student-owned 529 account was assessed like any other student-owned investment at the 35 percent rate then in effect for student assets. (For school years beginning in 2006, 2007, and 2008 the financial-aid laws contained an unintended loophole that effectively exempted student-owned 529 accounts from being reported on the FAFSA.)

Three other possible situations merit special attention:

+ First, if the 529 account owner is the grandparent or another third party, it is not reportable on the FAFSA. This may sound like good news, but be sure to read the discussion below concerning "untaxed income."

+ Second, if the 529 account owner is a legal trust established for the student's benefit, the special exception for student-owned 529 account described above presumably does not apply and the student's interest in the trust, including any applicable portion of the 529 account, will have to be reported as a student asset.

+ Third, the FAFSA must include as a parent asset the value of a 529 account the student's parent owns for someone else, such as a younger sibling. This result can be avoided by placing the ownership of the account in the name of the sibling or a custodian under the UTMA/UGMA, but most parents would not wish to transfer ownership and control of the account for what is likely a very small impact on financial-aid eligibility.

Should we be transferring assets out of mutual funds and into a 529 plan to improve our child's eligibility for financial aid?

If the mutual fund is currently in a UGMA/UTMA account or in the student's name directly, you should look into the possibility of transferring the money to a 529 plan, as you would be converting a 20 percent asset to a 5.64 percent asset. The transfer of a $10,000 investment, for example, could increase financial aid eligibility by as much as $1,436.

However, you need to weigh the consequences of liquidating the non–529 investments (a 529 plan can only accept cash). By triggering capital gains you are creating an immediate income tax liability, and if the gains are reportable to your child under the age of 24, the kiddie tax may require those gains to be taxed at your (the parent's) higher bracket. The reporting of gains on your tax return, or on your child's tax return, will also be included in the base-year income on the FAFSA filed in the following year, thereby reducing aid eligibility.

If you are the parent of a dependent student and the mutual fund is in your name, there is no longer any financial-aid advantage in moving the funds to a 529 with your child as owner. Either way, the account value will be included on the FAFSA as a parent asset.

Placing your college savings in a 529 plan can help you qualify for zero- or simplified-EFC status because the 529 plan will not cause you to report capital gains. If you or the student were to invest in mutual funds or other securities, any gains from the sale of those securities would require that you file Schedule D with your Form 1040, thereby disqualifying you from special EFC status.

Are the distributions from a 529 plan reportable as "untaxed income" on the FAFSA?

Tax-free distributions from a 529 savings account owned by the student or parent do not constitute untaxed income and, therefore, will not impact the EFC. This can provide a tremendous advantage to 529 plans as compared with mutual funds, municipal bonds, or other investments that generate reportable interest, dividends, or capital gains.

With respect to distributions from 529 accounts owned by grandparents or other third parties, the answer is decidedly different. Although a provision in the 2007 College Cost Reduction Act prevents such distributions from being treated as a "resource" that reduces financial need on a dollar-for-dollar basis, the distribution will have to be included in base-year student income on the FAFSA line that asks for "Money received, or paid on your behalf (e.g. bills), not reported elsewhere on this form." This result can be avoided by waiting until the year in which the student enters his or her final year of school before taking distributions from a grandparent-owned 529. A grandparent can also consider transferring 529 account ownership to the parent or student if the money is needed sooner.

How does a 529 account compare to ESAs and IRAs?

Beginning in 2006, Coverdell ESAs and 529s are treated alike in the federal financial-aid formula. An ESA for a dependent student is reported as a parent asset, and tax-free ESA distributions are not reportable as untaxed income.

In comparing a 529 plan to a traditional or Roth IRA, special care is needed. Although an IRA is generally considered to be a favored type of investment when it comes to the financial-aid formula, it may in fact have severe negative financial aid consequences to the unsuspecting family. Qualified retirement accounts, including IRAs, are excluded assets in the EFC computation and, as discussed in chapter 11, premature distributions from an IRA may now be taken penalty-free to pay for college. The problem is with the income side of the EFC computation. The entire amount of the IRA distribution—both principal and earnings—is reportable on the FAFSA. Aid-eligible families with retirement assets should not plan on tapping those accounts to pay for college until the year in which the last FAFSA is filed.

Of course, many families will never expect to qualify for financial aid regardless of who is credited with the assets and income. For them, the financial-aid implications of a 529 plan, or any other investment alternative, will be of little concern. Even those who do qualify may discover that financial aid means loans and work-study, not grants or scholarships. Their concerns about the financial-aid consequences of investment decisions should also be tempered.

Federally-Funded Student Aid

+ **Federal Pell Grants**—Non-discretionary grants awarding up to $5,645 for the 2013–14 award year to applicants with financial need.

+ **Federal Supplemental Educational Opportunity Grants** (FSEOG)—Up to $4,000 per year allocated by the institution to students with financial need.

+ **Federal Stafford Loans**—Student loans directly from the government available to all students, but subject to annual borrowing caps. Limited interest subsidy is available to students determined to have financial need.

+ **Federal PLUS Loans**—Similar to Stafford, but made to creditworthy parents of students. Also available to graduate students.

+ **Federal Perkins Loans**—Up to $5,500 per year ($8,000 for graduate study) of 5%-interest loans allocated by the institution on the basis of financial need.

+ **Federal Work-Study** (FWS)—Funds provided by government for an institution's part-time employment of students with financial need.

FIVE

Prepaid vs. Savings

Section 529 plans come in two basic forms: prepaid and savings. But categorizing any given program is not always simple. Some plans contain features that are common to both prepaid and savings programs. They act like a prepaid program under some conditions, and like a savings program under different conditions. Some states even combine their separate prepaid and savings programs into a single package, marketed to the public as one program with different options.

If your state operates a prepaid program, one of your first steps should be to check whether the program is accepting new enrollments. Several states, including Alabama, Colorado, Kentucky, Ohio, South Carolina, Texas, and West Virginia have temporarily or permanently suspended enrollment into their prepaid programs. Other states may follow suit if program financial solvency is further stressed by rising tuition levels.

What is a prepaid program?

A prepaid program is one involving the purchase of tuition credits or certificates that entitle the beneficiary to a waiver or payment of future qualifying college costs. In essence, future tuition is being purchased today. The price you pay now is not necessarily equal to current tuition levels, although current tuition is always a factor when a prepaid program establishes its prices.

There are three types of prepaid programs. The most prevalent is the state-sponsored **"contract" program**. In return for your upfront cash payment, or your commitment to a series of cash payments, you receive a promise from the program that it will pay for future tuition and mandatory fees at public colleges, universities, or community colleges located in the state. The contract may cover a period from one semester to five years, depending on the program's available packages and the amount of tuition you wish to purchase. If your beneficiary attends a private or out-of-state school, the program will determine the value of your contract under a pre-set formula and make payments in an amount not to exceed that value.

The second type of prepaid program, also state-sponsored, is a prepaid/savings hybrid that is sometimes referred to as a **"unit" program**. It typically involves the purchase of tuition units or credits that represent a fraction (e.g. 1%) of the average yearly tuition and mandatory fees at public institutions in the state. These units change in value each year as average in-state tuition and fees increase. They are redeemed in the future to pay for tuition and fees, and in most cases, they can be redeemed for other qualified expenses as well (room and board, books, supplies, and equipment).

Categorizing the unit program as either prepaid or savings remains a matter of debate; it makes little difference now that prepaid programs and savings programs are treated equally in determining student eligibility for federal financial aid (see chapter 4). In 2000, a time when prepaid programs were at a severe disadvantage in the federal formula, Pennsylvania reconfigured its unit-type prepaid program in an effort to secure more favorable treatment for its participants, and labeled it a "guaranteed savings" program.

The third type of prepaid program, referred to here as a **"voucher" program**, involves the voluntary participation of one or more educational institutions. In return for your contribution, you receive a certificate redeemable toward a specific percentage of tuition and mandatory fees at any of the participating institutions. Percentages are set at the time of contribution. For example, the program may provide that a $5,000 contribution is worth 50 percent of one year's tuition and mandatory fees at participating College A, and 30 percent at College B. If your child attends one of those participating institutions, the tuition bill is reduced by the stated percentage. If your child attends a non-participating institution, or decides not to go to college at all, you can request a return of your payments adjusted for interest or other factors as described in program materials.

The Massachusetts U.Plan, with its 80 Massachusetts private and public institutions, was the first to offer a voucher-type prepaid program. The U.Plan is not a true 529 plan, but because it involves the issuance of Massachusetts general obligation bonds, participants are not subject to federal and Massachusetts state income tax. Another pure voucher-type program is the Private College 529 Plan, the private-college prepaid program that launched in fall 2003.

Here is another way to think about the three different types of prepaid programs: A contract program works like a futures contract; a unit program like an index fund (the index being average tuition at selected schools); and a voucher program like a discount coupon. All three rely on the program trust fund, made up of participant payments or contributions, to generate an investment return sufficient to cover the program's liability—or in some cases, the school's liability—for future tuition payments and unit redemptions.

What is a savings program?

A 529 savings program is a more familiar type of tax-deferred investment, in several ways similar to a Roth IRA. Contributions are made to a trust fund that is invested in mutual funds and other financial instruments. The idea is that your account will grow in value over time to keep up with, or preferably surpass, the increasing price of a college education.

Before Congress enacted Section 529 in 1996, several states had prepaid tuition programs but only one state, Kentucky, had a pure savings program. Since 1996, a majority of the new 529 plans are savings programs.

There appear to be a couple of reasons for this phenomenon. One is that savings programs offer the potential for higher investment returns than prepaid or guaranteed savings programs. Accounts are usually invested in equity and bond mutual funds that have historically outpaced the increases in college expenses.

The other reason is that savings programs are easier and cheaper for a state to administer, especially when the outside vendor that manages the investments also agrees to handle much of the program administration and marketing. In recent years, several states have launched new or redesigned programs in which the program fund is charged a fee that is shared by the program manager and the state treasury, in effect making the program a source of revenue for the state.

What are the major differences between prepaid and savings programs?

Most people evaluating college-savings plans will, quite naturally, focus attention on the investment aspects of the programs being considered. After all, we all want our investments to do as well as possible. Historically, over long periods of time, stocks have outperformed many other investments, and certain types of common stocks have done better than others. On the other hand, stocks generally carry more investment risk than most other types of investments.

Nearly all 529 plans, of either variety, employ professional investment managers to maximize potential return within a certain level of risk. In a savings program, the investment management is applied directly to the assets in a participant's account. In a prepaid or guaranteed savings program, the investment management is applied to the program fund to ensure that the program will be able to pay for future tuition or unit redemptions. Because a participant will have no choice in the state's selection of investment managers, the participant must rely on the judgment of program officials.

While most savings programs offer the advantage of unlimited upside investment potential, prepaid and guaranteed savings programs offer the advantage of keeping up with inflation of college expenses, no matter how high those costs may go. A risk-tolerant saver may be more attracted to the savings program while a risk-averse saver may be more attracted to the prepaid or guaranteed savings program.

Here are some of the major differences between prepaid and savings programs:

1) In a savings program you own an interest in the program fund by virtue of your contributions into that fund. Your contributions are co-mingled with those of other participants, but the program administrator keeps track of each dollar you put in by setting up a separate account for you. With a prepaid program, you are purchasing the program's promise to deliver an agreed-upon bundle of benefits in the future. The amount you pay for that promise is determined by the program, as is the amount of any refund you may request later on. You should attempt to compare the price of the prepaid contract to the current tuition and fee levels at the institution your beneficiary is likely to attend. Is it the same, higher, or lower? Most state-sponsored prepaid programs are now charging more than the amount you would pay if your beneficiary were attending college this year. This "premium" is necessary for the program to cover administrative costs as well as to help build a reserve against potential shortfalls in the trust fund. A shortfall can occur if the program's obligation for future payments increases faster than the investment earnings in the trust. A premium causes the overall return of your investment in the prepaid contract to be somewhat less than the rate of tuition inflation. The price of the contract may also vary based on the age of your beneficiary. Prepaid programs often offer lower prices for younger beneficiaries because a longer time horizon allows for more predictable investment returns in the program trust fund.

2) Most prepaid programs have a specified enrollment period each year. Prepayment contracts must be purchased during the enrollment period, and the price of a contract is adjusted each year when the new enrollment period begins. Alternatively, some prepaid programs are now permitting year-round enrollment but setting new prices at certain times during the year. Savings programs do not have restricted enrollment periods and accept new accounts and contributions at any time.

3) Almost all state-sponsored prepaid programs require that either the account owner or the beneficiary meet state residency requirements. The majority of savings programs, however, are open to residents of any

state. Any family considering investing in a 529 plan should evaluate programs from the state where the donor lives, from the state where the designated beneficiary lives, and from states that offer 529 plans without residency requirements.

4) Most prepaid contracts are of limited duration. For example, the program may specify that the contract will be terminated, and a refund paid, if the benefits are not used within 10 years after the beneficiary's normal college matriculation date. Most savings programs, however, have no program-imposed limit on account duration and can remain open indefinitely, subject only to the requirement that there be a living beneficiary named on the account.

5) Most contract-type and voucher-type prepaid programs provide only for undergraduate tuition and mandatory fees, while savings programs and unit-type prepaid programs can generally be used for any costs that meet the definition of "qualified higher education expense" under Code Section 529. Unless the student is commuting from home, tuition and fees comprise less than 50 percent of the student's total cost of attendance at most in-state public institutions. However, nothing prevents a family from combining participation in a prepaid program with participation in a savings program.

6) All 529 plans allow distributions to pay for out-of-state colleges and universities. However, contract-type prepaid programs are generally designed for the child who eventually will be enrolling at an in-state public institution. For the beneficiary in a prepaid program who attends an in-state private school or an out-of-state school, the contract benefits must first be valued. Many programs use the weighted-average, credit-hour value of in-state public universities for this purpose. However, some prepaid programs compute a value by adding a fixed rate of interest to the contract purchase price. Also, most of these programs will limit the benefits paid to private and out-of-state institutions to the lesser of actual tuition and fees or the value of in-state tuition and fees. This means that a participant who moves out-of-state and then attends a public university in the new state will not receive a refund if the new state has lower in-state tuition than the old state. In this situation, the best move may be to cancel the contract and obtain a refund. The choice of college is not an issue in

most savings and unit-type prepaid programs because beneficiaries receive the same amount whether they attend an in-state public, in-state private, or out-of-state school.

7) Even if the beneficiary of a contract-type prepaid program chooses to enroll in an in-state public institution, the investment return will often depend on the institution attended and the number of credit hours taken. A student attending the most expensive public university in the state and taking the maximum number of credit hours covered under the contract receives a better deal than the student who attends the least expensive university or takes fewer credit hours than the program is obligated to cover. In some states, the range of tuition prices among public institutions is wide. The ultimate choice of school does not affect the investment return in a savings program or unit-type prepaid program.

8) Most prepaid programs make payments directly to the institution after receiving notice of pending tuition bills from the participant. Savings programs generally permit cash withdrawals by the account owner or beneficiary, and do not require documentation to substantiate the use of the withdrawn funds. (Some savings programs will ask on the withdrawal request form if the withdrawal is "qualified" or "nonqualified." The participant's response is not determinative for federal tax purposes.)

9) State-sponsored prepaid programs tend to have more transaction fees than savings programs. Perhaps this is because prepaid programs are more difficult to administer, or because they are operated by state agencies that are accustomed to imposing fees. All 529 plans will list the fees charged to participants, including fees for enrollment, annual maintenance, and change of beneficiary or account owner. Savings programs compete more directly with other investment alternatives available to the college saver, and seem more intent on keeping fees and transaction charges to a minimum.

10) Some prepaid programs require a minimum purchase of at least one semester's worth of tuition, but allow payments to be made over time. The installment payments include an interest component, although the full payments are included in the tax basis of the account and none of the extra payment is treated as interest expense for income tax purposes. Savings programs do not work this way and simply credit the account whenever a contribution is received.

11) State-sponsored prepaid programs, including both the unit-type and guaranteed savings programs, make actuarial assumptions in evaluating the soundness of the program trust fund and in setting prices for the upcoming enrollment period. Relevant factors used to calculate the liability for future payouts include the projected investment return on fund assets, tuition increases and enrollment trends at state schools, and the expected number of refunds. Although the bull market of the 1990s allowed several prepaid programs to build up large reserves, stock market losses and spiraling public tuition in subsequent years created significant financial challenges for many of these programs. Reserves began drying up and by the end of 2002 nearly all prepaid programs were showing deficits on their balance sheets. The financial situation was particularly difficult for newer prepaid programs that opened in the midst of the financial squeeze. This situation was repeated during the 2008-09 recession. Several states closed off their prepaid programs to new enrollment, and will reopen only when financial conditions improve or when the programs can be restructured to minimize the risk of loss.

12) Some prepaid programs and unit-type programs are backed by the full faith and credit of their sponsoring states, providing a safety net for participants should the program run out of funds. A few programs do not enjoy this guarantee, but do offer some added safety under laws that require their state legislatures to consider an appropriation if their 529 plan runs into financial difficulties. Still other programs have no backing or guarantees from the state whatsoever, although the ongoing commitment on the part of the state may be implied. Savings programs typically have no state guarantee, and should have no reason to need one.

It is reasonable to expect that over time we will see further blurring of the lines that distinguish prepaid and savings programs. We are already beginning to see savings programs offering some inflation-protection features normally associated with prepaid programs, including guaranteed investment options. At the same time, some prepaid programs are becoming more flexible and investment-oriented. It may be difficult to achieve, but there is no reason why the best features of each type of 529 plan cannot be successfully incorporated into a single program.

SIX

Comparing 529 Plans: A Checklist

Beyond the basic characteristics of the two types of 529 plans described in the previous chapter, numerous differences exist in program design among the various programs operating today. The task of sorting through all the choices can be somewhat daunting. Just understanding how the 529 plan in your home state works is difficult enough; shopping among competing 529 plans becomes even more confusing.

Your analysis should involve not only a comparison of each program's investments or tuition guarantees, but also many other aspects of the program. Your own family circumstances, investment objectives, risk tolerance, and financial knowledge will all play a large part in selecting an appropriate 529 plan. The "best" 529 plan for one family is not necessarily the best one for another.

How do you go about this selection process? This book and our companion website (www.savingforcollege.com) are certainly good first steps. Then be sure to obtain the official program materials for your own state's 529 plan. Finally, request information from other states' programs that interest you and that accept nonresidents.

Many individual investors rely on a professional financial planner or investment advisor in developing, implementing, and monitoring an investment plan. Before 2001, few financial professionals had the knowledge, experience, and interest in 529 plans to be of much help to you in this regard. But over the past twelve years, professionals have awakened to the benefits of 529 plans for their clients, and many programs have been adapted for sale through financial advisors.

Whether you use a financial advisor to help select a 529 plan, or search on your own, learn as much as you can about the program before you invest in it. Here are the primary information sources that may or may not be included in the materials that a program makes available to you:

State statute. Every state with a 529 plan will have a law on the books authorizing the program. Sometimes, more than one section of state law is involved, e.g., when special state tax treatment is provided for participants in the 529 plan.

Program rules. Usually, a state agency or program board is charged with implementing and overseeing the operation of the program and acting as trustee. This agency develops the official rules of the program as allowed by the statute. These rules are extremely important because they contain the program's operational details. The rules are prone to frequent change, however, so it is important to be sure that you are accessing the most current version.

Program description. All 529 plans now provide an extensive explanatory booklet that describes their rules. This document also explains the tax treatment of 529 accounts and contains appropriate disclaimers.

Investment prospectuses. If a 529 savings program invests in mutual funds, it may send you the prospectuses for those funds—the same SEC-registered prospectuses that any investor would receive. The 529 plan itself is not required to produce a prospectus because securities laws treat interests in a 529 plan as "municipal securities" exempt from Securities and Exchange Commission registration requirements.

Program booklet. You will usually find an attractive, glossy marketing piece that contains pictures of cute children and summarizes the key advantages of the program. This is often presented in a helpful FAQ (frequently asked questions) format. An enrollment/application form is generally provided with the program booklet.

Website. Every 529 plan has a website. The Internet has become an extremely important and useful way to convey information and is perfectly suited to these programs. The best websites will make available all the materials provided in the enrollment packet, plus higher-education information including college-cost calculators and links to state financial-aid programs. Many 529 plans now allow you to enroll on-line.

The remainder of this chapter describes many of the ways in which 529 plans may differ from one another, and suggests an approach for comparing the various programs. This approach takes the form of a three-step process:

Step 1: Eliminate any 529 plans that clearly fall outside your criteria for acceptability, as well as those that will not accept you due to their eligibility requirements.

Step 2: For each program being considered, ask yourself the question "How much will my invested dollar produce by the time my beneficiary is ready for college?" Your own investment objectives, future college plans, and risk tolerance will play a part here. Be sure to consider the level of fees and expenses, as well as any state-tax benefits and other financial incentives offered by the plan.

Step 3: If Step 2 does not produce a clear winner in your mind, make a comparison of the restrictive features in the programs. For example, some programs permit you to tranfer account ownership to someone else, while other programs do not. This feature may or may not be important to you; that is for you to decide. You can often circumvent a restriction by using multiple 529 plans, or by rolling over your 529 account to a less-restrictive 529 plan later on.

How much time will you need to complete this three-step process? It could be a lot, depending on how many possibilities you wish to explore. There are so many 529 plans to choose from and they differ in so many ways that your beneficiary could have completed college before you finally complete the exercise. That would not be a good thing. The tools available in this book, i.e., the checklist in this chapter, the program descriptions contained in Part II, and the online tools and information available at www.savingforcollege.com, can help shortcut the process.

Before making any final decisions, however, read and understand the official program materials of the programs you are most interested in. Contact the program administrators directly to obtain further explanation and clarification. For some important items (e.g., legal and tax questions), consider having a conversation with your attorney, accountant, or other professional advisor. The importance of a thorough due-diligence process cannot be overstated because it can greatly reduce the chances of being surprised or disappointed later on.

The following checklist is presented in three sections. It is organized in this manner so that you may more easily identify the 529 plans most likely to meet your needs. Revisit this checklist occasionally, as 529 plans are constantly making changes—usually improvements—to their program rules and investment options. Please note that this checklist excludes items that pertain exclusively to prepaid tuition programs. Please refer to chapter 5 for a discussion of how to compare features in prepaid plans.

Section 1: Required elements

The first section describes eligibility or user requirements that either the program or the investor may impose when determining program suitability. As you read through these, remember that certain items will be viewed as requirements by only some investors. For other investors, they may have no relevance or importance.

1) Are there any state residency requirements?

Most 529 savings programs do not require that you or the designated beneficiary reside in the sponsoring state, but a few do. Conversely, 529 prepaid programs generally restrict enrollment to those who meet state residency requirements. Of course, the Private College 529 Plan does not have state residency restrictions, because it is not state-run. The Massachusetts U.Plan is a non-529 prepaid program that accepts anyone who intends to send their child to a participating Massachusetts college or university.

Often, a 529 plan with restrictions will permit enrollment if either the account owner or the beneficiary is a state resident at the time of enrollment. If you are establishing an account for a grandchild living in a different state, you may want to consider the program offered in the state where your grandchild resides.

Questions regarding residency can arise in certain situations. Is there a minimum period of residency? What happens if the eligible resident moves out-of-state after the account is opened? What happens if enrollment is contingent on the state residency of the beneficiary, and you later change the beneficiary to someone who is not a state resident? How are the residency restrictions applied to military personnel stationed in the state, or those originally from the state but now stationed elsewhere?

Some 529 plans that impose residency restrictions will accept nonresidents who meet other conditions. For example, Nevada's prepaid program allows a nonresident alumnus of a Nevada postsecondary institution to enroll.

2) What are the other eligibility requirements?

Most 529 plans require that the individual account owner be of legal age (e.g. 18) and that an account funded with a minor's own money be maintained by an adult custodian or guardian on behalf of the minor. In addition, the program may be restricted to account owners who are U.S. citizens or resident aliens. The program may require that the beneficiary have (or obtain within a certain period of time) a Social Security number or a federal taxpayer identification number.

Most prepaid programs require that the beneficiary be below a certain age or grade level at the time of enrollment, making these programs unsuitable for older individuals who may be planning to attend college in the future.

3) Can the account owner and the beneficiary be the same person?

Although every 529 savings program permits you to establish an account for yourself, this may not always be feasible in programs that place age or grade limits on beneficiaries. Such restrictions are common in prepaid programs.

4) How does the program handle funds coming from an existing UTMA or UGMA investment account?

Many families have children with assets in a Uniform Transfers to Minors Act (UTMA) account or Uniform Gifts to Minors Act (UGMA) account. If you are the custodian of the account, and you wish to invest the child's assets in a 529 plan, you will need to determine if, and how, the program accommodates funds coming from UTMA/UGMA accounts. There are a few different ways this is being done.

- The program (e.g. New York) will permit the minor child to establish an account in his or her own name. A parent or legal guardian must execute documents and authorize decisions with respect to the account until the minor reaches the age of majority.
- The program will permit the account to be titled in the same way as any other account owned by the minor under the UTMA/UGMA. The custodian must notify the program administrator at the time the custodianship is terminated upon the child reaching legal age so that the account can be re-titled in the child's own name. The program generally prohibits a change in beneficiary, or any withdrawal that is not for the benefit of the minor, until the custodianship terminates.
- The program will title the account in the name of the adult acting as custodian but will provide a "check box" to indicate that the source of funds is an existing UTMA/UGMA account. The account will be restricted as to beneficiary changes and withdrawals until the custodianship terminates.
- The program will title the account in the name of the adult acting as custodian and will impose no special restrictions or requirements.

The program administrator in this instance adopts the position that it is the custodian's legal responsibility to ensure that the account is handled in accordance within UTMA/UGMA laws.

5) Will the program accept a corporation or a trust as account owner?

A corporate-owned 529 account can provide unique benefits as part of a bonus plan or nonqualified deferred compensation plan. However, owners of closely-held corporations are often disappointed to learn that a 529 plan does not promise a tax-advantaged way to distribute corporate profits. Contributions made from company funds to an employee's or owner's 529 account are generally treated the same as cash payments made to the employee or owner.

The trustee of an irrevocable trust, attracted to the investment and tax advantages of a 529 plan, may decide to establish an account with a 529 plan and invest the trust's cash in the account, naming as 529 account beneficiary the beneficiary of the trust. Or, the individual owner of a 529 account may want to name a trust as successor owner, to make certain that in the event of the owner's death the account is used in accordance with his or her wishes. (Passing ownership directly to an individual successor owner could be viewed as too risky since control of those funds, including the power to take distributions, rests entirely with the new owner.)

Anyone planning to install a non-natural entity as owner or successor owner should seek professional advice from an attorney and an accountant. Many legal and tax complications can arise in these situations.

6) Are interests in the 529 plan being sold through brokers?

If you rely on a financial advisor who earns commissions from the sale of investment products, chances are that the advisor will focus on 529 plans that pay a commission. This isn't necessarily bad. Most adviser-sold 529 plans are excellent programs and they often have the most flexible features. They have passed the scrutiny of your advisor's broker-dealer, and they provide a substantial amount of technical and administrative support to the financial advisor.

On the other hand, if you wish to conduct all the research and analysis on your own, or if you use a fee-only rather than commission-based financial planner, you will probably be more inclined to look for non-broker (i.e. direct-sold) 529 plans. You will generally incur lower expenses in direct-sold plans and your program selection will not be restricted to those that pay a commission.

With some advisor-sold 529 plans, a fee-based registered investment advisor (RIA) will have access to investments at net asset value, which means that the normal sales load is waived. The RIA will typically charge you a separate fee each quarter or year based on the amount of your assets he or she is managing.

Note that many direct-sold programs are prohibited by law from providing investment advice to you because they are not offered through licensed securities representatives or RIAs.

Several states restrict participation in their direct-sold 529 plans to residents, but make their advisor-sold 529 plans open to residents of any state.

7) What is the minimum contribution?

The issue here is your ability to make at least the minimum required contribution to the 529 plan. Some programs have no minimum contributions while others have minimum contributions of $1,000 or more. Many savings programs waive the initial lump-sum minimum contribution if you commit to an automatic investment plan. In a prepaid program, the minimum contribution is the lowest-priced tuition package. But many prepaid programs also offer a monthly payment plan, albeit at a higher total cost.

8) Does the program accept contributions through payroll deduction and/or electronic funds transfer from your checking or savings account?

To contribute through payroll deduction or electronic funds transfer, make sure the program you select will accommodate it. Even if a program accepts contributions through payroll deduction, your employer must be able to meet the requirements of the program in establishing the payroll deduction process.

Many programs now permit online enrollment and contributions. This is a welcome convenience and can save time in establishing and funding a 529 account.

9) Does the 529 plan affiliate with a rewards program?

Upromise is a consumer-rewards program with a college savings tie-in. With this free service you earn rebates by making purchases from participating vendors, and you are given the option to have your rebates automatically deposited into an account at a 529 plan managed by Upromise Investments. Several credit cards, including cards available through Fidelity Investments, Union Bank & Trust Company of Lincoln, Nebraska, and Sallie Mae Bank, also offer cash-back rebates that can be automatically directed into one or more 529 plans. Participants in the Pennsylvania 529 plan are eligible for free scholarships at a number of private colleges through an arrangement with SAGE Scholars (www. sagescholars.com).

10) Does the program place any restrictions on your ownership rights or give any of these rights to the beneficiary?

Most 529 plans permit you as account owner to change the designated beneficiary, determine when and for what purpose distributions are made, and cancel the account and request a refund. But Michigan's prepaid tuition program, the Michigan Education Trust, is irrevocable and generally prohibits any refunds until after the beneficiary reaches age 18. Ownership rights affect several aspects of participation in a 529 plan, including financial-aid treatment, creditor actions, and eligibility for Medicaid, Social Security disability, food stamps and other similar programs.

11) Is an account in the program protected from the claims of creditors under state law?

A 529 plan offering special asset protection for participant accounts under state law may appeal to individuals with creditor concerns. Many states offer this protection, although the degree of protection may vary. If you are participating in a 529 plan outside your own state, discuss with an attorney how the asset protection provided by that state applies to creditor actions in your own state.

12) Can a non-owner make contributions to an account in the program?

To establish an account that other persons, including your relatives, can contribute to without opening their own accounts, the 529 plan must accommodate non-owner contributions. Nearly all now do. New York was conspicuous in denying non-owner contributions in the past, but amended its laws in 2008 to permit them, although non-owner contributions are not eligible for the New York state-income tax deduction. Many 529 plans promote the idea of contributing to someone else's 529 plan using "gift" contribution certificates. Several unaffiliated websites—including Grad-Save.com and GiftofCollege.com—also offer a friends-and-family registry service. Be sure to read and understand their rules, procedures, protections, and fees.

13) Does the program permit the account owner to designate a successor owner?

If you as account owner of a 529 plan were to die, your 529 account does not terminate. Instead, account ownership passes to a successor. Most programs make it easy for you to designate a successor owner at the time of enrollment, and permit you to submit a change in your designation at any time. If you do not designate a successor owner, the program will either automatically install a new owner at the time of your death, or pass ownership to your estate. If passed automatically, the chain of possible successors might start with the program beneficiary or your spouse, depending on the rules of the program.

14) How complete and accurate are the program disclosures?

The quality and quantity of program disclosures can vary among different 529 plans. Interests in a 529 savings program are "municipal fund securities" exempt from federal regulation; however, those distributed through broker-dealers must conform to the rules of the Municipal Securities Rule-making Board, a self-regulatory organization responsible to the Securities and Exchange Commission. Some programs offer very extensive disclosures that answer most questions, while others are not quite so complete. All 529 savings programs have agreed to follow a set of disclosure principles first issued by the College Savings Plans Network in December 2004 and revised several times since then. Because of their structure, prepaid programs are not obligated to adopt those principles. With any 529 plan, check to see how current the program disclosures are and whether updated information is available on the official program website. You may also want to judge how knowledgeable and responsive the program call center is when you ask questions by telephone. If you are working with a financial advisor, be sure the advisor is willing and able to obtain education and technical support from the broker-dealer, program manager and/or distributor.

15) How does the program report account activity to its participants?

Every 529 plan sends you a statement of your account at least annually, and many will send it more frequently. Perhaps you want online access to your account. Not all programs provide that. If you establish your account through a financial advisor, it may not appear along with other investments on your monthly or quarterly statements. However, the investment industry is making strides in capturing both 529 and non-529 investments for investors in one place through their record-keeping systems. You should also read and understand a program's privacy policy. This is usually not a concern and your account information should be exempt from any state "open document" laws (but ask if you are not sure).

Sometimes privacy concerns stem from the requirement that all accounts with the same beneficiary be aggregated when applying the program's contribution limit. You may become privy to what other family members or friends are contributing when several people are contributing to separate accounts for the same beneficiary. Some programs will even print the unused contribution limit on monthly or quarterly account statements. (Most families will not be too concerned about this issue and will probably appreciate staying informed about the unused contribution limit.)

16) Has the IRS "qualified" the program?

A formal determination of qualified status from the IRS, although not required as a condition for a state to offer a 529 plan, can provide added comfort that the program is structured in compliance with Section 529 of the Code. Several programs applied for and received favorable determinations in the past. However, the IRS is no longer issuing such determinations[1] and states must rely on the legal opinions of their attorneys.

17) How does the program handle rollovers?

Although federal tax law permits you to roll over your account to another 529 plan without federal tax or penalty under certain conditions, not all 529 plans readily accommodate rollovers. Ideally, you will be able open an account with a new 529 plan and give authorization for a direct trustee-to-trustee rollover from your existing 529 account. The transfer is completed without your further involvement, and the Form 1099-Q you receive after the end of year will indicate that the transaction was a direct transfer between plans. Some savings programs charge a small fee on an outbound rollover. You must still comply with the requirements for qualified rollovers in order for it to be tax free (see chapter 3).

---

1. IRS Rev. Proc. 2013-04, IRB 2013-01 (Jan. 2, 2013)

If the 529 plan you wish to roll into does not agree to initiate and coordinate a direct trustee-to-trustee rollover, or your existing plan refuses to send the money directly to a new plan, you can still accomplish the rollover, but you will have to take a distribution and within 60 days recontribute the funds to a new 529 plan.

In prepaid programs, your decision to transfer your investment to another 529 plan (savings or prepaid) may require a full or partial cancellation of your contract, and the financial consequences may be more significant. Be sure to investigate this before signing up with a prepaid program. If you wish to roll over an existing 529 account to a prepaid program, you will need to find out if the prepaid program accepts rollover contributions. For example, Florida's prepaid program does not.

Section 2: Investment and expense characteristics

The second section of this checklist involves an evaluation of the investment and expense characteristics of the program to determine which programs best meet your college savings objectives.

18) Does the program offer a college-savings strategy consistent with your own objectives and preferences?

This is the essential issue for most investors. What do I get for the money I contribute? How will my investment perform? How much risk am I accepting? How does it compare to other 529 plans, and to other types of investments? You will need to carefully consider what happens to your money after it is contributed to the program, and make the decision to join only after you become comfortable with its investment approach.

19) Does the 529 plan provide a "guarantee" that your investment will keep up with the increasing costs of college?

A "yes" answer is the hallmark of a 529 prepaid program or guaranteed savings program, while a "no" answer indicates a 529 savings program. A savings program will not promise that your account will keep pace with any measure of increasing college costs (with very limited exceptions, such as Alaska's program that offers an option guaranteeing a minimum return equivalent to tuition increases at the University of Alaska, but only for beneficiaries who end up attending the University of Alaska). You have the potential to do better than the college cost inflation rate, but you also have the risk of seeing your account lag behind college costs.

20) Does the 529 savings program offer an "age-based" asset allocation strategy, a menu of "static" portfolios, or both?

An age-based or matriculation-based strategy is one in which your account is automatically moved to a more conservative asset allocation over time. Typically, the age of your beneficiary will determine the portfolio in the program into which your contributions are initially placed, although it is now common that a program will base the initial portfolio on the expected number of years to matriculation rather than age, or will simply allow you to choose your starting point from any of the program's age-based portfolios.

The idea of an age-based asset allocation strategy is that you will want to be more aggressively invested when your investment time horizon is long (e.g. for a young child), and so your account will be invested primarily in stock funds. Over time, your account will gradually be shifted out of stock funds and into fixed-income and/or money market funds. It finally comes to rest in the most conservative age-based portfolio until fully withdrawn.

Savings programs manipulate their age-based asset allocations through one of the following two mechanisms. The first is by establishing a series of portfolios where each portfolio has a target asset allocation among stock, bond, and money market funds that generally does not change over time. Your account is transferred ("migrated") from one portfolio to the next at scheduled intervals. The second approach is to assign your account to a portfolio targeted to a particular year of use. Instead of moving your account from one portfolio to the next, the manager adjusts the underlying investments of the portfolio to achieve new asset allocation targets over time. Only when the target year of use is reached is the account transferred to a final "resting" portfolio.

Is one approach better than the other? Not necessarily. The first, in which your account is transferred among increasingly conservative portfolios, is more mechanical yet more disciplined. You will know "going in" how your account is to be allocated among stocks, bonds, and money market funds at any point in the future. The second approach is less mechanical and gives the portfolio investment manager a greater amount of discretion in adjusting the asset allocation for changing market conditions.

A "static" option in a savings program is one in which your portfolio's targeted asset allocation does not change over time. It can be a 100% equity option, a 100% fixed-income option, or a pre-determined blend of different asset classes. Many of the static options are assembled as "funds of funds," combining two or more underlying mutual funds within a given portfolio. These portfolios are often labeled the "asset allocation" options. An increasing number of programs now offer individual-fund portfolios in addition to multi-fund and other options.

21) Does the program offer a principal-protected option?

If you have no tolerance for downside risk with your investments, consider a savings program with an interest-bearing investment option that protects the value of your principal. There are several different types of principal-protected options found among 529 plans. Be aware that the amount of interest you earn may not keep pace with increasing college costs.

Many 529 plans offer a money market option. A money market fund consists of short-term securities and is designed to maintain a level unit price, although its dividend/interest payout can swing dramatically over a short period of time.

Some programs (including most of the programs managed by TIAA-CREF) offer "guaranteed" options that not only protect principal but guarantee a minimum level of interest. The actual rate is declared on an annual or quarterly basis and can be higher than the minimum rate.

The investment is typically backed by a "funding agreement" with a life insurance company. Another variation found in the 529 marketplace is the "stable value" investment. This is a product that seeks to combine the stable share pricing of a money market fund with the higher returns of a bond fund. By leveling the yields of its underlying fixed-income securities, it also produces less variability in overall yield.

Over a dozen states are now offering FDIC-insured bank products in their 529 savings programs, including certificates of deposit and bank savings accounts.

22) What are the other characteristics of the underlying securities in the options available under a savings program?

This book does not purport to provide a technical analysis of investments. However, you should attempt to determine the investment fundamentals of portfolios in a 529 plan (or rely on a professional who can) and see that it fits well with your other investments (retirement accounts, etc.). Ask the following questions:

- How is the portfolio allocated among stocks, bonds, and money market funds?
- How much of the portfolio is invested in international stocks, junk bonds, large-cap, medium-cap, and small-cap stocks?
- Who manages the underlying mutual funds?
- What are the track records of those funds?
- Does the program require that you develop your own "portfolio" by allocating your contributions among individual mutual funds (or permit you to do so)?

Some 529 savings programs invest in mutual funds from one particular fund family (typically an affiliate of the 529 program manager), while others are "multi-manager," incorporating funds from two or more separate fund families. Under either model, the investment history of most 529 plans has not been long enough to make conclusive comparisons, although a detailed analysis of various portfolios can yield useful information. Many 529 plans now post 529 portfolio performance on their websites with the information updated either daily, monthly, or quarterly.

23) Does the program permit contributions to be allocated among multiple options?

If the answer is "no," you will have to open separate accounts for the same beneficiary if you wish to use more than one investment option. In plans that charge an account maintenance fee, multiple accounts may mean multiple fees (see #27 below).

24) How quickly does the program invest your contribution?

Not all 529 plans possess the administrative capabilities to ensure that your contribution is invested within a day or two of when your check is received. This can be of particular concern at certain times during the year, most notably late December when a large inflow of contributions can overwhelm processing capacities. The day on which your contribution is processed can also depend on the method you use in making your contribution. For example, it may take longer to process an initial contribution using an electronic funds transfer from your bank account than one made by check.

A delay means that you will not have the benefit (or possible detriment) of market activity during that time. A program that is not managed by an outside investment firm may lack the administrative resources needed to process investments on a daily basis. For example, in the Virginia529 inVEST plan, the investment of your contribution can take several days (the "pending settlement period").

25) How are earnings in the portfolio credited to your account?

The vast majority of savings programs use daily valuation. You own "shares" of the program trust fund and the price of those shares will reflect the daily share prices of the underlying funds, along with any investment earnings and program expenses posted to the trust fund. A small number of programs use balance-forward accounting for one or more of their investment options, where earnings are posted to individual accounts on a regular basis, but not updated daily.

26) Does the program charge an enrollment fee or sales charge?

Some 529 plans charge a small enrollment fee and others do not. Sometimes the enrollment fee is waived, or the amount reduced, in particular circumstances (e.g., for state residents or during special promotions). If you open multiple accounts for the same beneficiary, or for beneficiaries in the same family, the program may offer a discount off normal enrollment fees. Because it is a fixed charge, the effect of any enrollment fee on your overall return will depend on how much money you invest in the program.

If you are enrolling in a 529 plan through a financial advisor receiving commissions, there may be a sales charge or "load" depending on which "class" of shares or units you choose to purchase. The upfront load on an "A" unit may be as little as 1% or as much as 5.75% of your contribution. "B" units typically do not involve an upfront load, but incur a "deferred" sales charge if you liquidate your investment within a certain period of time. For example, a B unit may be subject to a 5% deferred sales charge if liquidated anytime during the first year, declining in steps to 1% in year five before it drops to zero. "C" units generally are not subject to an upfront sales charge, but are often subject to a 1% deferred sales charge for the first 12 months after purchase. The price you pay for a lower C-unit sales charge structure is higher ongoing annual expense compared to A units.

For investors with substantial sums to invest through a commission-based advisor, "breakpoint" pricing is often available for A units. The upfront sales load is reduced or eliminated for account balances above certain breakpoints or for purchase commitments above those breakpoints. Some 529 plans will include the mutual funds you have in taxable accounts or IRAs with the same fund family that manages the 529 plan when determining your eligibility for breakpoints, while other 529 plans will not aggregate those accounts. If you are looking to invest substantial sums in a 529 plan, be sure to investigate your eligibility for breakpoint pricing.

27) Does the program charge an annual account maintenance fee?

An account maintenance fee is a fixed-dollar amount charged against your account on a quarterly, semi-annual, or annual basis. These fees can vary from $10 to $50 per year. In some programs, the account maintenance fee is waived if you have a specified account balance or commit to an automatic investment plan.

28) What is the program's annualized expense ratio?

The expense ratio of a savings program typically consists of two components. The first is the total of any asset-based fees charged against the value of the program fund by the outside program manager and/or state agency in charge of administering the 529 plan. The second consists of the expenses of the underlying mutual funds, which can range from very low-cost index funds to relatively high-cost international equity or other specialized sector funds. In some savings programs there is a third source of expense—certain administrative costs charged to the program fund, such as the cost of an annual audit—although these expenses tend to have a relatively small impact.

Some program managers include, or "wrap," the underlying mutual fund expenses in the management fees they charge to the 529 plan, resulting in one "all in" expense ratio that remains constant over time. The advantage to this approach is that it presents a simple and easy-to-understand fee structure, and there is no incentive for the program manager to select mutual funds with high underlying fees. A possible disadvantage is that the investor with a conservative asset allocation may be paying the same expense as the investor with an aggressive asset allocation, despite the fact that bond and money market funds generally have lower expense ratios than stock funds.

Total asset-based expenses in direct-sold 529 savings programs currently range from less than 0.10% annually to over 2%. Programs distributed through commissioned-based advisors will charge additional annual asset-based fees used to compensate the advisor. An example of this would be a program that charges an extra 0.25% annual fee for A units (along with an upfront sales load discussed above), an extra 0.90% annual fee for B units that convert to lower-cost A units after six years, and an extra 0.60% annual fee for C units that do not convert. Actual expenses vary among programs.

Considering the valuable tax benefits available with a 529 plan, and the special effort required to design, market, and administer a plan, the total fixed-dollar and asset-based expenses associated with most programs are very reasonable. But with the wide range and variety of expenses, and the significant impact they can have on your overall investment return, you should place special emphasis on expenses when choosing a 529 plan.

29) Are there charges for other transactions?

Some programs may impose a charge on beneficiary changes, account owner changes, rollovers, and certain other requests.

30) Can you claim a state income tax deduction for any or all of your contributions to the program?

Thirty-four states and the District of Columbia offer a state income tax deduction or credit for contributions to 529 plans. Most require that you use the in-state 529 plan to be eligible for the tax benefit, and depending on your state income tax bracket and any limits placed on the amount of your deduction, this can be a powerful incentive for choosing your own state's program. Arizona, Kansas, Maine, Missouri, and Pennsylvania allow a deduction for contributions to any 529 plan, not just the home-state plan. Any of these five states may ultimately reverse course and restrict deductions to their in-state programs. Some other states, however, may eventually decide to extend their deductions to contributions made to out-of-state 529 plans.

Be sure you understand how the tax deduction in your state, if any, is structured. Here are some important questions:

- If the contributor is not the same as the account owner, which person claims the deduction?
- Is there a cap on the amount of deduction that can be claimed each year? If so, is the maximum deduction computed per contributor, per tax return, per beneficiary, or per account?
- Can contributions in excess of any annual deduction limit be carried over to future tax years?
- Does the account beneficiary have to be related in any particular way to the contributor? Can you claim a deduction for an account you establish for yourself?

If your state offers a state income tax deduction, you should recognize the circumstances under which you may be required to "recapture" the tax deduction in a future year. Most states require that you recapture prior deductions if you take a nonqualified distribution, and some states will apply the recapture to outbound rollovers as well. If you can claim a deduction for only a portion of your contributions, you will need to understand the ordering rules for recapture if only a portion of your account is withdrawn for non-qualified purposes. You may find, however, that your state has not yet fully explained how recapture applies in all situations.

31) Does the program offer any other financial incentives?

Providing a state income tax break is not the only way a state can encourage participation in 529 plans. Several states offer a partial match for contributions made by low-income and moderate-income residents into their 529 savings programs. New Jersey provides a first-year scholarship of as much as $1,500 to New Jersey beneficiaries attending a New Jersey public or private university. Kentucky guarantees that beneficiaries of accounts with at least $2,400 and open at least eight years can claim resident status for Kentucky public school tuition pricing no matter where they end up residing. A number of states will disregard balances in their own 529 plans when determining student eligibility for state-funded financial aid programs.

These are all examples of how states are striving to make their programs as attractive as possible.

32) What is the term of the program manager?

The fact that a particular financial services firm has been selected to manage a 529 plan does not mean that the program will be using that manager forever. Management contracts are subject to terms of anywhere from two to 30 years. At the end of the initial program term, the contract may be extended or, if the contract is re-bid, the manager may be replaced. Naturally, in the event the manager is replaced, the program will probably look much different under the new manager.

Besides manager changes, many other aspects of a program are subject to change at any time. Thus far, most changes we have witnessed have benefited participants, but there is no guarantee that it will always be that way.

33) How popular is the program?

As a general rule, you want to join a 529 plan that has proven to be popular with other investors, or at least one that has the prospect of becoming popular. Level of assets in the program can be an indicator of popularity, although you need to consider several factors: how long the program has been around in its current form; restrictions on participation such as state residency, age, etc.; population of the sponsoring state; and whether the program is being distributed on a nationwide basis through financial advisors.

Programs must attract a sufficient level of assets in order to generate the revenues needed to pay for administration, investment management, and oversight. If the program is unable to achieve critical size, it becomes more likely that changes will be made, and these changes can be dramatic. While a replacement or addition of a program manager or changes to the investment offerings can be positive, other alterations, such as an increase in fees and expenses to cover the costs of operation, can be negative. The worst result is where the state, or the firm hired as program manager, loses its enthusiasm for the program and scales back its resources or the amount of attention it devotes.

Although it is impossible to establish a strict standard, any program at least three years old that has not yet attracted $150 million in assets can be considered small. A large 529 plan would be one with over $1 billion in assets. The largest prepaid program in the country is Florida's with over $10 billion in assets. The largest savings program currently is Virginia's CollegeAmerica, managed by American Funds, with over $35 billion at the end of 2012.

Another way to gauge program popularity is to search for articles in the local and regional press. Often, the media are able to pick up on developments or concerns by keeping tabs with state and program officials. Occasionally, a state's 529 plan becomes fodder in the political wrangling that characterizes many state legislatures and official offices.

34) Does the program rely on a state subsidy?

Most states expect their 529 programs to generate revenues sufficient to cover operating costs. A few states still find it necessary to subsidize program operations. A state subsidy to the program can help keep costs low for the participant, but budget cuts in the future may cause an increase in the fees charged to your account. Louisiana is a good example of a state that keeps fees low by paying the administrative costs for its 529 savings program out of state coffers.

Section 3: Avoidable restrictions

This third section describes restrictions or hazards that may be evident in a program but can be avoided through a timely rollover to another 529 plan without those problems. The ability to roll over your account means an unacceptable provision in any particular program should not necessarily eliminate it from contention. You simply have to recognize the appropriate time to make the rollover, and any costs associated with the rollover. Watch out especially for the contingent deferred sales charges in advisor-sold 529 plans. These charges, typically associated with the purchase of B or C units, are avoided only by keeping your money in the 529 plan for a specified number of years.

35) Are there any penalties or fees for withdrawing your money from the program?

Some programs may charge a fixed dollar fee (e.g., $50) on a nonqualified distribution which can be avoided by first rolling over to another 529 plan.

36) Are distributions from the program exempt from your state's income tax?

For most people, qualified distributions from any 529 plan are exempt from their state income taxes, and they don't have to worry about this issue when choosing a 529 plan. Alabama is the lone exception; qualified distributions from an Alabama 529 plan are exempt from Alabama tax, but qualified distributions from a non-Alabama plan are not. Legislation has been introduced in the Alabama legislature to "fix" this problem, but it had not passed by the time this book went to press. An Alabama resident using an out-of-state 529 plan may wish to roll over to the Alabama 529 plan before taking distributions to pay for college.

Also consider that you may be living in a state that exempts a distribution attributable to the beneficiary's death, disability, or receipt of a scholarship, but only when the distribution is from the in-state 529 plan. (Such distributions are taxable nonqualified distributions for federal tax purposes, although the 10 percent penalty is waived.) Under certain circumstances, you may wish to roll over from an out-of-state 529 plan to your in-state 529 plan to take advantage of this particular exemption.

37) Are there any time or age limits on the use of the account?

If the 529 plan requires that the account be used within a certain number of years, for example, simply roll over the account to another state's program prior to reaching that point.

38) Is there a minimum time period before taking qualified or nonqualified distributions from your account?

While a few states in the past placed a several-month, or several-year, minimum holding period on contributions made to their 529 savings plans, nearly all of these restrictions have since been removed. All 529 savings programs will, however, deny or delay distribution requests made within the first several days after receiving a contribution to be certain that your check clears. Because of the different manner in which 529 prepaid programs operate, many of them will require that your account be open for a certain number of years before you can receive full benefits.

39) Are there other withdrawal restrictions that can be avoided by rolling over to another 529 plan?

Here are some examples:

- Your program has cumbersome substantiation requirements of education expenses that other 529 plans may not have.
- Your program requires that the account owner be treated as the recipient of any undocumented distributions while other 529 plans give you the option of directing the distribution to your beneficiary (thereby shifting the income to a lower tax bracket).
- Your program will only pay a qualified distribution directly to the beneficiary's school, and does not give you the option of having the qualified distribution made payable to the beneficiary.

* Your program has a minimum distribution amount or limit on frequency of distributions that other programs do not have.

40) Will the program approve a request to transfer ownership of the account?

There are a number of reasons why you may decide you want to transfer ownership of your 529 account to someone else. One possibility is that an account you own may be subject to the claims of your creditors. Another possibility is that you do not want your account considered a countable asset for Medicaid purposes. Finally, you may at some point decide that you just do not want to be responsible for the management of the 529 account and would like someone else to handle it. The last two possibilities are particularly relevant for grandparents.

Some 529 plans do not approve requests for a transfer of ownership prior to your death or incapacity, or a court order in a divorce or other legal proceeding. To accomplish such a change, you would have to first roll over your account to another 529 plan that does permit owner transfers.

41) How much can be contributed to an account in the program?

One of the requirements for qualification under Section 529 is that the program establishes procedures so that participants do not contribute more than needed for the beneficiary's future qualified higher education expenses. These maximum contribution limits can vary significantly among 529 plans, with some savings programs below $250,000 per beneficiary and others approaching $400,000.

If you plan on making very large contributions, you should be sure to understand how the limit is applied. In general, the maximum contribution limit refers to the account balance which, when reached, requires the program administrator to reject further contributions. In some plans, but not typically, the account balance limit is reduced once you begin taking qualified distributions. In no case will your account be prevented from growing in value beyond the stated limit.

Many 529 plans will increase their contribution account-balance limits periodically as the cost of college attendance rises. But what do you do if the 529 plan you are interested in does not permit you to contribute as much as you think you should invest for your beneficiary's future higher education costs? The answer would be to open accounts in more than one program. Although all accounts in the same state with the same beneficiary must be aggregated, the IRS does not require that a 529 plan consider balances in other states' programs when applying its limits. Although this may seem like an easy way to get around the individual state limits, exercise caution. You are looking for trouble if you open accounts in multiple programs simply as a way to shelter more assets than you can reasonably anticipate as the amount your beneficiary will need for college and graduate school. A state that determines that you are intentionally exceeding your investment need for higher education costs can terminate your account and possibly charge extra penalties. You may also subject yourself to extra scrutiny from the IRS.

SEVEN

Income Tax Planning with 529 Plans

The three major income tax benefits associated with 529 plans—tax-deferred growth, the tax exclusion for earnings withdrawn for qualified purposes, and the possible shifting of earnings to a low-income tax bracket when withdrawn for non-qualified purposes—are explained in detail in chapter 3. Once the basic federal rules are understood, the next step is to explore income tax planning opportunities associated with 529 plans. This chapter will help you do that. Below is a discussion of several income-tax planning considerations related to 529 plans.

In which years should I take distributions from my 529 account?

Naturally, you should take distributions in years when the earnings are excluded and avoid taking distributions that generate taxable income and incur the 10 percent penalty tax. This is not as easy as it sounds. A lot will depend on when the beneficiary is attending college, the expenses that will be incurred, the amount of money in your 529 account, the amount of untaxed earnings in the account, your tax brackets, and the other tax benefits that may be available to you and your beneficiary. Fitting all the pieces together in one plan for an optimal tax result can be challenging. Be sure to consider the following:

1) American Opportunity and Lifetime Learning credits

Avoid using your 529 account to pay for 100 percent of qualifying college costs in a year when you or your beneficiary will be claiming one of these credits. Otherwise, as explained in chapter 3, claiming the credit will cause some portion of your 529 distribution to be subject to income tax. Instead, consider using other non–529 resources to pay for some of the expenses and spreading your 529 distributions between years to effectively capture qualified expenses above the amount of expenses that are applied to the credit. It is important to realize that the type of credit you claim can make a significant difference. The American Opportunity credit "consumes" up to $4,000 of tuition and related expenses while the Lifetime Learning credit consumes up to $10,000 of these expenses.

Example: Steve has a 529 account worth $40,000 for his daughter Amy. It consists of $30,000 basis and $10,000 earnings. Amy incurs qualified higher education expenses totaling $25,000 each year for four years. Assuming no further growth in the account, Steve withdraws $25,000 from his 529 account in Year 1 and the remaining $15,000 in Year 2 to pay those expenses. However, because either Steve or Amy claims the maximum $2,500 American Opportunity credit, Amy's qualified higher education expenses for 529 purposes is reduced in each of those four years by the $4,000 used to generate the credit. The $25,000 in distributions for Year 1 now consists of $21,000 in qualified distributions and $4,000 in nonqualified distributions. (The $15,000 in distributions during Year 2 remain entirely tax-free because Amy has $21,000 in qualified expenses even after the $4,000 reduction for tax-credit expenses.) The recipient of the distributions (either Steve or Amy) has to report $1,000 in income for Year 1, calculated by multiplying the account's 25% earnings ratio times the $4,000 in nonqualified distributions.

To avoid this result, Steve could have limited his 529 account distributions to $21,000 for Year 1 expenses, and used $4,000 from an education loan or other non–529 source. He would then have had an extra $4,000 to withdraw from his 529 account for Year 2 expenses. But Steve failed to talk to his accountant in time. Fortunately, the 10 percent penalty tax is waived to the extent a nonqualified distribution is caused by the tax credit adjustment. Furthermore, by making Amy or her college the recipient of the distributions, the earnings will be reported on Amy's tax return and she may be in a lower tax bracket than Steve.

2) Above-the-line deduction for tuition and fees

The tax coordination rules here are different than with the American Opportunity or Lifetime Learning credit, but the result is similar. If you are eligible to claim this deduction, realize that the pool of deductible expenses is reduced by the earnings portion of distributions from a 529 account attributable to tuition and related expenses. Some taxpayers will not be affected by this adjustment because they will incur enough in tuition to claim the $4,000 maximum deduction even after the reduction for the distributed 529 earnings.

3) Financial aid eligibility

Chapter 4 explains how parent and student income from the base year (the year prior to filing the FAFSA aid application) will cause an increase in the student's expected family contribution (EFC) and a decrease in need-based financial aid. Any action that results in reportable income—e.g. a nonqualified distribution from a 529 plan, or a capital gain from the sale of mutual funds—should be delayed to the calendar year in which the student enters the final year of school, if possible, so as not to reduce the student's financial aid package.

How do distributions from a 529 plan affect my child's status as a dependent for tax purposes?

The use of a 529 plan may affect your ability to claim the beneficiary as a dependent on your tax return and take advantage of a $3,900 (in 2013) dependency exemption. One of the tests that must be met for a dependency exemption is the support test.

The support test requires that your child cannot have provided more than one-half of his or own support during the year (to be a qualifying child) or that you furnish more than one-half of the dependent's support during the year (to be a qualifying relative). Withdrawals from a 529 account owned by you, but paid to the student or to the institution, presumably count as your child's self-support and not as support furnished by you. The contributions you made to the 529 plan were considered completed gifts at the time of contribution, under the gift-tax provisions of Section 529. Furthermore, the designated beneficiary will be the one to receive the 1099-Q.

If these distributions do not count as your support, you may fail the support test, precluding you from claiming the student as a dependent. You would also lose the ability to claim the American Opportunity credit, the Lifetime Learning credit, and the tuition and fees deduction on your tax return for your child's eligible education expenses. The credit or deduction would have to be taken on the child's own tax return where it may not do any good.

You might have a better case for treating the distribution from your 529 account as support coming from you, and not from your child, if you have the distribution made payable to you. This way, Form 1099-Q identifies you as the recipient. You then simply use the money to pay your child's college expenses. Following this approach will not deprive you of the tax exclusion for the earnings distributed from your 529 account provided you are able to substantiate the qualifying expenses to the IRS.

It is important for you to realize that the IRS has not ruled or commented on the specific question of how the use of a 529 plan impacts the support test, and that the gift-tax treatment under Code Section 529 does not necessarily control the income-tax consequences. You should seek the advice of your tax professional.

Also note that failing the dependency tests is sometimes advantageous, especially if you lose some or all of the benefit of the dependency exemption due to the alternative minimum tax or the income phase-out rules. The student will be able to claim his or her own personal exemption that may save more in taxes on the student's return than you give up in lost tax savings on your return. For 2013, the phase-out of the dependent exemption begins for married taxpayers filing jointly at an adjusted gross income of $300,000 and the exemption is phased out completely at an adjusted gross income of $422,500. The phase-out range for a single taxpayer is $250,000 to $372,500.

How will use of a 529 plan affect my state income taxes?

State tax planning can be important in getting the most tax benefits from a 529 plan. Many states provide an income tax deduction for all or a portion of your contributions to a 529 plan. Most of these states require that you use the in-state 529 plan to earn the deduction, but a small number of states have laws that permit the deduction for contributions to any state's 529 plan. Be sure you understand the rules in the state where you live.

If state deductions are available but are subject to a maximum annual amount, consider spreading out your contributions over two or more years rather than contributing one amount higher than the deduction limit. This won't be necessary in a state that allows you to carry forward your excess contributions to future tax years.

Most states allowing a deduction for contributions will require recapture of those deductions if nonqualified distributions are taken in later years. This recapture will be in addition to the earnings portion of the nonqualified distribution reportable on the state return. Be sure to understand how the recapture rules work for the 529 plan in your state. For example, some states may require that a pro-rata amount of your deduction be recaptured anytime a nonqualified distribution is taken, while others will recapture your deduction only after total nonqualified distributions exceed your non-deductible contributions into the 529 plan.

Are there any tax benefits in opening multiple accounts for my child?

Establishing multiple 529 accounts in different 529 plans can provide you with an opportunity to better control the amount and timing of distributed earnings. Each 529 account will have a different earnings ratio depending on its investment history, making it possible to take withdrawals on a selective basis. This strategy is similar to selecting certain mutual fund shares to sell based on their unrealized gains or losses. A 529 savings account established ten years prior to college is probably going to have a higher earnings ratio than an account established one year prior to college.

It may also be possible to achieve this positioning by placing different types of investments into different accounts. For example, if you seek to diversify your college savings with a 50/50 blend of stocks and bonds, consider opening one 529 account with a 100% stock portfolio and a second account in a different 529 plan with a 100% bond portfolio. Your two accounts will develop different earnings ratios as determined by their respective investment performance.

In years with sufficient qualified expenses, you would normally decide to withdraw from the account with the highest earnings ratio because the earnings will be excluded from taxable income. Withdrawals from the account with the lowest earnings ratio should be targeted for any years in which you decide to take a nonqualified distribution.

Of course, if all distributions are being used to pay for college and tax-free anyway, there is no strategic value in maintaining separate accounts. It is only when there is a nonqualified distribution producing taxable income that this can become useful.

In a down market, the isolation of asset classes in separate accounts may produce the opportunity to claim a tax loss that might not exist with a single balanced account. You could liquidate the account showing a net loss while retaining the account showing a net gain. Chapter 12 explains how

529 losses may be deducted under certain conditions on your income tax return.

These strategies will not work for multiple accounts you maintain for the same beneficiary in the same state. The IRS requires that they be aggregated in determining the earnings ratio (see chapter 3).

Should I borrow money to invest in a 529 plan?

It could make sense to fund a college savings account with borrowed money. The interest paid on the debt may produce an income tax deduction for you at a high tax bracket, while the 529 earnings may escape taxation altogether.

The tax law contains a prohibition against deducting interest on debt used to produce tax-exempt income. If you borrow money to invest in tax-free municipal bonds, for example, the interest expense on the loan is not deductible.[1] A critical question is whether the exclusion of qualified 529 distributions invokes the prohibition against deducting interest on borrowings. The answer appears to be "no," simply because the distributions are not, per-se, exempt. Unless certain hurdles are cleared the distributed earnings become taxable. However, some caution is warranted as the IRS has not yet ruled on this specific issue.

Another question to be explored in considering whether to borrow is the character of the interest expense on the loan. If the interest were considered investment interest expense, it would be deductible as an itemized deduction. (But only to the extent you have investment income. Any excess investment interest expense is carried forward indefinitely and deducted against investment income in future years.)

It is doubtful, however, that the interest on debt used to fund a 529 contribution is investment interest, despite the fact that the debt proceeds are being deposited into an investment account with the 529 plan. The IRS can take a position that the debt was incurred for personal purposes, and not for investment purposes, because the contribution into the 529 plan is treated as a gift, and gifts are personal in nature. If this is

---

1. Code Section 265(a)(2)

correct, the interest on the debt is classified as nondeductible personal interest.

In order to avoid the characterization problem, the best way to borrow for 529 funding purposes is with a home equity loan. Interest on qualifying home-equity indebtedness of up to $100,000 is deductible on Schedule A of Form 1040, no matter what use is made of the borrowed funds. The home equity loan must be on a first or second home. The interest on home-equity indebtedness used for this purpose is not deductible for purposes of the alternative minimum tax (AMT), so be careful in determining whether you are subject to the AMT.

Once you are comfortable that your home-equity loan interest can be deducted, calculate the after-tax interest rate on your loan. A taxpayer in a 30% combined tax bracket with a 4% interest loan is paying 2.8% interest after-tax (70% times 4%). The after-tax interest rate can then be compared to the expected return of your 529 account—assuming you can count on distributions being tax-free. An investment return above 2.8% in the above example means the investor is coming out ahead.

Of course, there may be many other things to think about before borrowing for this purpose. Cash flow impact is one. The loan will need to be paid back over time, while your investment presumably stays in the 529 plan until the college years. Impact on your borrowing ability for other purposes could be another consideration. And finally, there is the risk that the college savings account may not perform as well as originally anticipated, and the leveraging strategy could lose money.

What can I do if the beneficiary of my 529 account graduates from college and I still have money left in the account?

You can either withdraw the money, with the earnings portion of any withdrawal subject to federal income tax and the 10 percent penalty, or you can leave it in the account to continue growing tax-deferred. If you leave it in, you can keep the same beneficiary on the account (despite having graduated) or you can change the beneficiary to a qualifying family member.

Let's say that you no longer want to maintain the 529 account and would like the excess funds distributed. If the account beneficiary is in a lower tax bracket, you may want to request that the distribution be made to the beneficiary so that the earnings are reported in the beneficiary's name and social security number. However, you need to be careful with this strategy. If your child is subject to the kiddie tax, you will not be able to take advantage of the lower tax brackets. The kiddie tax can apply to children as old as 23 (see chapter 11).

Regardless of the recipient of a nonqualified distribution, the 10 percent federal penalty will be owed on the earnings portion of the distribution unless it is eligible for one of the penalty exceptions explained in chapter 3.

Does a 529 account have to be for college?

The obvious attraction of tax-deferred earnings may cause some investors to consider putting money into a 529 savings plan account without actually intending to use the account to pay for higher education expenses. After all, if the account is later withdrawn, the added penalty is only 10 percent applied against the earnings portion of the distribution, and a few financial calculations may suggest that the tax deferral benefits can overcome the penalty after a sufficient number of years.

Naturally, this strategy would be viewed by many as an abuse of the tax laws. Although Section 529 does not contain any explicit language that would put the individual investor at risk, the statute does assign some responsibility to the state by defining a 529 savings plan as one "under which a person may make contributions to an account which is established for the purpose of meeting the qualified higher education expenses of the designated beneficiary of the account." If investors establish accounts for a different purpose—namely the deferral of income—the tax-qualified status of the program may be in jeopardy. Some states, but certainly not all, have developed program rules that permit the program administrator to reject contributions or terminate accounts if it is determined that the account was established for a purpose other than the payment of the named beneficiary's qualified higher education expenses. The Pension Protection Act of 2006 also gives the Treasury Department additional authority to issue anti-abuse regulations in the future.

It can be argued that concerns about abuse are overblown. Many individuals are returning to school at a later age, even after retirement, and funding a 529 plan for that purpose is entirely appropriate. Even those who now have only a vague interest in returning to school may later decide to act on it once they have funds tucked away in a 529 plan account. Furthermore, the strategy of "overfunding" a 529 account for reasons of tax deferral can easily backfire. In a political environment that rewards taxable investors with low tax rates on capital gains and certain other types of investment income, the risk of having highly-taxed income and penalties on a future nonqualified 529 distribution is sufficient to cause the overwhelming majority of investors to limit their 529 contributions to truly-anticipated future college costs.

EIGHT

Estate Planning with 529 Plans

The estate and gift tax rules surrounding 529 plans are unique and the planning considerations are anything but straightforward. In fact, the gift tax provisions contained in Section 529 fly in the face of the general gift tax rules contained elsewhere in the Internal Revenue Code.

The law provides that a contribution into a 529 plan after August 5, 1997 is treated as a completed gift from the donor to the account's designated beneficiary. Further, the gift is considered a gift of a "present interest" that qualifies for the $14,000 gift tax annual exclusion, despite the fact that in nearly all 529 plans the designated beneficiary never has rights to the money.[1] The portion of the contribution covered by the $14,000 exclusion is also excluded for purposes of the generation-skipping transfer tax.

Section 529 goes one step further and provides an election that allows the donor to treat a contribution of more than the annual exclusion amount as occurring ratably over five years for gift tax purposes. This means you can contribute as much as $70,000 in 2013 to the account of

---

1. The annual gift exclusion amount is adjusted for cost of living increases, in increments of $1,000. In 2013, the exclusion amount was increased from $13,000 to $14,000.

one designated beneficiary without creating a taxable gift, assuming you make no other gifts to that beneficiary during the five-year period 2013–2017. Although not contained in the statute, the IRS takes the position that if a contribution of more than $70,000 is made to a 529 plan, the averaging election applies only to the first $70,000 and the remainder is treated as a gift in the year of contribution. The five-year election is made on the federal gift tax return, Form 709.

The value of the 529 account is excluded from your gross estate, with one possible exception. If you make the five-year election but then die before the first day of the fifth calendar year, the portion of the contribution allocated to calendar years beginning after your death is included in your estate.

Besides the five-year election, what is so unique about these rules?

The most startling aspect of the Section 529 gift and estate rules is that you can continue to exercise nearly complete control over your account. The account owner can change the designated beneficiary to another qualifying family member at will. Further, you will have the option to simply terminate the account and receive a refund of the account value, subject to income tax and a federal 10 percent additional tax on the earnings. While this rescission may defeat the purpose of removing value from an estate, it certainly provides the level of control and flexibility that many individuals seek when talking to advisors about gifting and other estate-reduction strategies.

If you change the designated beneficiary to a qualified family member, no further gift is involved, unless the new beneficiary belongs to a lower generation than the former beneficiary.[2] If the new designation crosses the generation boundary, the former beneficiary is treated as making a gift to the new beneficiary subject to all the normal gift tax rules. In this situation, the special five-year election can be made by the former beneficiary, if necessary, to minimize or avoid gift tax consequences.

---

2. The rules for determining the assignment of generation to any particular individual are contained in Code Section 2651.

Under usual estate and gift tax principles, the level of control enjoyed by the account owner would most assuredly cause the contribution to be treated as an incomplete gift and the value of the account to remain in his or her gross estate. In fact, this was precisely the treatment accorded contributions to a 529 plan from the time Section 529 was signed into law on August 20, 1996 until August 5, 1997, when it was amended by the Taxpayer Relief Act of 1997. A contribution made to a 529 plan during that one-year span was not treated as a gift. The subsequent withdrawal to pay for educational expenses was not treated as a gift either, because it was deemed to be a direct payment of tuition, and direct payments of tuition (and medical care) on behalf of another individual are not counted as gifts.[3]

How much can I remove from my estate by using a 529 plan?

Most 529 savings programs accept contributions of $300,000 or more for each child, grandchild, or other beneficiary. Contributions of this magnitude are sure to exceed the gift tax annual exclusion, even with the five-year election, and the excess will be a taxable gift. Your $5.25 million (in 2013) lifetime exemption for gifts can be employed to shelter such large contributions. To the extent you dip into your lifetime exemption for gifts, the amount of exemption for your estate (also $5.25 million) is reduced. Grandparents making substantial contributions for grandchildren must also consider the generation-skipping transfer (GST) tax. The GST exemption follows the same schedule as the estate tax exemption.

Many contributors to 529 plans will attempt to stay within the bounds of the annual exclusion. This can still add up to a substantial sum, especially with the five-year election. Consider the wealthy couple with four children. With each parent contributing $70,000 to the 529 plan account of each child in 2013, this couple can effectively remove $560,000 from their combined estates in one day without using up a single dollar of their

---

3. Code Section 2503(e) describes the exclusion for certain transfers of educational and medical expenses.

lifetime exemptions. Not only is the value of their 529 accounts removed from their taxable estates, they are invested in portfolios that can appreciate over time without the drag of income taxes. And so the estate tax savings will grow even more substantially. That's effective estate planning!

Why should I contribute to a 529 plan when I can make direct tuition payments to reduce my estate?

A grandparent may be planning to make use of the unlimited gift tax exclusion under Code Section 2503(e) for the direct payment of tuition to an educational institution. To the extent that tuition is paid with non–529 assets, the funds in a 529 plan may not be needed for college. Note, however, that the exclusion for direct payment of education expenses applies only to tuition, while a 529 plan may allow funding for all qualified higher education expenses.

There are other reasons to consider funding a 529 plan now even if you intend to make direct payments of tuition out of other funds in the future. For one, you may not live long enough to pay the tuition, and the funds you intend to target for education funding thus become subject to tax in your estate. You may be better off by funding the 529 plan and removing mortality risk as a factor.

Furthermore, you may decide that there is little harm done by funding a 529 account and later deciding to make direct tuition payments from other resources in lieu of distributions from the 529 account. An over-funded 529 account can be redirected to another beneficiary in the family, or simply refunded subject to income tax and the 10 percent penalty.

You may even have a case for arguing that the distribution of funds from a 529 plan to the beneficiary is a qualified distribution, even if tuition is paid directly from non-529 sources. The beneficiary would simply receive the distributed 529 funds without tax or penalty, to be used for any purpose. This argument rests on the fact that Section 529 contains no "tracing" rules. However, the IRS may in the future seek to impose rules restricting the free movement of 529 funds in this manner.

What happens if I am making other direct gifts to the beneficiary?

Before funding a 529 account, be sure to count up your other annual-exclusion gifts to that beneficiary. These gifts reduce the amount of annual exclusion that you can apply to 529 contributions. For example, if you normally make a cash gift of $2,000 each year to your grandchild, you will have only $12,000 left in your 2013 annual exclusion. You should limit your 529 contribution under the five-year election to $60,000 unless you are willing to exceed the exclusion amount and use part of your $5.25 million dollar lifetime exemption.

How do I make the five-year election?

You are required to file Form 709 Gift (and Generation-Skipping Transfer) Tax Return in any year that you wish to make the five-year election for your contributions to 529 plans. Form 709 is due on April 15, just like your federal income tax return, but is filed separate from your Form 1040. Make your election by checking Box B on Schedule A of Form 709. Attach an explanation to the return stating the beneficiary's name, your total 529 contributions on behalf of the beneficiary, and the amount for which the election is made.

You need only file Form 709 in the year of election. You will not have to file it for each subsequent year of the election period as long as you have no taxable gifts or generation-skipping transfers to report in those years.

If you and your spouse agree to split your gifts, one-half of your 529 plan contributions will be considered made by each of you. The five-year election, if desired by both spouses, must be made on separate gift-tax returns. Gift splitting can help keep your 529 contributions under the $14,000 annual exclusion amount (or the $70,000 five-year averaging maximum) when you and your spouse do not make equal contributions for a particular beneficiary. See the Form 709 instructions for information on the gift-splitting election.

If my child's grandparent makes contributions to a 529 account on which I am account owner, who has made the gift to my child, the grandparent or me?

Although the IRS has not yet ruled on this particular question, the gift appears to be from the contributor—the grandparent in this case—to the designated beneficiary, even if the contributor is not the account owner. Because the contributor will not retain the rights of ownership in this situation, he or she should consider establishing his or her own account instead. Some grandparents do not desire ownership and prefer to leave responsibility for the 529 account to the beneficiary's parents. In fact, it may help prevent any future problems if the grandparent ends up requiring long-term care and applying for Medicaid benefits.

What happens if the designated beneficiary dies?

Most 529 plans provide that upon the beneficiary's death, the account owner can either direct a distribution to the beneficiary's estate or substitute a new qualifying family member for the deceased beneficiary and continue the account. If nonqualified distributions are made to the beneficiary's estate, or to a substitute beneficiary, the earnings are taxable to that recipient but the 10 percent penalty tax is waived.

The IRS' 1998 proposed regulations suggest the value of the account is included in the deceased beneficiary's gross estate, despite the fact that he or she never had any control or ownership of that asset. Some tax attorneys argue that a beneficiary's gross estate should include the 529 account only where the beneficiary has rights of ownership, e.g. where the beneficiary is also the account owner.

Any future regulations are expected to contain different rules, according to the Advance Notice of Proposed Rulemaking issued by the IRS in January 2008:

  ♦ The distribution of the entire account to the estate of the beneficiary within six months of death will result in the inclusion of the account in the deceased beneficiary's gross estate.

- A change in designated beneficiary to a new beneficiary who is a member of the family of the deceased beneficiary and in the same or higher generation will result in the account not being included in the deceased beneficiary's gross estate.
- The distribution of all or part of the account to the account owner, or the failure of the account owner to name a new beneficiary by the due date for filing the deceased beneficiary's estate tax return, will result in the account not being included in the deceased beneficiary's gross estate. The account owner will be liable for income tax on the earnings distributed or deemed distributed.

Most beneficiaries of 529 accounts are young family members with few assets, so the inclusion of the asset value in the estate will usually not create a tax problem.

Other issues to be resolved

There remain a number of other questions regarding the Section 529 gift and estate tax rules that were not adequately addressed by the IRS' 1998 proposed regulations. These include the following:

- What are the gift-tax consequences when the account owner, rather than the beneficiary, receives a distribution out of a 529 account? Nothing in the proposed regulations suggests that the beneficiary reports a gift back to the account owner; nor does it appears that the initial gift, recorded at the time of contribution, is canceled or reversed. If the account owner takes the refund proceeds and re-invests in another 529 account for the same beneficiary, assuming it is not a rollover, he or she has apparently made a second gift with essentially the same dollars.
- Is there a gift-tax consequence to a transfer of account ownership? A literal reading of Code Section 529 indicates there is not. However, an estate reduction strategy involving the transfer of 529 account ownership, followed by a distribution to the new account

owner, will be deemed abusive. See chapter 12 for more discussion.

♦ Assume a contributor dies after making the five-year averaging election, and is required to include a portion of the contributions in his or her gross estate. Can the marital deduction be applied to reduce the taxable estate if account ownership is left to the contributor's spouse? You'll have to rely on an attorney's advice.

NINE

529 Plans vs. Coverdell ESAs

The Coverdell education savings account, known until mid–2001 as the Education IRA, is a direct competitor to the 529 plan, each providing families of the college-bound the opportunity for tax-free earnings. Major improvements were made to the ESA beginning with the 2002 tax year, including an increased annual contribution limit as well as the removal of a provision that prevented families from claiming the tax benefits of ESA distributions and Hope or Lifetime Learning credits in the same year. Further, the list of qualifying expenses was expanded beyond college to include primary and secondary school ("K–12") expenses, a change championed by the late Senator Paul Coverdell.

Whereas the "old" Education IRA was not easy to recommend, the new Coverdell ESA is attractive to many parents, especially those intending to send their children to private schools for grades K–12. Although many of its improvements were scheduled to expire at the end of 2012, the American Taxpayer Relief Act of 2012 made them permanent. However, a close examination will still uncover several important differences between Coverdell ESAs and 529 plans.

What is a Coverdell education savings account?

A Coverdell ESA is a trust or custodial account created exclusively to pay the qualified education expenses of a named beneficiary. Many banks, savings and loan associations, brokerage firms and mutual fund companies now offer Coverdell ESAs in addition to traditional IRAs and Roth IRAs. However, a Coverdell ESA does not require that the contributor have earned income, and does not impact your ability to contribute to a traditional or Roth IRA. Annual contributions to Coverdell ESAs may not exceed $2,000 per child and, unless the child has "special needs," may not be made after the child reaches age 18. The $2,000 contribution limit is applied on a calendar-year basis across all Coverdell ESAs for the same child. You have until April 15 to make contributions counted towards the previous year's $2,000 limit. A special provision enacted in 2008 for families of soldiers killed in action permits the rollover of a Military Death Gratuity to a Coverdell ESA without regard for the $2,000 annual contribution limit.

Any individual, including your child, can contribute to a Coverdell ESA as long as the contributor's modified adjusted gross income (MAGI) is less than $110,000 ($220,000 if filing a joint return).[1] An individual's ability to contribute up to $2,000 for any child is reduced on a ratable basis as modified AGI rises above $95,000, and is phased out completely at $110,000. For joint filers the phase-out range is $190,000 to $220,000. If you are above the income limits, there is nothing to prevent you from making a gift to someone else—probably the child—who is within the limits, followed by a contribution of your gifted funds into the Coverdell ESA. A corporation that makes contributions to a Coverdell ESA is not subject to the income limits.

What is the federal income tax treatment of a Coverdell ESA?

Although your contributions to a Coverdell ESA are not tax-deductible, any withdrawals from the account are exempt from federal tax to the extent the

---

1. MAGI means the adjusted gross income increased by certain exclusions relating to income earned abroad or received from certain American territories or possessions.

beneficiary incurs qualified education expenses during the year. Qualified education expenses include qualified higher education expenses (QHEE) and qualified elementary and secondary education expenses (QESEE). See chapter 3 for the definition of QHEE. QHEE must be reduced by any other tax-free educational benefits, including scholarship and fellowship grants and employer-provided educational assistance.

The following three categories of elementary and secondary school expenses are included in QESEE:

1) tuition, fees, academic tutoring, special needs services in the case of a special needs beneficiary, books, supplies, and other equipment which are incurred in connection with the enrollment or attendance of the designated beneficiary;

2) room and board, uniforms, transportation, and supplementary items and services (including extended day programs) which are required or provided by the school in connection with such enrollment or attendance; and

3) any computer technology or equipment or Internet access and related services, if such technology, equipment, or services are to be used by the beneficiary and the beneficiary's family during any of the years the beneficiary is in school.

If withdrawals from a Coverdell ESA exceed the qualified education expenses incurred by the beneficiary during the year, the earnings portion of the excess withdrawal is includable in the beneficiary's gross income, and an additional 10 percent penalty tax is imposed on the earnings. The earnings portion is computed by the beneficiary in the same manner that a 529 plan administrator computes the earnings portion of a 529 account distribution (see chapter 3). IRS Publication 970 (available at www.irs. gov) contains complete instructions for computing the earnings portion of withdrawals and maintaining a record of the tax basis of the account. In 2003, the IRS changed the form used for reporting Coverdell ESA withdrawals to the same form (Form 1099-Q) used for reporting 529 distributions, and proposed that the Coverdell ESA provider, rather than the individual taxpayer, keep track of tax basis. However, in Notice 2003–53, the IRS gave Coverdell administrators a reprieve by permitting Forms 1099-Q to be filed showing only gross distributions and the value of the account, and not requiring a breakdown between earnings and basis. At the time this book went to press, the reprieve was still in place.

The 10 percent penalty tax is computed on Form 5329 and paid with the beneficiary's federal income tax return. Exceptions to the penalty exist for withdrawals made on account of the beneficiary's death, disability, or receipt of a tax-free scholarship (to the extent of the scholarship value).

A state is not required to follow the federal rules described above for purposes of the state income tax, although it appears that every state except Pennsylvania currently conforms to federal treatment of the Coverdell ESA.

What is the federal gift and estate tax treatment of a Coverdell ESA?

Just like contributions to a 529 account, your contributions to a Coverdell ESA are considered completed gifts from you to the beneficiary and are eligible for the gift tax annual exclusion. Because the annual Coverdell ESA contribution limit is below the gift tax annual exclusion amount, the special five-year election (see chapter 8) normally does not come into play. However, in the rare instance where the beneficiary of the Coverdell ESA is changed to a lower-generation family member, the deemed gift rule described for 529 plans applies, and the five-year election is available if the balance at the time of the change exceeds the gift tax annual exclusion amount.

What happens if the account is not spent by the time the beneficiary graduates from college?

Any balance left in a Coverdell ESA when the beneficiary turns age 30 must be distributed within 30 days. The earnings portion is subject to income tax and the 10 percent penalty tax. The age limit does not apply to "special needs beneficiaries." Subject to the policies of the financial institution serving as trustee or custodian of the Coverdell ESA, a change in designated beneficiary may be made before age 30 without incurring tax or penalty, as long as the new beneficiary is a member of the family and under the age of 30. The definition of "member of the family" follows the definition contained in Section 529 (see chapter 3). A rollover of a withdrawal from a Coverdell ESA within 60 days into another Coverdell ESA for the beneficiary or member of the beneficiary's family under the age of 30 is permitted, but only once in a 12-month period.

A balance in a Coverdell ESA may also be withdrawn tax-free and penalty-free in a year when equal or greater contributions are made to a 529 plan for the same beneficiary. This option provides you with significant flexibility if you start out investing with a Coverdell ESA and later decide that you are better off in a 529 plan. It can also extend the deferral of earnings beyond age 30.

Who makes the decisions about investments, withdrawals, and beneficiary changes in a Coverdell ESA?

These aspects are governed by the adoption agreement used by the Coverdell ESA trustee or custodian. The IRS has made available two "model" agreements for use by financial institutions, Form 5305-EA for custodial accounts and Form 5305-E for trust accounts. Since the Coverdell ESA is established for a minor, a "responsible individual" must be named to the account. Forms 5305-EA and 5305-E generally require that the responsible individual be the beneficiary's parent or legal guardian (presumably to guard against multiple account contributions that exceed the $2,000 annual limit). However, the custodian or trustee may establish policies that permit someone besides a parent or guardian to be the responsible individual.

The contributor who opens the account makes the initial investment selection and names the responsible individual. He or she also indicates whether the responsible individual is permitted to change the designated beneficiary to another qualifying family member, and whether control of the account passes to the beneficiary when he or she reaches the legal age of majority. After the account is established, the responsible individual makes decisions as to investments, withdrawals, and beneficiary changes.

Which is better—the 529 plan or the Coverdell ESA?

Ignoring other investment alternatives, any family saving for a child's college education must decide whether their first $2,000 of savings goes into a 529 plan or into a Coverdell ESA. (Beyond $2,000 in annual contributions, the Coverdell ESA is generally not an option.) Factors to consider include the following:

- **K–12 expenses.** A Coverdell ESA can be withdrawn tax-free for qualifying elementary and secondary school expenses while a 529 account cannot be used for that purpose without incurring tax and a 10 percent penalty on the earnings. A family planning to send a child to a private school may find this feature of the Coverdell ESA very attractive. Even for children who will be attending public grade schools, the ability to use the Coverdell ESA for home computer purchases and certain other expenses may be seen as a significant advantage. Anyone home schooling his or her children must be careful; some states do not recognize this type of education as a "school."
- **Investment options and flexibility.** The financial institution that serves as custodian or trustee of a Coverdell ESA can offer the same types of investments found in individual retirement accounts (IRA), including self-directed investment accounts. Contributions may not be invested in life insurance. You may roll assets from one Coverdell ESA to another Coverdell ESA only once in a 12-month period, but the law does not restrict the number or frequency of investment changes within your current Coverdell ESA. The menu of investment options available in a 529 plan is more limited and you are permitted only one investment change or reallocation within a 529 account in any calendar year.
- **Fees and expenses.** Because Coverdell ESAs generally require less effort to administer, expenses are often lower than with an equiva-

lent amount invested in a 529 plan. Fees can vary significantly from one ESA sponsor to another, however.

- **Account ownership.** In nearly all 529 plans, you remain the owner of the account and can revoke it at any time. That is not the case with Coverdell ESAs. Distributions from a Coverdell ESA are paid directly to the beneficiary or to a guardian on behalf of the beneficiary, and should not revert to the contributor or responsible individual. If the beneficiary of a Coverdell ESA dies, the account is paid out to the beneficiary's estate unless another qualifying family member is substituted as beneficiary.

- **Financial aid.** Coverdell ESAs and 529s are treated alike in the federal financial aid formula (see chapter 4). Beginning with the 2009–10 award year, if owned by a dependent student, the account value is reportable on that student's FAFSA as a parent asset, representing a significant advantage over bank accounts and other types of student-owned investments. If owned by an independent student, the Coverdell ESA or 529 account is reportable on the FAFSA as the student's asset.[2]

- **State tax benefits.** Your state may offer you a state income tax deduction for some or even all of your contributions to a 529 plan. Currently, there are no states permitting a deduction for Coverdell ESA contributions.

- **Deduction for tuition and fees.** Section 222 of the Internal Revenue Code favors the 529 plan in prescribing coordination with the above-the-line deduction for tuition and fees. Deductible tuition and fees must be reduced by both the principal and earnings portion of any Coverdell ESA distribution used to pay those expenses, but only by the earnings portion of any 529 distribution used for the same purpose.

- **Excise tax.** If contributions to all Coverdell ESAs for a child exceed $2,000 in a year—or are made after the child reaches age 18 or by

---

2. Who "owns" a Coverdell ESA? Unlike a 529 account, which clearly has an owner separate and distinct from the beneficiary, a Coverdell ESA is maintained by an institutional custodian or trustee on behalf of the beneficiary, similar to an UGMA or UTMA account, suggesting that the student is the owner of the ESA in every case. The person named as "responsible individual" has no rights to the Coverdell ESA other than the right to direct investments and, in some accounts, to change beneficiaries.

a taxpayer who is not eligible based on modified adjusted gross income—the excess contributions are subject to a 6 percent excise tax for each year until corrected. The excise tax is computed on Form 5329 and is filed alone or, if the child is required to file an income tax return, with the child's Form 1040. An excess contribution can be corrected for the year in which it arises by removing the contribution, along with all earnings attributable to the contribution, by May 31 of the year following the year of contribution. The earnings portion of a corrective withdrawal is subject to tax on the child's tax return for the taxable year for which the contribution was made, but the 10 percent penalty is not imposed. An uncorrected excess contribution will be treated as a new contribution in the following year. With a 529 plan, the investor need not worry about federal penalties on excess contributions. Rather, the programs themselves will establish and monitor contribution limits. Any contributions beyond those limits will not be accepted by the 529 plan, or will be returned when discovered, but in any event will not subject the plan participant to a penalty.

♦ **Tax reporting.** With both the Coverdell ESA and 529 plans, the taxpayer determines the tax treatment of distributions and maintains records of qualifying expenses in the event of an IRS audit. The 529 plan administrator will keep track of your basis and compute the earnings portion of distributions when it reports them on Form 1099-Q. But with a Coverdell ESA, you may need to keep track of basis yourself. The IRS has proposed a change that would require Coverdell ESA administrators to keep track of basis, but has postponed the implementation of that change.

♦ **Asset protection.** The Bankruptcy Abuse Prevention and Consumer Protection Act of 2005 extended special protections to Coverdell ESAs and to 529 plans. The entire account[3] is exempt from the bankruptcy estate for assets contributed at least two years prior to the bankruptcy filing, while a maximum $5,000 is exempt for assets contributed between one and two years prior to filing.

---

3. The bankruptcy exclusion cannot exceed the amount needed to provide for the beneficiary's qualified higher education expenses, subject to a cost-of-living adjustment.

The account beneficiary must be a child, stepchild, grandchild, or step-grandchild of the debtor. In non-bankruptcy actions, assets in Coverdell ESAs may be better protected from creditors than assets in 529 accounts. Speak to your attorney about the laws in your state, and if you invest in an out-of-state 529 plan, how any special protections in that state might apply to you.

+ **Transfer of assets.** An advantage of the Coverdell ESA is that you can transfer Coverdell ESA assets to a 529 account without federal tax. You cannot transfer tax-free from a 529 plan to a Coverdell ESA. You may even plan for future ESA-to-529 transfers at the time you fund a Coverdell ESA. For example, in order to maximize state tax benefits in a state that caps its annual deduction for contributions to its 529 plan, you may decide to "park" your savings beyond the deduction amount in a Coverdell ESA until a later year when the transfer of those savings into the 529 plan will yield a state tax deduction. The untaxed earnings portion of the Coverdell ESA withdrawal will be recorded as earnings in your 529 account and reported as such when future distributions are made from the 529 plan. To take advantage of the ability to transfer Coverdell ESA assets, you are required to provide the 529 plan administrator with documentation that shows the earnings portion of the Coverdell ESA withdrawal.

Can I regain direct ownership of the assets in my child's Coverdell ESA by transferring these assets to my 529 account, as long as I name my child the beneficiary of the 529 account?

Although you satisfy the literal requirements for a tax-free and penalty-free transfer, you may be violating state laws designed to protect the ownership rights of your child in the Coverdell ESA. This situation is similar to assets that are owned by a minor through a custodial arrangement (UTMA or UGMA). Seek the advice of your attorney in this situation as you may be required by law to establish the 529 account in such a way as to protect the minor's ownership rights.

TEN

529 Plans vs. U.S. Savings Bonds

Under certain conditions, an owner of U.S. savings bonds may redeem those bonds and exclude the interest from income if the proceeds are used for qualified higher education expenses. These rules are contained in Section 135 of the Internal Revenue Code. Eligible bonds include Series EE bonds issued after 1989 and all Series I bonds, but only when purchased by an individual who was at least 24 years old on the first day of the month in which the bond was purchased. These eligible bonds are sometimes referred to as education savings bonds.

Savings bonds are attractive to many savers because they are backed by the full faith and credit of the U.S. government, their interest is exempt from state and local income taxes, and they are easy to purchase. Electronic bonds can be purchased directly over the Internet (www.savingsbonds. gov). They are issued in face values as low as $25. In the past, paper EE bonds were sold by financial institutions at one-half their face value, but as of January 1, 2012 paper EE bonds are no longer available.

There are limits on how much you may invest in savings bonds in any particular year. The maximum annual investment is $10,000 for electronic

Series I bonds, and $10,000 for electronic Series EE bonds. Paper I bonds may be purchased using your IRS tax refund, but are issued with a $50 minimum denomination and are subject to a $5,000 annual maximum purchase.

A Series EE bond purchased today will earn interest at a fixed rate, with rates for new issues adjusted each May 1 and November 1. Accrued interest is added to the value of the bond. EE bonds issued before May 1, 2005 are subject to different terms.

Series I bonds (known simply as I Bonds) were first issued in September 1998 and are also sold at face value. Interest is composed of a fixed rate of return plus a variable semiannual inflation rate based on the Consumer Price Index. The 30-year fixed rate on I Bonds issued between November 1, 2012 and April 30, 2013 is 0.00%. These particular bonds have an initial composite annual earnings rate of 1.76%, but adjust on each 6-month and 12-month anniversary of the issue date for a new inflation figure. The issue date is the first day of the month in which the bond was purchased.

Series EE and I bonds earn interest for up to 30 years and are redeemable after twelve months, although you forfeit three months of interest if you redeem a bond within five years of its issuance.

In order to exclude any bond interest under the Section 135 education exclusion, your income must be below a certain level in the year of redemption. In 2013, the exclusion is phased out for joint filers and surviving spouses with modified adjusted gross income between $112,050 and $142,050. The phase-out range for single taxpayers is $74,700 to $89,700. These limitations are adjusted each year for inflation. Note that your income, for purposes of the limitation, includes the entire amount of interest on redeemed savings bonds without regard to the potential exclusion. Married taxpayers filing separately do not qualify for the education exclusion.

For many taxpayers, it will be difficult to predict future income levels at the time of a bond purchase, so the bond owner may end up not being able to take the tax break anticipated at purchase. The rule requiring that you be at least 24 years old is designed to prevent you from avoiding the income limitation through issuance of bonds directly in your child's name.

The entire amount of bond redemption proceeds is compared to qualified higher education expenses in determining the amount of interest excluded from your gross income. If the redemption proceeds exceed qualifying expenses, the amount of excludable interest is reduced pro rata. The exclusion is figured on Form 8815, to be filed with your Form 1040 for the year you redeem the bonds.

"Qualified higher educational expenses" are defined differently for the bond income exclusion than for 529 plans and Coverdell education savings accounts. For the bond income exclusion, qualified higher education expenses include only tuition and fees for the bond owner or the bond owner's spouse or dependent. (A grandparent will not be able to take advantage of the exclusion except in the unusual situation where the child is the grandparent's dependent.) Also treated as qualified expenses are contributions made to a 529 plan or Coverdell ESA that names you, your spouse or your dependent as beneficiary. Qualified expenses exclude any costs for sports, games, or hobbies, unless they are incurred as part of a degree program. Total qualified expenses must be reduced by the tuition used in determining the American Opportunity credit or Lifetime Learning credit, by tax-exempt scholarships, and by qualified distributions from a 529 plan or Coverdell ESA.

Distributions from a 529 plan or Coverdell ESA can also impact your ability to take advantage of the education bond exclusion if the distributions cause your beneficiary to fail the support test for tax dependency. Chapter 7 discusses this issue with respect to 529 plans. (Coverdell ESA withdrawals are presumably included in the student's self-support.) If your child no longer qualifies as a dependent, your redemption of savings bonds to pay for the child's college expenses will be taxable.

For the college saver who appreciates the investment characteristics of savings bonds, this set of rules makes planning interesting, to say the least. And to use the bonds in conjunction with a 529 plan or Coverdell ESA is particularly challenging. After reducing your child's total tuition and related expenses by your 529 plan and Coverdell ESA distributions, there will likely be little, if any, qualified expenses to use against bond redemption proceeds. It appears the tax coordination rules will not permit you to attach your 529/ESA distributions first to non-tuition, qualified higher education expenses, such as room and board, leaving the tuition and fees for use against bond redemption proceeds.

Which is better for college savings—savings bonds or a 529 plan?

If you have to choose, the 529 plan will be the preferred vehicle for many, although a number of variables should be considered. Certainly, your anticipated future income level is an important factor because the tax break on savings bond redemptions is lost for higher-income taxpayers. If you own savings bonds but never find a way to fit within the education exclusion, the interest will be subject to federal income tax (but not state income tax) when you redeem the bonds. Your income level will not prevent you from taking advantage of the tax exclusion on 529 plan distributions.

Another obvious consideration is the gross investment return available from a U.S. savings bond versus a 529 plan. Over a long investment horizon, a 529 savings account invested in a portfolio of equity and debt securities is likely to outperform a savings bond. But the level of market risk is higher, too. A conservative investor may be more attracted to savings bonds no matter how long the targeted investment horizon happens to be, but that investor could also choose a 529 savings plan with an option that guarantees principal and interest.

A 529 prepaid program will outperform a savings bond if the value of benefits under the contract, based on future tuition increases, exceeds the interest earnings on the bond. Recent history has shown tuition inflation on average to be significantly higher than increases in the Consumer Price Index. Whether the interest premium on savings bonds, if any (the fixed rate on I Bonds purchased from November 2012 through April 2013 is zero), can close the tuition inflation gap is a question that has no certain answer.

Yet another variable is the amount of money you have available for investment. A 529 savings program can be used for certain educational expenses, such as room and board, that savings bonds cannot cover under the education exclusion.

I already have a significant investment in eligible U.S. savings bonds, but I am interested in 529 plans too. What are my options?

Since it is difficult to effectively combine the tax exclusion for savings bonds with other education tax incentives, you need to decide whether the bond education exclusion is your best bet. Fortunately, you may not need to make this decision now. The tax law permits you to claim the education exclusion on your redemption of qualifying savings bonds to the extent contributions are made to a 529 plan or Coverdell ESA that names you, your spouse, or your dependent as beneficiary. In essence, the contribution to a 529 plan or Coverdell ESA constitutes a qualified higher education expense for purposes of the education savings bond exclusion. It is important to remember, however, that you must satisfy the income requirements in the year of redemption in order to take advantage of the opportunity.

The ability to make this transfer out of savings bonds without triggering tax provides a significant degree of flexibility. In fact, you may decide to purchase qualifying savings bonds with the intent of making the transfer to a 529 plan or ESA in a future year.

Here are some situations in which the transfer should be considered:

* You currently own qualifying U.S. savings bonds and your income is within the limits this year, but the bonds are targeted for college expenses in a future year, and you expect your income to be too high in that year. By redeeming the bonds now and transferring the proceeds into a 529 plan or Coverdell ESA, you succeed in "locking in" the tax exclusion on bond interest no matter what your income level is in the future. However, the strategy will backfire if you end up taking nonqualified distributions from your 529 account after transferring the bond proceeds into the account. Not only will the deferred bond interest become subject to tax, but it will incur the 10 percent penalty tax as well.
* Similarly, you may be unsure of your ability to claim the future college student as your dependent under the various dependency tests. You may decide to make the tax-free transfer from savings bonds to a 529 plan this year while your child still qualifies as a dependent.

With a 529 plan, the dependency status of your child should no longer matter.

♦ You intend to use your qualifying savings bonds to pay college expenses for a currently enrolled child. Even though your income is within the bond exclusion limits, you discover that you will not be able to take full advantage of the exclusion because you lack sufficient qualified expenses. This can easily occur, for instance, when the tuition is absorbed by the American Opportunity or Lifetime Learning credit, or when it is reduced by qualified distributions from a 529 plan or Coverdell ESA. You will save taxes by first directing the bond redemption proceeds to a 529 plan or Coverdell ESA and then taking distributions for college expenses. Section 529 plan and Coverdell ESA withdrawals can be used to pay for certain expenses (i.e. room and board, books, supplies, and equipment) that are not considered qualified expenses under the education bond exclusion.

♦ Because Coverdell ESAs can be used for certain elementary and secondary school expenses that are not counted for the education bond exclusion, the transfer of bond redemption proceeds into a Coverdell ESA for this purpose may offer an added benefit.

I am a grandparent who owns post–1989 savings bonds and I would like to use these bonds to pay for my grandchild's college costs. Can I take advantage of the education bond exclusion?

Unfortunately, unless your grandchild is also your dependent, you do not qualify for the education bond exclusion. You will have to report the interest income on your tax return in the year you redeem the bonds even if you use the proceeds to fund a 529 plan or Coverdell ESA for the grandchild. However, there appears to be a loophole if you establish a 529 account, naming yourself as beneficiary, and redeeming eligible bonds to fund that account. You meet the literal requirements for the education bond exclusions by naming yourself beneficiary of the 529 account. Sometime later, you change the beneficiary of the 529 account to your grandchild. Be sure to discuss this strategy with your own tax professional before attempting it.

Why should I worry about qualifying for the education bond exclusion when I can avoid tax by purchasing the bonds in my child's name and reporting the accrued interest on her tax return each year?

This alternative strategy no longer works as well as it used to. Although by adopting this method of reporting your child can effectively shelter the annual bond interest accrual with her standard deduction ($1,000 in 2013), if she is subject to the kiddie tax any unearned income in excess of twice her standard deduction will be taxed at your marginal tax rate. The kiddie tax now affects children as old as 23 (see chapter 11). Your decision to report your child's accruing bond interest each year on her tax return applies to all future years unless you receive permission from the IRS to begin deferring the interest.

Also be sure to consider other aspects of placing investments in the name of your child, such as gift-tax consequences and student financial-aid impact.

Some parents who otherwise qualify for the education bond exclusion discover too late that the savings bonds were originally issued in the child's name, violating the requirement that the bonds be issued to an individual at least 24 years old. If they do not elect annual reporting of interest, the entire amount of accrued interest is taxable to the child upon redemption. It may be possible, however, to re-register the bonds in the name of the parent. Go to www.savingsbonds.gov for more information about correcting mistakes in the registration of your bonds. Also see IRS Publication 550, available online at www.irs.gov.

ELEVEN

529 Plans vs. Other Investment Alternatives

Besides 529 plans, Coverdell education savings accounts, and U.S. savings bonds, a number of other tax strategies and financial products have been popular over the years among families seeking to save for future college costs. While these alternatives may not be directly or exclusively geared to college savings, they are easily adapted for this purpose. This chapter will discuss several of these options in comparison to the 529 plan.

IRA Withdrawals Used for Higher Education Expenses

Before the Taxpayer Relief Act of 1997, an IRA withdrawal taken before the owner turned 59½ years of age and used to pay for education expenses would incur a 10 percent penalty on premature distributions. The changes made in 1997 now allow a premature IRA distribution to be taken without penalty if used to pay for the qualified higher education expenses of the taxpayer or the taxpayer's spouse, child, or grandchild. Qualified higher education expenses include the same categories of expense applicable to 529 distributions, but are reduced by the proceeds from the tax-free redemption of qualified U.S. savings bonds.

Many individuals have assets in individual retirement accounts and it is nice to know that those assets are accessible not only for retirement, but also in the event they are needed for college expenses. Note, however, that any *earnings* in an IRA will still be taxable when withdrawn for college. The *principal* portion of a distribution from a traditional IRA will also be taxable to the extent you claimed deductions for your contributions to the IRA.

A Roth IRA can be more effective than a traditional IRA when tapped for college expenses. Because contributions to a Roth IRA are not deductible, the principal will always come out tax-free. Best of all, Roth IRA distributions are first considered a nontaxable return of principal; earnings come out only after the principal is exhausted. A viable strategy is to withdraw principal for college expenses and leave the earnings to grow in the Roth IRA. Once you turn 59½ and have held the Roth IRA for at least five years, all distributions, including earnings, are tax-free.

Which investment vehicle should I use—an IRA or a 529 plan?

For many people, the answer would be the IRA, and more specifically, the Roth IRA. The Roth IRA offers federal income tax benefits equivalent to the 529 plan—even better, if you qualify for the Saver's Credit.[1] In addition, the Roth IRA withdrawn in retirement can be used for any purpose without negative consequences, whereas the 529 plan is tax-free only if used to pay qualified higher education expenses. Consider also that for

---

1. The federal Saver's Credit is targeted to low and moderate income taxpayers making contributions to a qualified retirement plan (e.g. 401k) or IRA. The credit is worth 50%, 20%, or 10%—depending on income level—of the taxpayer's contributions in any year, with a maximum annual credit of $1,000 ($2,000 for joint filers). In order to claim the credit, the taxpayer must be at least 18 years old but cannot be a full-time student or the tax dependent of another taxpayer. A single taxpayer must have income below $29,500 to claim the credit in 2013, and a married couple filing jointly must have income below $59,000.

many people the objective of funding retirement is a higher priority than funding college. Borrowing is almost always an option for college expenses but not for retirees with inadequate financial resources.

So why not forget about the 529 plan and just concentrate on using the Roth IRA? If you are not already contributing the maximum amount to a Roth IRA, perhaps you should. But the Roth IRA is subject to income limitations, just like the Coverdell ESA. Furthermore, the annual contribution limit in 2013 is only $5,500 ($6,500 under a catch-up provision for anyone age 50 and above). It also requires that you have earned income at least equal to the amount of the contribution.

For federal financial-aid purposes, an IRA or Roth IRA is a mixed blessing. The IRA balance will not be counted as part of the expected family contribution. But if IRA withdrawals were taken during the previous year, the financial aid application requires that any untaxed principal, in addition to taxable earnings that show up on the Form 1040, be added to the student's or parents' income in the formula.

You will probably find that the IRA is not the total solution to saving for your child's college expenses. Even if it were large enough to cover the cost, tapping it for college means it will not be there for your retirement. A 529 plan will probably still provide the best means to save for the largest portion of future college expenses.

Should I be funding a 529 account instead of making contributions to my employer's 401(k) plan?

Unlike an IRA, a 401(k) cannot be tapped directly for college expenses before you retire. If the plan permits you to take a loan, you could use the loan proceeds to pay college expenses, but the loan must be repaid.

Choosing between a 529 plan and your employer's 401(k) plan will depend on your own particular circumstances. As discussed above, the importance of saving for retirement may turn out to be your overriding concern and you will want to maximize any opportunity you have to contribute to qualified retirement plans. An analysis of your current and projected future tax situation can also help in your decision. With a 401(k) you are making "pre-tax" contributions—i.e. you receive an upfront tax break on your contributions—but you pay income tax down the road on the full amount of each distribution. Similar to a Roth IRA, contributions to a 529 plan are made with after-tax dollars, and qualified distributions are tax-free.

If your state offers a tax deduction for contributions into its 529 plan, you may decide that is reason enough to direct some dollars into that program. However, in most cases it will be unwise to do so if it means you will be giving up an employer match of your 401(k) contributions.

Investments in Your Child's Name

Traditional investment planning for college-bound families often includes the transfer of income-producing assets from parent to child in order to take advantage of the child's low tax bracket. When the child is under 24 years old, this planning must consider the impact of the so-called "kiddie tax." If the child is subject to the kiddie tax, investment income above $2,000 (in 2013) is taxed at the parents' top marginal tax rate. The first $1,000 of the child's investment income is fully sheltered by the standard deduction and the next $1,000 is taxed at the lowest 10 percent income tax bracket. IRS Form 8615 is used to compute the kiddie tax.

Before 2008, the kiddie tax was no longer imposed once the child reached age 18. But now it can affect individuals as old as 23 (see box on page 147). If your child has taxable investments, liquidating those investments for college and triggering capital gains may result in a tax liability based on your capital gains rate (probably 15%) rather than your child's capital gains rate (possibly 0%). Thus the decades-old strategy of gifting large amounts of money or investment securities to your child as a way to save taxes is no longer very effective.

Gifting assets to your child can also hurt his or her financial aid eligibility. As discussed in chapter 4, a student's investment assets—other than a 529 plan, Coverdell ESA, or IRA—are counted heavily in the calculation of the student's expected family contribution, or EFC. Furthermore, when investment assets are sold to pay for college the gain reported on the child's federal income tax return can reduce financial aid eligibility for the following year by as much as 50 percent of the gain.

Kiddie Tax Rules

Congress in 2008 changed the kiddie tax rules, a consequence of ongoing efforts in Washington to raise tax revenues for other initiatives. Individuals subject to the kiddie tax are required to apply their parents' marginal tax rate to unearned income (e.g. interest, dividends, capital gains, and other non-wage income) that exceeds twice the minimum standard deduction amount. In 2013, the minimum standard deduction amount is $1,000, placing the kiddie-tax threshold at $2,000. Earned income is not subject to the kiddie tax, and as much as $6,100 in earned income can be sheltered by the child's standard deduction.

Before 2006, the added tax burden was imposed only on children under the age of 14. In May 2006, Congress delayed the age of kiddie-tax emancipation from 14 to 18, retroactive to the beginning of that year. Beginning with 2008, the kiddie tax was expanded once again, to include individuals falling into any one the following three groups (with an exception for those filing a joint return or not having a living parent on the last day of the tax year):

♦ Children age 17 or under as of December 31.

♦ 18-year-olds who do not have earned income (i.e. wages) exceeding one-half of their total support.

♦ 19-to–23 year-olds who are full-time students and do not have earned income exceeding one-half of their total support.

Example: Ellen is 16 years old and does not have a job. Her parents had made gifts to a UTMA account for Ellen in previous years and in 2013 the account generates $1,200 in interest income and

$3,500 in long-term capital gains. Ellen's parents are in the 35% tax bracket. Ellen is claimed as a dependent on her parent's tax return.

♦ Under the kiddie-tax rules, the first $1,000 of Ellen's interest income is free from tax, shielded by the standard deduction for a dependent.

♦ The next $1,000 of investment income is taxed in Ellen's own tax bracket. This consists of the remaining $200 in interest income, taxed at the lowest 10% ordinary-income rate, and $800 of capital gains, which is taxed at 0% under the special rate for capital gains applicable to taxpayers in the 10% and 15% ordinary-income brackets. The remaining $2,700 of capital gains is taxed at her parents' 15% capital-gains tax rate.

♦ Ellen's total federal tax is $425.

Life Insurance and Annuities

Families are sometimes advised to invest in annuity contracts or life insurance because these assets are generally not reportable on the financial aid application. Life insurance has attractive tax features, including tax-deferred build-up of value and tax-free death benefits. Universal life insurance policies can work especially well as a college savings vehicle. They are flexible and allow parents to adjust the level of premium payments, borrow against cash value, and make partial withdrawals. A related product, variable universal life, allows the policy owner to select the underlying investments from a menu of mutual funds and provides more upside potential in the cash value build-up. If a cash-value policy is used as a college savings vehicle, it is important to start early in the child's life to allow time for the policy to build in value. A careful review of the prospectus is necessary to understand all costs and restrictions.

Annuities are insurance products sometimes chided for their low investment return as affected by mortality and expense charges, as well as for the penalties charged on withdrawal or surrender in the first five to ten years. There is an additional problem for most college parents in that annuity payments received prior to the age of 59½ are subject to a 10 percent federal tax on top of the income tax. A 529 plan will generally provide a better tax outcome when used for college expenses.

Treasury Inflation-Indexed Securities

The U.S. government promotes its Treasury Inflation-Protected Securities (TIPS) as an appropriate investment for college savings. These bonds are sold in $1,000 denominations and the principal value is adjusted upwards each year for inflation as measured by the CPI. TIPS are sold with terms of 5, 10, or 30 years. The bond's redemption value at the end of its term includes the annual inflation adjustments. The coupon rate paid semi-annually on these bonds is lower than a comparable-term regular Treasury bond, but the rate is applied to the inflation-adjusted value, so the interest paid to the bondholder increases each year. Even if you are satisfied with the yield, the tax treatment of these bonds is a disadvantage. Investors must pay federal tax each year not only on the interest payments, but also on the value increase from the inflation adjustment.

The inflation protection offered by TIPS and the tax advantages of a 529 plan might seem like an attractive combination for the safety-conscious investor interested in hedging tuition inflation. In fact, 529 savings programs in several states now offer investment options featuring TIPS, allowing you to take advantage of the benefits while avoiding the tax problems.

Zero Coupon and College Savings Bonds

Zero coupon bonds are bonds that do not pay interest but are issued at a discount to face value. The size of the discount determines the effective interest rate on the bond if held to maturity. Zero coupon bonds can be useful for college saving because maturities can be matched to the college years, and holders do not have to deal with the reinvestment of interest (unlike interest-paying bonds). The price of a zero coupon bond sold prior to maturity is affected not only by the amount of unearned interest, but also by market conditions at the time of sale. In a period of rising interest rates, the relative value of the bond will decrease.

There are several types of zero coupon bonds, each with unique tax and investment characteristics. Zero Coupon Treasury bonds are U.S. Treasury bonds or notes that have been stripped of their coupons and sold at a discount to face value. Corporations issue zero coupon bonds that provide a higher return on investment because they are subject to the risk of default (principal and earned discount could be lost). Banks may issue zero coupon certificates of deposit that are FDIC-insured up to $250,000.

Most zero coupon alternatives, including those mentioned above, suffer a disadvantage: although you don't receive the interest until redemption, you are required to report each year's earned discount in taxable income. Zero coupon municipal bonds do not present this problem because, except for the individual who has to pay state tax on an out-of-state bond, their interest is tax-exempt for federal and state purposes.

Several states have issued bonds that are specifically targeted to families saving for college. These are essentially zero coupon municipal bonds although they are often given the name of college savings bonds, baccalaureate bonds, or similar. There have been few, if any, recent issuances of these bonds due to the popularity of 529 plans.

Mutual Funds

Five main advantages are commonly cited for the use of taxable mutual funds, as opposed to 529 plans, for college savings. They are (1) potential for superior investment performance, (2) ability to direct the investments, (3) low tax rates on capital gains and dividends, (4) lower fees and expenses, and (5) ability to use the investment for any purpose without penalty. Each of these factors is examined below.

The first supposed advantage, potential for superior investment performance, is valid only when comparing taxable mutual funds to the prepaid variety of 529 plan. The 529 savings programs provide the college saver with returns directly linked to the investments in the 529 portfolios, and these investments are often the same equity mutual funds that would be attractive to the non–529 college saver. In fact, they may be even better. Taxable mutual funds are sometimes deliberately managed to achieve a "tax-efficient" result, creating a risk that investment decisions are based on tax considerations. The manager of a 529 savings program has no reason to be concerned with the tax consequences of investment activity and can focus entirely on making the best investment decisions within its asset guidelines and investment policy.

The second noted advantage of taxable mutual funds, the ability to direct investments among different funds at the discretion of the owner, will never be totally matched by 529 plans absent a change to the law. By definition, a 529 plan cannot allow the account owner to direct the investments. In actuality, the increasing number of 529 savings programs, the ever-expanding menu of investment options available, and the ability to change your investment option every year or roll over your account to another state's program once every 12 months,[2] together provide as much flexibility as most investors will ever need.

Perhaps more relevant, however, is the question of whether the ability to direct investments is an advantage or a disadvantage. Most states have hired professional money managers for their 529 plans to determine the mix of investments that should produce the best balance of risk and return for any particular beneficiary's college savings. The "age-based" options available in most 529 savings program continue to be the most popular options, offering a mechanism that automatically shifts the account to lower-risk investments as the beneficiary approaches college age, and preventing the novice investor from doing damage to his or her own savings. Of course, the age-based approach does not produce an asset allocation and investment approach that takes into account all the other components of your financial situation. A professional investment advisor or financial

---

2. See chapter 3 for a discussion of the investment flexibility now permitted under IRS Notice 2001–55.

planner can provide valuable services even if you select the age-based option, and will seek to incorporate the 529 investment into your total financial picture in an effective way.

The third perceived advantage of taxable mutual funds, low tax rates on capital gains and dividends, will generally not stand up to close scrutiny. A 2003 study published by the TIAA-CREF Institute compared after-tax accumulations of an investment in a 529 plan and a portfolio of equivalent investments (stock mutual funds) in a taxable account.[3] Assuming the investor is in the 25% federal tax bracket and a 6% state tax bracket, and that the expenses are the same under both alternatives, the study found that after 18 years the 529 investor winds up with a balance 12% higher than that of the mutual fund investor.

But what about the expenses in a 529 plan (the fourth objection listed above)? Most 529 plans charge management fees and/or account maintenance fees and these charges will reduce your overall investment return. The TIAA-CREF Institute study included a second set of calculations which assumed 529 plan expenses were 0.47% higher than taxable mutual fund expenses. The result: the advantage of the 529 plans over the 18-year investment horizon was reduced from 12% to 8%. But since that study was published, expenses in many 529 plans have dropped to a level well below 0.47%. Also, the study found that the advantage of a state income tax deduction in certain 529 plans can overcome the disadvantage of 529 program expenses.

The fifth objection is the flexibility to use mutual funds for any purpose. An investor withdrawing funds from a 529 plan for a purpose other than college suffers the consequence of reporting the earnings as ordinary income and paying an additional 10 percent penalty tax. In most cases, the investor who ends up using his 529 money for non-educational expenditures would have been better off investing in taxable mutual funds. The risk of winding up in this situation should be assessed prior to making the decision to use a 529 plan. If you do use a 529 plan, and ultimately find yourself in the position of withdrawing funds that will not be used for college, you should consider the option of directing the withdrawal to your child, not to yourself, in an effort to lessen the tax cost.

---

3. TIAA-CREF Institute, *The 2003 Tax Law's Impact on College Savings Plans, Quarterly (Summer 2003)*

Uniform Gifts or Transfers to Minors Act

The Uniform Gifts to Minors Act (UGMA), adopted in some form in all 50 states, allows assets to be transferred to a custodian for the benefit of a minor child. The child receives direct ownership of the assets upon reaching the age of majority (18 or 21) as determined under state law. The Uniform Transfers to Minors Act (UTMA), a more recent alternative to the UGMA, and available in nearly all states, works in essentially the same manner. The UTMA account is preferable in several respects, because it may stay open for a longer period of time (up to age 25 in some states), and because it can hold certain types of assets, such as real estate interests, that the UGMA account cannot. UGMA/UTMA accounts do not provide the level of control available to the donor in a 529 plan, where assets may be kept out of the hands of the beneficiary indefinitely.

Dividends, interest, or capital gains realized in an UGMA/UTMA account will be taxed to the minor beneficiary and may be subject to the kiddie tax if the child is under age 24. However, the donor, not the child, will recognize the income from an UGMA/UTMA account if it is used to satisfy the donor's legal obligation to support the minor.

You also need to be careful about the estate tax treatment of UGMA/UTMA accounts. While a contribution to a 529 plan is removed from your gross estate, UGMA/UTMA transfers will be included in your gross estate if you die while serving as custodian. To avoid this risk, you would name someone else—perhaps your spouse—as custodian at the time the account is established, thereby relinquishing your control over its management.

Can I transfer my child's existing UGMA/UTMA assets into a 529 plan?

Yes, if you are custodian and decide that a 529 plan is a better way to save, you can liquidate the current investments and reinvest the proceeds in a 529 plan. The sale of investments may generate a tax on capital gains. See checklist item #4 in chapter 6 for a description of the different ways 529 plans accommodate contributions from an existing UGMA/UTMA account. Ultimately, it is your responsibility as custodian to comply with state law in handling UGMA/UTMA funds. Some parents will be disappointed to learn that a transfer of assets to a 529 plan will not result in a transfer of ownership rights from the minor to the parent. The minor will assume direct ownership of the 529 account at the age of majority or other age established under the law. For this reason, consider spending down current UGMA/UTMA assets for the benefit of the minor, and replacing those funds by contributing your own money into a 529 plan. If you do have a 529 account for a minor under the UGMA/UTMA, establish a different account for any of your own funds.

Irrevocable Trust

A gift to an irrevocable trust allows you to maintain some level of control over the assets by dictating the terms of the trust agreement. The trust agreement could provide that your beneficiaries will receive trust corpus and income only under certain conditions. However, there are several problems with this approach. Any income retained in the trust is taxed not to you or to the trust beneficiary, but to the trust itself, at tax brackets that escalate very quickly. Also, your transfer to the trust is considered a gift of a "future interest," and does not qualify for the $14,000 gift tax annual exclusion.

You can deal with the gift tax problem by establishing a "Crummey" trust. A Crummey power allows the beneficiary to withdraw the current year's gift within a limited time period, often 30 days following the contribution of funds to the trust. The beneficiary is not expected to exercise this right. When properly drafted and executed, the transfer of property to a Crummey trust qualifies for the $14,000 gift tax annual exclusion as a gift of a present interest. Income generated by the trust may be taxed to the trust, to the beneficiary with Crummey withdrawal rights, or to the distributee of the income, depending on the circumstances.

A 529 plan offers the asset control that individuals establishing Crummey trusts are attempting to achieve, without all the complications. A

Crummey trust can invest in life insurance policies, however, which is not possible with 529 plans.

Section 2503(c) Minor's Trust

Another way to qualify the gift-in-trust for the $14,000 gift tax annual exclusion is to establish the trust under Code Section 2503(c). The so-called "minor's trust" provides the trustee total discretion to expend trust corpus and income for the benefit of the minor before he or she turns 21; the beneficiary receives any remaining balance upon reaching age 21. The estate tax and income tax consequences are variable depending on a number of factors. Section 529 plans are better than Section 2503(c) trusts for most college savers.

Section 2503(b) Income Trust

This trust requires all income to be distributed at least annually. The "income interest" will qualify for the $14,000 gift tax annual exclusion as a gift of a present interest, valued under IRS tables, while the "remainder interest" is a gift of a future interest and will not qualify for the annual exclusion. There is no requirement that the trust terminate when the beneficiary turns 21. Again, the 529 plan is superior to the 2503(b) trust in that the entire interest may be retained in the 529 plan until you decide to withdraw it, the earnings are tax-deferred and potentially tax free, and the entire contribution (not just the income interest) qualifies for the gift tax annual exclusion.

Family Partnership

A family partnership or family limited liability company can be formed to hold securities and other investments that may be targeted for college savings or any other purpose. This can be a very useful tool for transferring assets to the next generation and can provide a way to shift income, reduce a large estate, and even provide some level of creditor protection. For gift and estate tax purposes, a valuation discount may be available for the fractional partnership interest gifted to the child. This may of course be challenged by the IRS, which looks for a "business purpose" and has a particular problem with family partnerships consisting only of marketable securities and no other business assets. In addition to all the potential tax advantages of a family partnership, you can also maintain effective control of the portion of the assets that are gifted away by transferring limited partnership interests and retaining the general partnership interest. The general partner has the authority to make decisions for the partnership, including the timing and amount of distributions to the partners.

The disadvantage of family partnerships is that they must be carefully crafted and they require significant effort for annual recordkeeping and tax reporting. In addition, the Internal Revenue Code contains certain income tax provisions targeted directly at family partnerships. A full explanation of the advantages and disadvantages of a family partnership is beyond the scope of this book and anyone interested in this option should consult an attorney. Due to the expense of setting up and maintaining family partnerships, they are usually only recommended when significant assets are at stake. A 529 plan, on the other hand, is a much simpler and much less expensive way to set up a college savings program for your family.

TWELVE

Managing Your 529 Account

A parent—let's call him John—decides to use a 529 plan but wants to keep it as simple as possible. He begins by establishing an investment account, or purchasing a prepaid tuition contract, for each of his children in his state's 529 plan. As the years go by, he pays little attention to the accounts, confident they will be there to help pay for the colleges his children ultimately decide to attend. When the college bills finally roll in, John taps the entire value of each account or prepayment contract for that purpose.

For John, as well as for many others, this uncomplicated approach will produce the desired results, and even the most restrictive 529 plan can be an appropriate choice. Realize, however, that federal tax law offers a significant degree of flexibility to those utilizing 529 plans as a savings vehicle. From a planning perspective, this flexibility can be extremely attractive. It means that you are not locked into the decisions made when the account is first established. As circumstances change, you can make adjustments to ensure that the benefits of your college savings accounts are maximized.

Most 529 plans allow you to change some aspect of your account. Well-timed moves can sometimes save federal and state income taxes, estate taxes, and generation-skipping transfer taxes, and can enhance eligibility for federal financial aid as well. Even if you change nothing substantial, you may still have to make some decisions along the way in order to take full advantage of 529 plans.

The flexibility allowed under federal tax law is not fully incorporated into all 529 plans. As demonstrated in chapter 6, some programs may limit your maneuverability. Understand these limitations before selecting a 529 plan and making contributions.

Basic Account Management

Let's assume that you have decided which 529 plan to use. You used the checklist in chapter 6 or sought the guidance of your financial planner. You've read through the official program materials and understand how the program works. If it is a savings program with different investment options, you have selected the option, or combination of options, that best suits you. What else do you need to think about? There are at least three questions you face between now and the time your child graduates from college.

1) When should you make your contributions?

It may not be wise to throw every available penny into a 529 plan at your first opportunity. You may be able to do better by spreading your contributions over time to obtain the most benefit from your investment and save as much in taxes as possible. Here are some reasons why:

+ Capital gains tax. If you have to liquidate other investments to fund your 529 account, carefully consider the tax consequences. Properly timing the sale can make a difference in how much income tax you pay. Chapters 7 and 11 cover this topic in more detail.

- State tax benefits. If your state offers an income tax deduction for your contributions, or perhaps a matching grant, consider how the timing of your contributions can affect the size of the benefit. For instance, if you live in a state like New York that puts an annual cap on the amount of the deduction you can claim for contributions to its 529 plan, and does not allow you to carry over excess contributions to future years, you may want to spread your contributions over more than one year to capture a greater tax benefit.
- Gift tax. If you decide to contribute more than $14,000 to a 529 plan for a particular beneficiary, or if you are making other gifts to that individual, be careful to formulate a gifting strategy. One of your objectives may be to stay within the gift tax annual exclusion. Making the special five-year election may help you do this. For example, if you wish to maximize your contributions while staying within the gift tax annual exclusion amount so as not to use up any of your $5.25 million lifetime exemption, and it is already late in the 2013 year, consider making a $14,000 contribution this year, and waiting until the beginning of next year before contributing another $70,000. By holding off on the five-year election until 2014 you have funded your account with $84,000 in contributions free from the gift tax, rather than $70,000. (However, you will have consumed your annual exclusions going into year six rather than year five.)
- Account expenses. Consider how the timing of your contributions might affect your overall program cost. Some of the 529 savings programs charge an annual account maintenance fee, but will waive the fee if you sign up through a payroll deduction plan, agree to automatic monthly or quarterly contributions from your checking or savings account, or maintain a specified minimum account balance. With some prepaid tuition programs, the price of a prepayment contract will vary based on the age of the child, usually with older children being more expensive, but in some programs the opposite being true. Prices of prepayment contracts also usually increase over time, and procrastination can be expensive. However, you could be better off waiting until next year if you determine that the price of a prepayment contract will not increase by very much and you can

set the money aside in an interest-earning account in the meantime. In many prepaid programs, you will also need to decide whether to purchase a higher-priced contract under an installment payment plan (total payments will be more than the lump-sum cost of the contract), or a lower-priced contract now with the intent to buy additional semesters or tuition units in future years.

* Market risk. Investing in a 529 savings program is similar to investing in mutual funds. Although the concepts of modern portfolio theory are beyond the scope of this book, some experts recommend "dollar cost averaging" as a way to manage the risk of a volatile stock market. This involves making contributions at regular intervals. (A number of 529 plans now offer a dollar-cost-averaging mechanism that allows the investor to pre-program the movement of a large initial contribution into equity-based options over time.) Remember also that your college savings accounts are probably just one piece of your total investment "pie" and that you should be balancing your asset allocation across all investments. If you do not feel comfortable managing your own investments, seek the help of an investment professional.

2) When should you take distributions to pay for college costs?

In a 529 prepaid program you may not have a great deal of flexibility in the timing of your benefits because payout procedures are likely to be standardized. But this does not mean you should forget entirely about timing opportunities. The date the program makes payments to your child's school will determine the year in which the expenses are considered paid under any other tax provisions including the American Opportunity credit, the Lifetime Learning credit, and the above-the-line tuition and fees deduction. A payment of second-semester bills in January rather than December can make a significant difference in your tax liability.

With the 529 savings programs, and with most of the unit-type prepaid or guaranteed savings programs, you will have much more latitude in the timing of distributions. It is up to you to decide how to allocate your account between academic years, and when to request distributions. It appears under the current tax rules that you must carefully coordinate any cash withdrawals from your 529 savings account to fall within the same calendar year as your payment of qualifying expenses. To determine the tax consequences of your withdrawals, you will need to compare the beneficiary's total qualified expenses to total 529 withdrawals. If you pay for college costs this year, but receive your 529 plan distribution next year, you may find that you have a tax problem. The IRS may eventually develop new rules that permit some crossover in matching expenses with cash withdrawals, but any such rules would add to your recordkeeping burdens.

Keep in mind that the coordination of various tax incentives for higher education can make for very complex planning. As an example, consider that Section 529 qualified higher education expenses are reduced by expenses used to determine the American Opportunity or Lifetime Learning credit. Since the American Opportunity credit is calculated on up to $4,000 in qualified expenses, but a Lifetime Learning credit is calculated on as much as $10,000 in qualified expenses, you may find that it is better to target the 529 withdrawals to the American Opportunity credit years rather than to the Lifetime Learning credit years. The effect on the dependency support test of taking distributions from a 529 and using them for a child's education expenses is another item to be planned for. See chapter 7 for a more extensive discussion of these considerations.

3) When should you take a nonqualified distribution?

Consider taking a nonqualified distribution whenever the tax and financial aid consequences will turn out better for you than the use of your account for qualified higher education expenses. Because you will be subject to income tax and a 10 percent penalty, this tactic is not often recommended, but here are some possible scenarios where a nonqualified distribution may be beneficial:

- In many prepaid programs, the value of the contract for beneficiaries attending college out-of-state is limited to actual tuition at the institution being attended. A beneficiary who is enrolled in the prepaid program but later relocates to another state may find that public university tuition in the new state is lower than tuition in the old state. In this situation, canceling the contract might be better than using it to pay tuition at the lower rate.

+ A refund of the account might make sense when its use for qualified expenses would severely impact a grant award from the school (this would not be the case with federal financial-aid awards, as discussed in chapter 4). You will not necessarily know this until your child is close to college age and you assess the prospects for financial aid. Before applying for admission, you should ask your child's targeted colleges about their policies concerning families with 529 accounts.

+ If your account has lost value—the balance is less than cumulative net contributions—a termination and liquidation of the account may produce an income tax benefit. The loss is deductible on your tax return as a miscellaneous itemized deduction. Discuss this strategy with a tax professional before claiming such a deduction. Many taxpayers will be unable to gain tax relief from miscellaneous itemized deductions because of the 2-percent-of-adjusted-gross-income floor, or because of the alternative minimum tax.

If a nonqualified distribution produces an unwanted result, and you have no immediate need for the funds, consider simply leaving the account alone. Unless the state imposes a time restriction, an account in a 529 savings program will continue to grow tax-deferred until you decide to take distributions, and that can be many years down the road.

4) Who should be the recipient of the distribution?

Typically, you will want the 529 plan administrator to make the distribution payable to the designated beneficiary or to the school. This way, the Form 1099-Q will be issued to the beneficiary, with nothing reported on Form 1040 provided the beneficiary incurs sufficient qualified higher education expenses. By directing the payment directly to the school, you also eliminate the risk of mismatching the year of the withdrawal and the year of the qualified expenses, but you may be creating a risk that the school will adjust your child's financial aid when it receives a check from the 529 plan. (So find out from the school first!)

As discussed in chapter 3, a distribution to you, the account owner, should also qualify as tax-free to the extent the designated beneficiary on your account incurs sufficient qualified higher education expenses. However, the Form 1099-Q will be issued to you and a checkbox on the form will indicate that you were not the beneficiary, raising a potential red flag with the IRS that could complicate your life.

If any portion of the distribution is taxable because the designated beneficiary has not incurred sufficient qualified higher education expenses, your decision as to who receives the distribution becomes even more critical, because it will determine who receives the Form 1099-Q and is responsible for reporting and paying tax on the income.

It is also possible that your choice of distributee will make a difference in determining whether you may claim your child as your dependent. See chapter 7 for further explanation.

5) Should funds be withdrawn if the beneficiary receives a scholarship?

Qualified higher education expenses (QHEE) must be adjusted to exclude tuition paid for with a tax-free grant or scholarship. If you withdraw more than the adjusted amount QHEE, the excess constitutes a nonqualified distribution. Although the earnings portion of a nonqualified distribution is taxable, a distribution made on account of a tax-free scholarship, to the extent of the scholarship, is not subject to the 10 percent penalty (see IRS Form 5329). The IRS has not indicated whether the distribution must occur in the same year as the receipt of the scholarship in order to be eligible for the penalty waiver—some tax experts feel it is permissible to look for scholarships received in prior years whenever a nonqualified distribution is taken.

If the beneficiary is in a low tax bracket, directing a scholarship distribution to that beneficiary may be much less costly than ending up with too much money in your 529 plan and ultimately taking a nonqualified distribution that is subject to the 10 percent penalty. Check to see if the beneficiary will be subject to the kiddie tax (see chapter 11) before making this decision, as the earnings may end up being taxed at your bracket rather than the student's.

A similar decision must be made when you or your child can claim the American Opportunity or Lifetime Learning credit. As discussed in chapter 3, qualified higher education expenses for Section 529 purposes must be adjusted to exclude the tuition used to claim the credit. As with the scholarship exception, the taxable earnings that arise from this adjustment are not subject to the 10 percent penalty. In some situations, directing the nonqualified distribution to the beneficiary can work out nicely. The parents' income may be too high to claim the American Opportunity or Lifetime Learning credit, but they can push the credit onto their child's tax return (provided they forego the dependency exemption) where the credit may be sufficient to wipe out any income tax resulting from the nonqualified distribution.

Managing Multiple Accounts

Here are several reasons to think about opening multiple accounts for the same beneficiary:

1) *To gain state tax deductions.* If you live in Virginia, for example, multiple accounts for the same beneficiary may lead to a larger tax deduction than just one account. If you live in any other state that offers a deduction for contributions, but places an annual cap on the amount of deduction, be sure to study the tax rules to determine if you are maximizing the benefit.

2) *To diversify your investments.* While some savings programs give you ample opportunity to diversify your investments within one account by spreading your contribution among different investment options, others require that you establish multiple accounts to use more than one of

the available investment options. Further diversification can be achieved by establishing accounts in different 529 plans.

3) *To combine a prepaid program with a savings program.* Because prepaid programs typically cover tuition and fees only, it is becoming more common among those using prepaid programs to open a separate account with a savings program to pay for books, equipment, supplies, and room and board.

4) *To contribute an amount higher than the state's maximum contribution limit.* If the 529 plan you've chosen has a contribution cap of $300,000 and you intend to invest $350,000, you would have to open accounts in multiple states. However, you should not attempt to use multiple states as a way to deposit more than you can reasonably justify as necessary for your beneficiary's higher education expenses.

5) *To take advantage of a limited benefit.* Some states provide a tax deduction, or a partial match, for your contribution, subject to a dollar limit. While the incentive may persuade you to direct your first dollars into that program, you may decide to use a different 529 plan for contributions beyond the amount that secures the maximum benefit.

6) *To start the clock running.* Even if a particular 529 plan is not your first choice, you may want to open a small account in it if there are any benefits that require a minimum period of participation. For example, a 529 plan may require that your account be open for a minimum period of time before taking qualified distributions (this is not common). Or perhaps your state offers a program that allows your beneficiary to "vest" as a state resident for tuition if you have been in the 529 plans for a certain number of years. This can be a valuable benefit if your family moves out of state and sends a child back to a public university in that state.

7) *To reduce income taxes.* See chapter 7 for a discussion of how multiple accounts can be used to your advantage by permitting selective withdrawals based on each account's "earnings ratio."

Multiple accounts can mean multiple account maintenance fees, however, and in some programs will cause you to miss out on the fee waiver given to large accounts. Multiple accounts will also result in more statements and other collateral material coming your way from the programs.

Account Management Beyond the Basics

Advanced account management involves making changes to your account after you have established it. There are three basic categories of change, any one of which should be considered in the appropriate circumstances:

1) *Changing the designated beneficiary.* A beneficiary change can be made in most 529 plans simply by filling out a change form and submitting it to the plan administrator. Sometimes a fee will be charged. To avoid termination of the original account, and the triggering of income tax and penalty, the new beneficiary must qualify under the Section 529 definition of "member of the family" (see chapter 3). As an alternative to a complete change of beneficiary, the owner may be able to accomplish a partial change by establishing a separate account for the new beneficiary and transferring some funds from the first account to the second through a rollover.

2) *Changing the account owner.* Most 529 plans allow the original account owner to transfer ownership of an account to another person. These programs generally do not require that the new account owner be a member of the family or have any other specific relationship to the original owner. However, some programs do not accept a request to change account owner prior to the original owner's death or incapacity, while still others spell out procedures in limited circumstances, such as when the account owner and spouse are separated or divorced. For the most part, a change in account ownership is a tax-neutral event. However, this is an area that invites IRS scrutiny and can create tax uncertainties, especially when questions surrounding the generation-skipping transfer tax arise, or where a non-individual account owner such as a corporation, trust, or other entity is involved.

3) *Transferring balances between 529 plans.* Section 529 allows a tax-free rollover from one state's 529 plan to another state's at any time as long as the beneficiary of the receiving account is a different member of the beneficiary's family. In addition, a same-beneficiary rollover can be transacted once in any 12-month period. If your 529 account has lost value, and you wish to recognize the loss for tax purposes, you should avoid making

contributions to another 529 plan for the same beneficiary or for any other member of the beneficiary's family for at least 61 days following the liquidation of the loss account, so as to avoid rollover treatment.

The following strategies demonstrate the flexibility of 529 plans.

Strategy #1: When you are uncertain about college

Let's say you are attracted to the tax advantages and investment approach of a 529 plan, but have no specific plans to use your savings for your own or someone else's education. You, your children, your grandchildren, or some other family member might need education funds in the future, but you do not want to irrevocably commit your savings to that purpose. Consider establishing an account and naming yourself as beneficiary. If you later decide to fund a relative's college or graduate-school education, you can then change the beneficiary designation.

> *Example:* Joyce is a 50-year old grandmother with $30,000 invested in bank certificates of deposit. She is already funding her 401(k) account and Roth IRA to the maximum extent allowable, and has substantial assets in those retirement plans. Joyce decides to open an account in a 529 savings plan using the $30,000 received when her CDs mature so that she can now take advantage of tax deferral. She names herself as beneficiary of the account, with the idea of taking post-graduate classes in the future, although having no specific plans to do so. Ten years later, Joyce abandons the idea of returning to school and decides to change her 529 account beneficiary designation from herself to her grandson, who is now 11 years old. She makes the five-year averaging election so that the value of the gift (now $70,000) is covered by her gift tax annual exclusions. The account will continue to grow tax-deferred until Joyce withdraws the funds for her grandson's college expenses.
>
> Alternatively, Joyce can name her grandson as initial beneficiary of the account even if she thinks she may want to use the funds for her own education in the future. The advantage of this approach is that the value of the account is removed from her

taxable estate now, along with future earnings and appreciation. Joyce never gives up ownership and retains the right to use the account for non-educational purposes, subject to income tax and 10 percent penalty on the accumulated earnings.

With her substantial assets and a desire to shelter as much as she can from income tax and estate taxes, Joyce may decide to establish two sizable accounts: one for herself and another for her grandson. She can, for example, contribute $70,000 in 2013 to a 529 plan for her grandson and make the special five-year election for gift tax purposes. Instead of waiting until 2018 to make an additional gift-tax-free contribution to that account, she establishes a second account with herself as beneficiary. Joyce's contributions to this account can now grow tax deferred and in 2018 she can simply change the beneficiary to her grandson and remove another $70,000—or more, if inflation adjustments cause the gift tax annual exclusion to be increased—from her estate without using any of her $5 million (plus inflation adjustments) lifetime exemption.

The 529 plan administrators can refuse to accept Joyce's contributions or they can terminate the account if they determine that Joyce does not intend to use the 529 account to pay the higher education expenses of the designated beneficiary.

Strategy #2: For the family that may qualify for financial aid

Chapter 4 describes how an interest in a 529 plan may impact the student's eligibility for financial aid. Let's assume you own three accounts in a 529 plan, one for each of your three children. When your oldest child enrolls in college and files the FAFSA application, all three accounts would be reportable on the FAFSA as parent assets, assessed at a maximum 5.64% rate in determining the expected family contribution (EFC). So before the FAFSA is filed, you change the registration of the 529 accounts for your two younger children to a UTMA custodian. These accounts are now considered the siblings' assets and excluded from the older child's FAFSA. CAUTION: Do not request an owner change to a grandparent or other third party in an effort to remove assets from the FAFSA unless you are fully aware of the potential negative consequences. You no longer have any rights to the 529 account, and you expose the assets to a number of risks and uncertainties, e.g. the new owner dying, being sued, or being required to spend down the account to receive Medicaid benefits. In addition, a college financial aid administrator who feels the change in ownership was improper may use "professional judgment" to include the value of the accounts as a parent asset when determining the student's expected family contribution.

Strategy #3: For those in states offering benefits to residents in the 529 plan

If you have more to invest than your state allows as an income tax deduction, and you do not want to delay any contributions to a future year, you should consider contributing the excess amount to another state's 529 plan. In the following year, roll over to your home-state program to claim another state tax deductions. Note, however, that this particular strategy won't work if your state is one of several that restrict the deduction to non-rollover or "virgin" contributions.

If an out-of-state 529 plan is more attractive than your home state 529 plan, but your state offers a deduction for in-state contributions, you may want to direct your contributions to the in-state 529 plan and later roll over to the out-of-state 529 plan. This strategy won't work in states that require "recapture" of your deduction on outbound rollovers.

Planning for state income tax savings can be an uncertain exercise, particularly where 529 plans are concerned. Obtain the advice of a tax professional in your state.

Avoid Abusive Change Strategies in Estate Tax Planning

The rules surrounding 529 plans offer unique opportunities to reduce or eliminate estate tax, gift tax, and generation-skipping transfer tax. They also give rise to strategies that some individuals believe will allow for a large tax-free intergenerational transfer of wealth that cannot be accomplished through traditional gifting techniques. These strategies pose a challenge to the IRS as it attempts to regulate the use of Section 529, and they pose a risk to taxpayers who use them without adequately considering the consequences of an IRS challenge. For example, consider the following "loophole":

> *Example:* John wants to contribute $280,000 to a 529 plan for his son Freddy while avoiding gift taxes. He can contribute only $70,000 this year under the special five-year election without creating a taxable gift. However, John also has three nieces, so he decides to establish and fund with $70,000 a 529 account for each niece. The five-year election shelters these contributions from gift tax. John figures that he can change the beneficiary designation on those three accounts to his son whenever he wants without further consequences. Because the cousins are the same generation as his son, the changes in beneficiary are not gifts (see chapter 9).

This maneuver is an end run around the gift tax annual exclusion limits, and the IRS will probably not be happy with it. But how can this apparent abuse be distinguished from a situation where John truly intends to help fund the future college expenses of his nieces, and only because of unforeseeable circumstances does he find it necessary to later change the beneficiary to his own son?

There are similar "opportunities" to leverage the annual exclusion through other family members. For instance, John conceivably could have established 529 accounts for his own five brothers and their wives using the available annual exclusions to place hundreds of thousands of dollars into tax-deferred investment accounts, removing these assets from his estate without incurring gift tax. The substitution of his son as designated beneficiary on these accounts would be deemed a gift from these extended family members to John's son due to the difference in generations, but the gift tax annual exclusions of each of those relatives can be used to avoid gift tax consequences.

To carry this to its absurd conclusion, consider how you might try to create a tax problem for your least favorite relative.

Example: Ed never forgave his brother Sean for taking, and then losing, his baseball card collection 40 years ago and now sees an opportunity to make him pay for it. In 2013, Ed contributes $70,000 to a 529 plan, designating Sean as the account beneficiary and electing five-year treatment to avoid any gift tax consequences. As owner of the account, Ed immediately changes the beneficiary from Sean to Ed's son, Kyle. Sean is never aware of his brother's actions, which according to the IRS' proposed regulations create a gift from Sean to his nephew Kyle (Kyle belongs to a lower generation than Sean). Sean understandably fails to make the five-year election, and so has unwittingly made a taxable gift that utilizes part of his $5.25 million lifetime exemption. Ed lets Sean know about his maneuvers after it is too late to do anything about it, and Sean realizes that he has now lost some of his lifetime exemption, or even worse, has failed to report a taxable gift and now is subject to gift taxes, interest, and possible penalties.

Although donative intent is not required for the federal gift tax to apply, it seems unfair that an unsuspecting donor would end up stuck with a gift tax liability. Perhaps the final regulations under Section 529 should require that the original intended beneficiary "accept" the designation before the gift of a 529 contribution can be considered completed. Rules similar to the qualified disclaimer provisions of the Internal Revenue Code could accomplish this. In the above example, Sean would have had the opportunity to smell the trap and refuse the position of designated beneficiary.

The ability to change account owner can also lead to abuse. The mere act of transferring ownership appears to have no federal income tax or gift tax consequences. This follows the tax logic underlying Section 529, provided the 529 account is ultimately expended for the beneficiary's qualified higher education expenses. But what happens if the new account owner requests a refund of the account balance? Is there a gift tax consequence? If the answer is no, then the opportunity presents itself to transfer wealth without making a gift.

Example: Shirley is a wealthy grandmother making maximum annual exclusion gifts to her son Todd and her grandson Timmy. Todd is wealthy in his own right and making his own annual exclusion gifts to Timmy. To bypass Todd's generation and funnel more of the family wealth to her grandson, Shirley establishes a 529 account for Todd, using the money she normally gifts directly to him. Shirley then transfers ownership of the 529 account to Timmy so Timmy becomes the account owner with his father as the beneficiary. Timmy simply requests a refund from the 529 plan and receives the money without any gift tax (although generation-skipping transfer tax may still be a concern).

Example: Charlie is another wealthy individual who plays cards in Shirley's bridge club. When Charlie hears what Shirley has done with her 529 account, he decides he can go even further in transferring millions of dollars to his children simply by opening dozens of 529 accounts and naming a different friend or neighbor as designated beneficiary to each account. He fully funds each account with $70,000 under the five-year election, avoiding gift taxes. He changes the ownership of the accounts to his children, who then request refunds of the millions in assets without further transfer tax consequences.

An often-heard phrase is "if it's too good to be true, it probably is." Section 529 of the Internal Revenue Code challenges that notion, especially in the area of estate and gift taxes. There is no question that the law provides unique and unconventional benefits, but Congress has signaled its concern about the potential for tax abuse with 529 plans, and the IRS is sure to challenge any transactions similar to Shirley's and Charlie's. The best advice is to stay within reasonable bounds and remember that 529 plans are intended to be a tax-advantaged college savings vehicle, not a tax shelter.

State by State Comparisons

This section of the book contains a brief description of every 529 plan. Although a substantial effort has been made to be accurate as possible in these descriptions, they have not been approved or verified by program officials, and they are not a substitute for the official plan disclosures, application forms, and other materials available from the plan sponsors. You should read and understand the official program materials before making a decision to invest in a 529 plan.

Be aware that many states are contemplating or are in the process of making changes to their 529 plans. Please visit www.savingforcollege.com to keep up on these changes and view updated program details.

PRIVATE COLLEGE 529 PLAN

The only Section 529 qualified tuition program that operates without state involvement is the Private College 529 Plan. "PC529" offers families the opportunity to lock in tuition costs by purchasing tuition certificates at current tuition rates, redeemable at any of its more than 270 participating private colleges.

SPONSOR:	Tuition Plan Consortium LLC, a non-profit membership organization of participating colleges and universities
PROGRAM MANAGER:	OFI Private Investments Inc., an affliate of OppenheimerFunds, Inc.
529 PROGRAM TYPE:	Prepaid
TELEPHONE:	888–718–7878
WEB SITE:	www.PrivateCollege529.com

Enrollment: Enrollment is open year-round. Prices are reset each July 1. There are no state residency requirements.

Time/age restrictions: A Tuition Certificate must be held a minimum 36 months before it can be redeemed for tuition. It must be used by the 30th anniversary of its purchase or it will be canceled for the refund amount. Ownership may not be transferred except in the case of death or other involuntary transfer.

Program benefits: Tuition Certificates purchased through this program may be redeemed for a pre-determined percentage of tuition at any of more than 270 participating institutions. The particular college to be attended does not have to be identified at the time of certificate purchase. Refunds requested for any reason (including attendance at a non-participating institution) provides a return of your contributions adjusted by program fund investment performance, but not to exceed plus-or-minus 2% on an annualized basis.

Minimum contributions: $25 to open, $500 within two years.

Maximum contributions: $215,950231,350 per beneficiary, adjusting each year on July 1.

Enrollment or application fee: None

ALABAMA

In 2010, Alabama's prepaid program (PACT) was closed to new enrollments due to funding deficits. The state's two savings programs, CollegeCounts 529 Fund and CollegeCounts 529 Fund Advisor Plan, are managed by Union Bank & Trust Company, and each features a menu of investment options utilizing funds from well-known fund companies.

STATE AGENCY: Board of Trustees of CollegeCounts 529 Fund chaired by the State Treasurer for the savings programs; Prepaid Affordable College Tuition Program Board of Directors for the prepaid tuition program

State income tax treatment: Contributions to an Alabama 529 plan, including rollover contributions, of up to $5,000 per year by an individual filer, and up to $10,000 per year by married taxpayers who each make their own contributions, are deductible in computing Alabama taxable income. The contribution deadline is December 31. Qualified distributions and rollovers from an Alabama 529 plan are excluded from Alabama taxable income. Alabama is currently the only state that requires its residents to pay tax on qualified distributions received from out-of-state 529 plans. Proposed legislation would exclude such distributions. Under the Alabama recapture rules, a nonqualified withdrawal from an Alabama 529 or rollover to a non-Alabama 529 plan, plus 10 percent of the amount of the withdrawal, must be included in Alabama taxable income to the extent of prior Alabama tax deductions.

Maximum contribution limit: A contribution will not be accepted if it would cause the total of all Alabama 529 account balances for the same beneficiary to exceed $350,000.

CollegeCounts 529 Fund

529 PROGRAM TYPE: Savings
PROGRAM MANAGER: Union Bank & Trust Company
DISTRIBUTOR: Union Bank & Trust Company
TELEPHONE: 866–529–2228
WEB SITE: www.CollegeCounts529.com

Enrollment: Enroll directly with the program.

Investment options:

Option type	# of options	Underlying investments	Expense ratio [1]
Age- or enrollment-based	3 tracks	Vanguard mutual funds	0.32%–0.34%
Static multi-fund	6	Vanguard mutual funds	0.32%–0.33%
Individual fund	19	Mutual funds from Vanguard, Fidelity, PIMCO, and T. Rowe Price	0.30%–0.91%

[1] 0.25% plan fees plus underlying fund expenses.

175

Minimum contributions: No minimum contribution required.

Account maintenance fee: $12 annually. The fee is waived for Alabama residents.

- Added feature: The CollegeCounts 529 Rewards Visa Card contributes 1.529% of qualifying purchases to your account.

CollegeCounts 529 Fund Advisor Plan

529 PROGRAM TYPE:	Savings
PROGRAM MANAGER:	Union Bank & Trust Company
DISTRIBUTOR:	Northern Trust Securities, Inc.
TELEPHONE:	866–529–2228
WEB SITE:	www.CollegeCounts529advisor.com

Enrollment: Purchase through a financial advisor (unit classes A and C). Unit class F is available through fee-based financial planners.

Investment options:

Option type	# of options	Underlying investments	Unit classes	Expense ratio [1]	Maximum sales charge	
					Initial	Contingent deferred
Age- or enrollment-based	3 tracks	Mutual funds from PIMCO, BlackRock, T. Rowe Price, Northern Funds, Fidelity, American Century, William Blair Funds, Lazard, Neuberger Berman, Templeton, Touchstone, ING, Credit Suisse, DFA, Lord Abbett, and Cohen & Steers	A	0.44%–1.28%	3.50%[2]	0.00%
			C	0.44%–1.53%	0.00%	0.00%
			F	0.44%–1.03%	0.00%	0.00%
Static multi-fund	6		A	0.90%–1.28%	3.50%	0.00%
			C	1.15%–1.53%	0.00%	0.00%
			F	0.65%–1.03%	0.00%	0.00%
Individual fund	24		A	0.44%–1.87%	3.50%[2]	0.00%
			C	0.44%–2.12%	0.00%	0.00%
			F	0.44%–1.62%	0.00%	0.00%

[1] 0.42% plan fees plus underlying fund expenses and distribution/servicing fees.
[2] None on BlackRock Cash Funds 529 Porfolio or PIMCO Short-Term 529 Portfolio.

Minimum contributions: No minimum contribution required.

Account maintenance fee: $12 annually. The fee is waived for Alabama residents.

- Added feature: The CollegeCounts 529 Rewards Visa Card contributes 1.529% of qualifying purchases to your account.

Prepaid Affordable College Tuition (PACT) Program

529 PROGRAM TYPE: Prepaid
TELEPHONE: 800–252–7228
WEB SITE: www.treasury.alabama.gov

Enrollment: Currently closed to new enrollments.

Time/age restrictions: The beneficiary must be in the 9th grade or below and under the age of 18 at the time of enrollment. Contract benefits must generally be used within 10 years of the beneficiary's projected college entrance date.

Contract benefits: The program has four-year and one-year options. The four-year option pays for four years or 128 semester hours of undergraduate tuition and fees at Alabama public colleges and universities. The one-year option pays for one year or 32 semester hours of undergraduate tuition and fees at Alabama public colleges or universities. A beneficiary attending a private or out-of-state institution receives the weighted-average tuition and mandatory fees charged by public four-year institutions in Alabama for the previous fall term, not to exceed actual tuition and mandatory fees incurred.

Program status: A settlement that would reduce tuition payments for current plan participants, thereby enhancing the program's financial strength, is before the Alabama Supreme Court for approval.

Statutory state backing: None

ALASKA

The T. Rowe Price College Savings Plan is a nationally-marketed, direct-sold 529 savings program utilizing T. Rowe Price mutual funds. The University of Alaska College Savings Plan does not receive national attention, yet offers equivalent investment options plus a unique, cost-saving option called the ACT Portfolio that invests in a conservative blend of equity and fixed-income index funds and provides a tuition guarantee for beneficiaries attending UA. Alaska also offers an advisor-sold 529 plan, the John Hancock Freedom 529 program, which utilizes a multi-manager approach in its investment portfolios.

STATE AGENCY: Education Trust of Alaska

State income tax treatment: Alaska does not have a personal income tax.

Maximum contribution limit: A contribution will not be accepted if it would cause the total of all Alaska 529 account balances for the same beneficiary to exceed $320,000.

Other considerations:

- Under Alaska law, accounts in an Alaska 529 plan are exempt from claims by the account holder's or the beneficiary's creditors and are not subject to involuntary transfer or alienation (with an exception relating to certain valid child support orders).

T. Rowe Price College Savings Plan

529 PROGRAM TYPE:	Savings
PROGRAM MANAGER:	T. Rowe Price Associates, Inc.
DISTRIBUTOR:	T. Rowe Price Investment Services, Inc.
TELEPHONE:	800–369–3641
WEB SITE:	www.price529.com

Enrollment: Enroll directly. This program is not sold through financial advisors. There are no state residency requirements.

Investment options:

Option type	# of options	Underlying investments	Expense ratio[1]
Age- or enrollment-based	1 track		0.69%–0.88%
Static multi-fund	2	T. Rowe Price mutual funds	0.86%–0.88%
Individual fund	3		0.27%–0.89%

[1] 0.20% plan fees plus underlying fund expenses. The Money Market Portfolio may waive fees to maintain a 0.00% yield.

Minimum contributions: With lump-sum contributions, the minimum initial contribution is $250, and the minimum subsequent contribution is $50. With the automatic investment plan, the minimum contribution level is $50 per portfolio per month.

Account maintenance fee: $20 annually. The fee is waived for account balances of $25,000 or greater, for account balances of $75,000 or greater when combined with all other Alaska 529 accounts owned by the same person regardless of the beneficiary, and for accounts in the automatic investment plan.

University of Alaska College Savings Plan

529 PROGRAM TYPE: Savings
PROGRAM MANAGER: T. Rowe Price Associates, Inc.
DISTRIBUTOR: T. Rowe Price Investment Services, Inc.
TELEPHONE: 866–277–1005
WEB SITE: www.uacollegesavings.com

Enrollment: Enroll directly. This program is not sold through financial advisors. There are no state residency requirements.

Investment options:

Option type	# of options	Underlying investments	Expense ratio[1]
Age- or enrollment-based	1 track		0.69%–0.88%
Static multi-fund	2	T. Rowe Price mutual funds	0.86%–0.88%
ACT Portfolio	1		0.31%
Individual fund	3		0.27%–0.89%

[1] 0.20% plan fees (none for ACT Portfolio) plus underlying fund expenses. The Money Market Portfolio may waive fees to maintain a 0.00% yield.

Minimum contributions: With lump-sum contributions, the minimum initial contribution is $250, and the minimum subsequent contribution is $50. With the automatic investment plan, the minimum contribution level is $50 per portfolio per month.

Account maintenance fee: $20 annually. The fee is waived for account balances of $25,000 or greater, for account balances of $75,000 or greater when combined with all other Alaska 529 accounts owned by the same person regardless of the beneficiary, for accounts in the automatic investment plan, and for accounts with any amount invested in the ACT Portfolio option.

Added features: The program offers a minimum-return guarantee on investments in the ACT Portfolio for any beneficiary attending the University of Alaska. A non-Alaska beneficiary is also eligible for a waiver of Alaska's nonresident tuition surcharge.

John Hancock Freedom 529

529 PROGRAM TYPE: Savings
PROGRAM MANAGER: T. Rowe Price Associates, Inc.
DISTRIBUTOR: John Hancock Distributors LLC
TELEPHONE: 866–222–7498
WEB SITE: www.johnhancockfreedom529.com

Enrollment: Purchase through a financial advisor. There are no state residency requirements.

Investment options:

Option type	# of options	Underlying investments	Unit classes[1]	Expense ratio[2]	Maximum sales charge	
					Initial	Contingent deferred
Age- or enrollment-based	1 track	Mutual funds managed by T. Rowe Price, Jennison, Franklin Templeton, Robeco, OppenheimerFunds, Davis, John Hancock, American Funds, Dimensional Fund Advisors and PIMCO	A	1.28%–1.45%	5.25%	0.00%
			B	2.03%–2.20%	0.00%	5.00%
			C2	2.03%–2.20%	0.00%	0.00%
Static multi-fund	4		A	1.19%–1.55%	5.25%	0.00%
			B	1.94%–2.30%	0.00%	5.00%
			C2	1.94%–2.30%	0.00%	0.00%
Static multi-fund	3	John Hancock Funds II Lifestyle Funds	A	1.49%–1.57%	5.25%	0.00%
			B	2.24%–2.32%	0.00%	5.00%
			C2	2.24%–2.32%	0.00%	0.00%
Individual fund	8	Mutual funds from T.Rowe Price, Jennison, Franklin Templeton and American Funds	A	1.31%–1.57%	5.25%	0.00%
			B	2.06%–2.32%	0.00%	5.00%
			C2	2.06%–2.32%	0.00%	0.00%
JH Money Market Portfolio	1	T. Rowe Price Summit Cash Reserves Fund	-	0.58%	0.00%	0.00%

[1] B units automatically convert to A units on the 15th day of the first month in the seventh year.
[2] 0.40% plan fees (0.30% for JH Money Market Portfolio) plus underlying fund expenses and distribution/servicing fees.

Minimum contributions: With lump-sum contributions, the minimum initial contribution is $1,000 per portfolio, and the minimum subsequent contribution is $50 per portfolio. With the automatic investment plan, the minimum contribution level is $50 per month per portfolio.

Account maintenance fee: $25 annually. The fee is waived for account balances of $25,000 or greater, for account balances of $75,000 or greater when combined with all other accounts owned by the same person regardless of the beneficiary, and for accounts in the automatic investment plan.

ARIZONA

Arizona offers two direct-sold 529 savings programs, one managed by College Savings Bank offering FDIC-insured options, and another managed by Fidelity Investments featuring its mutual fund portfolios that include age-based, indexed and actively managed optios along with a bank savings option. A third 529 savings program, managed by Waddell & Reed and featuring Ivy Funds, is an advisor-sold option that includes age-based, static portfolios and individual fund portfolios.

STATE AGENCY: Arizona Commission for Postsecondary Education

State income tax treatment: Contributions to any Arizona or non-Arizona 529 plan of up to $750 per year for a single or head-of-household taxpayer, and $1,500 per year for a married couple filing jointly, are deductible in computing Arizona taxable income. The contribution deadline is December 31. Qualified distributions from Arizona and non-Arizona 529 plans are excluded from Arizona taxable income. Arizona follows federal tax-free treatment of rollovers. Under the Arizona recapture rules, the principal portion of nonqualified withdrawals from a 529 plan must be included in Arizona taxable income to the extent of prior Arizona tax deductions. Nonqualified withdrawals for this purpose do not include withdrawals made as the result of the beneficiary's death or disability, withdrawals made on account of the beneficiary's receipt of a scholarship, or rollovers.

Maximum contribution limit: A contribution will not be accepted if it would cause the total of all Arizona 529 account balances for the same beneficiary to exceed $374,000.

Other considerations:

* Participation in an Arizona 529 plan does not affect the beneficiary's eligibility for financial aid programs administered by the state of Arizona.

Arizona Family College Savings Program (College Savings Bank)

529 PROGRAM TYPE: Savings
PROGRAM MANAGER: College Savings Bank
DISTRIBUTOR: College Savings Bank
TELEPHONE: 800–888–2723
WEB SITE: http://arizona.collegesavings.com

Enrollment: Enroll directly or through contracted partners including certain financial advisors and financial institutions within the state of Arizona. There are no state residency requirements.

Investment options: Four types of FDIC-insured options are available: (1) the CollegeSure® CD is a variable rate certificate of deposit from College Savings Bank, with a maturity ranging from one to 22 years, that is credited with interest each year based on the previous year's college inflation rate, as measured by the change in the College Board's Independent College 500® Index (IC 500®) less an issue margin, and is subject to a maximum interest rate which is equal to the first year's interest rate plus an interest rate cap (the issue margin and interest rate cap are determined on the contribution date); (2) the InvestorSure® CD is a five-year certificate of deposit that pays

70% of the average increase in the S&P 500 Index at maturity based on a formula and is guaranteed not to lose principal; (3) Fixed Rate CDs are available in 1- and 3-year maturities. (4) The Honors™ Savings Account is a high yielding, variable rate savings account available exclusively online.

Minimum contributions:

CollegeSure® CD: With lump-sum contributions, the minimum initial contribution is $250. With the automatic investment plan, the minimum contribution level is $25 per month via electronic funds transfer, or $25 per payroll via payroll deduction. Deposits under $250 are held in an interest bearing savings account, and each time the balance reaches $250, a CD purchase is made.

InvestorSure® CD: With lump-sum contributions, the minimum initial contribution is $250. With the automatic investment plan, the minimum contribution level is $25 per month via electronic funds transfer, or $25 per pay period via payroll deduction. Deposits under $250 are held in an interest bearing savings account, and each time the balance reaches $250, a CD purchase is made on the next CD issue date.

Fixed Rate CD: With lump-sum contributions, the minimum initial contribution is $250. With the automatic investment plan, the minimum contribution level is $25 per month via electronic funds transfer, or $25 per pay period via payroll deduction. Deposits under $250 are held in an interest bearing savings account, and each time the balance reaches $250, a CD purchase is made.

Honors™ Savings Account: The minimum contribution is $250 and must be contributed by electronic check through the state 529 program website or the College Savings Bank website.

Account maintenance fee: No asset-based fees. Service-based and other fees may apply.

Ivy Funds InvestEd Plan

529 PROGRAM TYPE:	Savings
PROGRAM MANAGER:	Waddell & Reed, Inc.
DISTRIBUTORS:	Waddell & Reed, Inc.
TELEPHONE:	1-800-877-6472
WEB SITE:	www.ivyfunds.com

Enrollment: Purchase through a financial advisor. There are no state residency requirements.

Investment options:

Option type	# of options	Underlying investments	Unit classes	Expense ratio [1]	Maximum initial sales charge
Age- or enrollment-based	1 track	Waddell & Reed Advisor Funds	A	0.98%–1.17%	4.25%–5.75%
Static multi-fund	3				
Individual fund	16	Ivy Funds	E	0.78%–2.36% [2]	5.75%[3]

[1] Underlying fund expenses and distribution fees.
[2] 0.78%–1.67% with waiver of management and/or distribution fees through July 31, 2013.
[3] 2.50% for Limited-Term Bond Fund and 0.00% for Money Market Fund.

Minimum contributions: With lump-sum contributions, the minimum initial contribution is $500. With the automatic investment plan, the minimum contribution level is $50 per portfolio per month via electronic funds transfer or $25 per pay period via payroll deduction.

Account maintenance fee: $20 annually. The fee is waived for account balances of $25,000 or greater and for Arizona residents.

Fidelity Arizona College Savings Plan

529 PROGRAM TYPE:	Savings
PROGRAM MANAGER:	Fidelity Investments
DISTRIBUTOR:	Fidelity Brokerage Services LLC
TELEPHONE:	800–544–1262
WEB SITE:	www.fidelity.com/arizona

Enrollment: Enroll directly. This program is not sold through financial advisors. There are no state residency requirements.

Investment options:

Option type	# of options	Underlying investments	Expense ratio [1]
Age-based (index)	1 track		0.31%–0.35%
Age-based (active)	1 track		0.67%–1.01%
Static multi-fund (index)	3	Fidelity Investments mutual funds	0.30%–0.35%
Static multi-fund (active)	3		0.56%–1.01%
Individual fund	5		0.25%–0.57%
Age-based (multi-firm)	1 track	Mutual funds from Fidelity Investments, Acadian, Artisan, Aston, BlackRock, Causeway, Credit Suisse, Eaton Vance, Harbor, Invesco, JPMorgan, MFS, Nataxis, OppenheimerFunds, PIMCO, Royce, Western Asset, and William Blair	0.94%–1.40%
FDIC-insured	1	Wells Fargo Bank, N.A.	0.05%–0.50%

[1] 0.15% (index), 0.20% (active), or 0.35% (multi-firm) plan fees plus underlying fund expenses. Fees on Bank Deposit Portfolio are variable.

Minimum contributions: With lump-sum contributions, the minimum initial contribution is $50, and the minimum subsequent contribution is $25. With the automatic investment plan, the minimum contribution level is $15 per month or $45 per quarter.

Account maintenance fee: None

- Added feature: Accounts can be linked to the Fidelity Investments 529 Rewards American Express Card.

ARKANSAS

Arkansas' direct-sold 529 savings program is managed by Upromise Investments and features age-based and static portfolio options utilizing Vanguard mutual funds. An advisor-sold savings program, the iShares 529 Plan, was added in 2007 as the first 529 plan to exclusively feature exchange-traded funds (ETF).

STATE AGENCY: The Arkansas 529 Plan Review Committee

State income tax treatment: Contributions to an Arkansas 529 plan of up to $5,000 per year by an individual filer, and up to $10,000 per year by a married couple, are deductible in computing Arkansas taxable income. The contribution deadline is December 31. Qualified distributions from Arkansas and non-Arkansas 529 plans are excluded from Arkansas taxable income. Under the Arkansas recapture rules, the principal portion of rollovers and non-qualified withdrawals from this plan must be included in Arkansas taxable income to the extent of prior Arkansas tax deductions.

Maximum contribution limit: A contribution will not be accepted if it would cause the total of all Arkansas 529 account balances for the same beneficiary to exceed $366,000.

Other considerations:

- Under Arkansas law, an account in an Arkansas 529 plan, or any legal or beneficial interest in an account, shall not be subject to attachment, levy, or execution by any creditor of an account owner or designated beneficiary.
- Arkansas law exempts accounts in an Arkansas 529 plan when determining eligibility for Transitional Employment Assistance, Medicaid, and food stamps, provided that the federal rules for these programs permit such an exemption.
- Accounts in an Arkansas 529 plan can be linked to the Upromise Rewards Service.

GIFT College Investing Plan

529 PROGRAM TYPE:	Savings
PROGRAM MANAGER:	Upromise Investments, Inc.
DISTRIBUTOR:	Upromise Investments, Inc.
TELEPHONE:	800–587–7301
WEB SITE:	www.thegiftplan.com

Enrollment: Enroll directly. This program is not sold through financial advisors. There are no state residency requirements.

Investment options:

Option type	# of options	Underlying investments	Expense ratio
Age- or enrollment-based	3 tracks		
Static multi-fund	5	Vanguard mutual funds	0.75% [1]
Money market	1		
FDIC-insured	1	Sallie Mae High-Yield Savings Account	0.55% [2]

[1] 0.75% plan fee includes underlying fund expenses.
[2] 0.55% plan fee.

Minimum contributions: With lump-sum contributions, the minimum initial contribution is $25, and the minimum subsequent contribution is $10. With the automatic investment plan, the minimum contribution level is $10 per month via electronic funds transfer or $5 per pay period via payroll deduction. Through the free Ugift service, friends and family are invited to make contributions of at least $10 each directly to a child's account.

Account maintenance fee: $20 annually. The fee is waived for Arkansas residents.

Added feature: Under the "Aspiring Scholars Matching Grant Program," matching grants of up to $500 annually are provided to eligible Arkansas families, based on household income level. For adjusted household income of $30,000 or less, the matching rate is $2 for each $1 contributed. For income of $30,001 to $60,000, the matching rate is $1 for each $1 contributed. Applications for matching grants are accepted each year between January 1 and April 30.

iShares 529 Plan

529 PROGRAM TYPE:	Savings
PROGRAM MANAGER:	Upromise Investments, Inc.
DISTRIBUTORS:	Upromise Investments, Inc. and BlackRock Fund Distribution Company
TELEPHONE:	888-529-9552
WEB SITE:	www.iShares529.com

Enrollment: Purchase through a financial advisor in a fee-based account. There are no state residency requirements.

Investment options:

Option type	# of options	Underlying investments	Expense ratio
Age- or enrollment-based	1 track		0.55%–0.65% [1]
Static multi-fund	4	iShares ETFs	0.59%–0.64% [1]
Individual fund	16		0.50%–1.02% [2]
FDIC-insured	1	Sallie Mae High-Yield Savings Account	0.35% [3]

[1] 0.40% plan fees plus underlying fund expenses.
[2] 0.35% plan fees plus underlying fund expenses.
[3] 0.35% plan fees.

Minimum contributions: With lump-sum contributions, the minimum initial contribution is $500 and the minimum subsequent contribution is $50. With the automatic investment plan, the minimum contribution level is $50 per month via electronic funds transfer or $25 per pay period via payroll deduction.

Account maintenance fee: $10 annually. The fee is waived for account balances of $20,000 or greater.

CALIFORNIA

TIAA-CREF manages California's 529 savings program, ScholarShare. ScholarShare is a direct-sold plan featuring two age-based options; one using actively managed mutual funds and one using index mutual funds. It also offers 17 static investment options. Among the static portfolio options is a socially responsible investment option, as well as one that protects principal. California no longer offers an advisor-sold 529 plan.

STATE AGENCY: ScholarShare Investment Board

State income tax treatment: California does not offer a personal income tax deduction for contributions to 529 plans. However, qualified distributions from all 529 plans used for qualified higher education expenses at eligible educational institutions are California state and federal tax-free

Maximum contribution limit: The current maximum account balance limit for ScholarShare is $350,000 per beneficiary. The ScholarShare Investment Board is considering an increase to this limit at the March 2013 board meeting.

ScholarShare College Savings Plan

529 PROGRAM TYPE:	Savings
PROGRAM MANAGER:	TIAA-CREF Tuition Financing, Inc.
DISTRIBUTOR:	TIAA-CREF Tuition Financing, Inc.
TELEPHONE:	800–544–5428
WEB SITE:	www.scholarshare.com

Enrollment: Enroll directly. This program is not sold through financial advisors. There are no state residency requirements.

Investment options:

Option type	# of options	Underlying investments	Expense ratio [1]
Age-based (index)	1 track		0.19%–0.27%
Static multi-fund (index)	6	TIAA-CREF institutional mutual funds	0.19%–0.29%
Individual fund	4		0.18%–0.30%
Age-based (active)	1 track	Mutual funds from T. Rowe Price, TIAA-CREF, DFA, and PIMCO mutual funds	0.35%–0.61%
Static multi-fund (active)	6		0.34%–0.62%
Principal protection	1	TIAA-CREF Life Insurance Funding Agreement	0.05%–0.50%

[1] 0.10% plan fees plus underlying fund expenses, except no fee on principal protection option.

Minimum contributions: With lump-sum contributions and non-payroll automatic contributions, the minimum initial contribution is $25 per investment portfolio, and the minimum subsequent contribution is $25 per investment portfolio. Under a payroll deduction plan, the minimum contribution level per investment portfolio is $15 per payroll.

Account maintenance fee: None

COLORADO

Colorado offers three direct-sold 529 savings programs and one advisor-sold plan. Its largest direct-sold plan is the Direct Portfolio College Savings Plan, managed by Upromise Investments, which utilizes Vanguard mutual funds. The Stable Value Plus College Savings Program offers a stable-value investment through MetLife Insurance Company, and the Smart Choice College Savings Plan offers two FDIC-insured options through FirstBank. The Scholars Choice College Savings Program is managed by Legg Mason and is sold through financial advisors. Colorado's Prepaid Tuition Fund is not included in the descriptions below; it was closed to new enrollment in 2002 and is being allowed to wind down.

STATE AGENCY: CollegeInvest, a division of the Colorado Department of Higher Education

State income tax treatment: Contributions to a Colorado 529 plan in any taxable year, to the extent of the contributor's Colorado taxable income, are deductible in computing Colorado taxable income. Rollovers from another 529 plan are not eligible for the deduction. Qualified distributions from Colorado and non-Colorado 529 plans are excluded from Colorado taxable income. Under the Colorado recapture rules, the principal portion of rollovers and nonqualified distributions from a Colorado 529 plan must be included in Colorado taxable income to the extent of prior Colorado tax deductions. Nonqualified distributions for this purpose do not include withdrawals made as the result of the beneficiary's death or disability or withdrawals made on account of the beneficiary's receipt of a scholarship.

Maximum contribution limit: A contribution will not be accepted if it would cause the total of all Colorado 529 account balances for the same beneficiary to exceed $350,000.

Other considerations:

- For middle- to lower-income Colorado residents, a dollar-for-dollar match of up to $500 in contributions is provided for accounts in any of Colorado's 529 savings programs with an eligible beneficiary (a dependent under age 13 at the time of initial application). Applications are accepted each year between September 1 and December 31. The match can extend for a maximum five years. Matching grants for future years are subject to continued funding by the sponsor.
- A $2,000 scholarship is available to any full-time student who is a Colorado resident, has maintained or has had a parent/guardian maintain a CollegeInvest account for at least two years, and can substantiate an expected family contribution (EFC) of $25,000 or less. The scholarship is renewable each year up to a total of four years or $8,000. Applications are accepted January 1 through July 31.
- Under Colorado law, moneys credited to or expended from the Colorado savings trust fund by or on behalf of an account owner, depositor, or designated beneficiary of a savings contract are exempt from all claims of creditors of the account owner, depositor, and designated beneficiary.

Direct Portfolio College Savings Plan

529 PROGRAM TYPE:	Savings
PROGRAM MANAGERS:	Upromise Investments, Inc. and The Vanguard Group
DISTRIBUTORS:	Upromise Investments, Inc. and Vanguard Marketing Corporation
TELEPHONE:	800–997–4295
WEB SITE:	www.collegeinvest.org

Enrollment: Enroll directly. This program is not sold through financial advisors. There are no state residency requirements.

Investment options:

Option type	# of options	Underlying investments	Expense ratio [1]
Age- or enrollment-based	3 tracks		
Static multi-fund	5	Vanguard mutual funds	0.46%
Individual fund	3		

[1] 0.46% plan fee includes underlying fund expenses. Shown net of current 0.04% voluntary waiver of state administrative fee.

Minimum contributions: The minimum initial contribution is $25, and the minimum subsequent contribution is $15.

Account maintenance fee: $20 annually. The fee is waived for Colorado and Wyoming residents, for accounts with balances greater than $10,000, and for account owners electing electronic delivery of all plan documents.

Added feature: Accounts can be linked to the Upromise Rewards Service.

Scholars Choice College Savings Program

529 PROGRAM TYPE:	Savings
PROGRAM MANAGER:	Legg Mason, Inc.
DISTRIBUTOR:	Legg Mason Investor Services LLC
TELEPHONE:	Clients & Operational Questions: 888–572–4652
FINANCIAL ADVISOR SALES QUESTIONS:	800-544-7835
WEB SITE:	www.scholars-choice.com

Enrollment: Purchase through a financial advisor. There are no state residency requirements.

Investment options:

Option type [3]	# of options	Underlying investments	Unit classes[1]	Expense ratio [2]	Maximum sales charge	
					Initial	Contingent deferred
Age- or enrollment-based	2 tracks		A	0.66%–1.14%	3.50%	0.00%
			B	1.36%–1.84%	0.00%	2.50%
			C	1.16%–1.64%	0.00%	0.00%
			0	1.09%	0.00%	0.00%
Static multi-fund	5	Mutual funds managed by Legg Mason-affiliated companies and Thornburg	A	0.78%–1.21%	3.50%	0.00%
			B	1.48%–1.91%	0.00%	2.50%
			C	1.28%–1.71%	0.00%	0.00%
			0	1.09%	0.00%	0.00%
Individual fund	5		A	0.96%–1.60%	3.50%	0.00%
			C	1.46%–2.10%	0.00%	0.00%
			0	1.09%	0.00%	0.00%
Money market	1	Western Asset Institutional Cash Reserves	A,B,C,0	1.09%	0.00%	0.00%

[1] B units automatically convert to A units at the end of the 8th year. As of 9/12/11, B shares are closed to investments.
[2] 0.10% plan fees plus underlying fund expenses and distribution/servicing fees. Does not reflect current 0.04% voluntary reduction in state administrative fee.
[3] The U.S. Treasury Zero-Coupon Bond Target Maturity Portfolios were discontinued on April 15, 2013.

Minimum contributions: The minimum initial contribution is $250 and the minimum subsequent contribution is $50. The minimum initial contribution is waived for employer-sponsored arrangements and systematic electronic funds transfers at the time of account opening.

Account maintenance fee: $20 annually. The fee is waived for Colorado residents and for account balances of $2,500 or greater.

Stable Value Plus College Savings Program

529 PROGRAM TYPE:	Savings
PROGRAM MANAGER:	MetLife Insurance Company
DISTRIBUTOR:	MetLife Insurance Company
TELEPHONE:	800-478-5651
WEB SITE:	www.collegeinvest.org

Enrollment: Enroll directly. This program is not sold through financial advisors. There are no state residency requirements.

Investment: A stable value investment under a funding agreement with MetLife Insurance Company. The interest crediting rate is declared annually.

Minimum contributions: $25

Account maintenance fee: None

Smart Choice College Savings Plan

529 PROGRAM TYPE:	Savings
PROGRAM MANAGER:	FirstBank Holding Company
DISTRIBUTOR:	FirstBank
TELEPHONE:	800-964-3444
WEB SITE:	www.collegeinvest.org

Enrollment: Enroll through a FirstBank branch location or online at www.efirstbank.com. There are no state residency requirements.

Investment: Two FDIC-insured options are offered, the One-Year Time Savings Account and the Money Market Savings Account.

Minimum contributions: No minimums.

Account maintenance fee: None

CONNECTICUT

Connecticut offers a direct-sold 529 savings program without residency restrictions, managed by TIAA-CREF, and an advisor-sold savings program restricted to Connecticut residents, managed by Hartford Life.

STATE AGENCY: Connecticut State Treasurer

State income tax treatment: Contributions to a Connecticut 529 plan of up to $5,000 per year by an individual filer, and up to $10,000 per year by a married couple filing jointly, are deductible in computing Connecticut taxable income. The contribution deadline is December 31. Contributions in excess of annual limits may be carried over and taken as deductions for up to five years. Rollover contributions are not deductible. Qualified distributions from Connecticut and non-Connecticut 529 plans are excluded from Connecticut taxable income. A beneficiary receiving a nonqualified distribution from the Connecticut 529 plan may subtract from Connecticut income any earnings reported on the federal income tax return. Rollovers and nonqualified distributions do not require recapture of prior Connecticut deductions.

Maximum contribution limit: A contribution will not be accepted if it would cause the total of all Connecticut 529 account balances for the same beneficiary to exceed $300,000.

Connecticut Higher Education Trust (CHET)

529 PROGRAM TYPE:	Savings
PROGRAM MANAGER:	TIAA-CREF Tuition Financing, Inc.
DISTRIBUTOR:	Connecticut State Treasurer's Office
TELEPHONE:	888–799–2438
WEB SITE:	www.aboutchet.com

Enrollment: Enroll directly. This program is not sold through financial advisors. There are no state residency requirements.

Investment options:

Option type	# of options	Underlying investments	Expense ratio
Age- or enrollment-based	3 tracks	Mutual funds from TIAA-CREF, DFA, Templeton, GE, T. Rowe Price, Thornburg and GMO	0.37%–0.43%
Static multi-fund	4		0.29%–0.87%
Individual fund	3		0.32%–0.38%
Principal protection	1	Funding agreement with TIAA-CREF Life Insurance Company	0.00%

[1] 0.19% plan fees plus underlying fund expenses. None for the Principal Plus Interest Option.

Minimum contributions: $25 per investment option, or $15 per investment option per pay period via payroll deduction.

Account maintenance fee: None

CHET Advisor College Savings Plan

529 PROGRAM TYPE:	Savings
PROGRAM MANAGER:	Hartford Life Insurance Company
DISTRIBUTOR:	The Hartford Financial Services, LLC
TELEPHONE:	877-407-2828
WEB SITE:	www.HartfordInvestor.com

Enrollment: Purchase through a financial advisor (unit classes A and C). Unit class E is available through fee-based financial planners. The account owner must have a Connecticut mailing address or be a Connecticut resident on active duty in the U.S. armed forces.

Investment options:

Option type	# of options	Underlying investments	Unit classes	Expense ratio[1]	Maximum sales charge	
					Initial	Contingent deferred
Age- or enrollment-based	1 track	Hartford mutual funds; ETFs managed by Invesco and State Street	A	1.12%–1.29%	3.00%–5.50%	0.00%
			C	1.87%–2.04%	0.00%	1.00%
			E	0.87%–1.04%	0.00%	0.00%
Static multi-fund	5		A	1.16%–1.35%	3.00%–5.50%	0.00%
			C	1.91%–2.10%	0.00%	1.00%
			E	0.91%–1.10%	0.00%	0.00%
Individual fund	10	Hartford mutual funds	A	1.08%–1.57%	3.00%–5.50%	0.00%
			C	1.83%–2.32%	0.00%	1.00%
			E	0.83%–1.32%	0.00%	0.00%
Money market	1		A	1.07%[2]	0.00%	0.00%
			C	1.82%[2]	0.00%	0.00%
			E	0.82%[2]	0.00%	0.00%

[1] 0.32% plan fees plus underlying fund expenses and distribution/servicing fees.
[2] Expense ratio is 0.52% net of plan manager and distribution fees currently being waived.

Minimum contributions: With lump-sum contributions, the minimum initial contribution is $50, and the minimum subsequent contribution is $25. With the automatic contribution plan, the minimum contribution level is $25.

Account maintenance fee: None

DELAWARE

Delaware's 529 savings program is managed by Fidelity Investments. Two sets of age-based and static investment options are available, one investing in actively-managed Fidelity mutual funds and the other investing in Fidelity index funds. A bank savings option is also available.

STATE AGENCY: Delaware State Treasurer

State income tax treatment: Contributions are not deductible on Delaware income tax returns. Qualified distributions from Delaware and non-Delaware 529 plans are excluded from Delaware taxable income.

Maximum contribution limit: A contribution will not be accepted if it would cause the total of all Delaware 529 account balances for the same beneficiary to exceed $350,000.

Delaware College Investment Plan

529 PROGRAM TYPE:	Savings
PROGRAM MANAGER:	Fidelity Investments
DISTRIBUTOR:	Fidelity Brokerage Services, LLC
TELEPHONE:	800–544–1655
WEB SITE:	www.fidelity.com/delaware

Enrollment: Enroll directly. This program is not sold through financial advisors. There are no state residency requirements.

Investment options:

Option type	# of options	Underlying investments	Expense ratio [1]
Age-based (index)	1 track		0.31%–0.35%
Age-based (active)	1 track		0.67%–1.01%
Static multi-fund (index)	3	Fidelity Investments mutual funds	0.30%–0.35%
Static multi-fund (active)	3		0.56%–1.01%
Individual fund	5		0.25%–0.57%
Age-based (multi-firm)	1 track	Mutual funds from Fidelity Investments, Acadian, Artisan, Aston, BlackRock Causeway, Credit Suisse, Eaton Vance, Harbor, Invesco, JP Morgan, MFS, Nataxis, OppenheimerFunds, PIMCO, Royce, Western Asset, and William Blair	0.94%–1.40%
FDIC-insured	1	Wells Fargo Bank, N.A.	0.05%–0.50%

[1] 0.15% (index), 0.20% (active), or 0.35% (multi-fund) plan fees plus underlying fund expenses. Fees on Bank Deposit Portfolio are variable.

Minimum contributions: With lump-sum contributions, the minimum initial contribution is $50, and the minimum subsequent contribution is $25. With the automatic investment plan, the minimum contribution level is $15 per month or $45 per quarter.

Account maintenance fee: None

Added feature: Accounts can be linked to the Fidelity Investments 529 Rewards American Express Card.

DISTRICT OF COLUMBIA

The District of Columbia's 529 savings program is sold nationally through financial advisors but is also available on a load-waived basis to District of Columbia residents and to employees at companies with at least 300 employees using a payroll deduction plan. It features a menu of age-based and static portfolio options featuring Calvert mutual funds but containing funds from other fund families as well.

STATE AGENCY: District of Columbia College Savings Program Trust

D.C. income tax treatment: Contributions to the DC 529 College Savings Program of up to $4,000 per year by an individual filer, and up to $8,000 per year by married taxpayers who each make contributions to their own account, are deductible in computing District of Columbia taxable income. The contribution deadline is December 31. Contributions in excess of annual limits may be carried over and taken as deductions for up to five years. Rollovers from another 529 plan are not eligible for the deduction. Qualified distributions from D.C. and non-D.C. 529 plans are excluded from District of Columbia taxable income.

Maximum contribution limit: A contribution will not be accepted if it would cause the total of all District of Columbia 529 account balances for the same beneficiary to exceed $260,000.

DC 529 College Savings Program

529 PROGRAM TYPE:	Savings
PROGRAM MANAGER:	Calvert Investment Management Co., Inc.
DISTRIBUTOR:	Calvert Investment Distributors, Inc.
TELEPHONE:	800–987–4859 (D.C. residents); 800–368–2745 (non-residents)
WEB SITE:	www.dccollegesavings.com

Enrollment: Purchase through a financial advisor. Direct enrollment (load-waived) is available for D.C. residents and persons employed at companies of 300 or more enrolling through a payroll deduction plan.

Investment options:

Option type	# of options	Underlying investments	Unit classes	Expense ratio [1]	Maximum initial sales charge
Age- or enrollment-based	1 track	Mutual funds from Calvert and funding agreement with Acacia Life	A	0.66%–1.34%	2.75% - 4.75% [2]
Individual fund	6	Mutual funds from Calvert and State Street	A	0.50%–1.97%	3.75% - 4.75% [2]
Stable value	1	Funding agreement with Acacia Life	-	0.15%	0.00%

[1] 0.15% plan fee plus underlying fund expenses.
[2] Waived for District of Columbia residents enrolling directly.

Minimum contributions: With lump-sum contributions, the minimum initial contribution is $100, and the minimum subsequent contribution is $25. With the automatic investment plan, the minimum contribution level is $25 per month via electronic funds transfer or $15 per pay period via payroll deduction.

Account maintenance fee: $30 annually ($15 annually for D.C. residents). Also a $25 enrollment fee is charged to D.C. nonresidents.

FLORIDA

The Sunshine State offers both a 529 prepaid program and a savings program. The Florida Prepaid College Plan has a Florida residency requirement and is the largest prepaid plan in the nation. It is unique among contract-type prepaid programs in offering a dormitory option in addition to its various tuition and fees packages. The Florida 529 Savings Plan is a board-managed 529 savings program available to residents of any state that hires outside investment managers to separately manage the program's portfolios.

STATE AGENCY: Florida Prepaid College Board

State income tax treatment: Florida does not have a personal income tax.

Maximum contribution limit: A contribution will not be accepted if it would cause the total of all Florida 529 account balances for the same beneficiary to exceed $394,000.

Other considerations:

- Under Florida law, assets in a Florida or non-Florida 529 plan are not liable to attachment, levy, garnishment, or legal process in the state in favor of any creditor of or claimant against any program participant, purchaser, owner or contributor, or program beneficiary.

Florida 529 Savings Plan

529 PROGRAM TYPE: Savings
PROGRAM MANAGER: Florida Prepaid College Board
DISTRIBUTOR: State-distributed
TELEPHONE: 800–552–4723
WEB SITE: www.myfloridaprepaid.com

Enrollment: Enroll directly. This program is not sold through financial advisors. There are no state residency requirements.

Investment options:

Option type	# of options	Underlying investments	Expense ratio
Age- or enrollment-based	1 track	Portfolios separately managed by Columbia Management, Quantitative Management, Fiduciary Management, and Northern Trust Investments	0.75%[1]
Actively-managed portfolios	3		
Equity index portfolio	1		
Money market	1	Florida PRIME, operated by Florida State Board of Administration	

[1] 0.75% plan fee includes underlying fund and investment manager expenses.

Minimum contributions: With lump-sum contributions, the minimum initial contribution is $250, and subsequent contributions can be any amount. With the automatic investment plan, the minimum contribution level is $25 per month.

Account maintenance fee: There is a one-time enrollment fee of $50 (or $80 for both Florida 529 plans). There is no ongoing annual account maintenance fee.

Florida Prepaid College Plan

529 PROGRAM TYPE:	Prepaid
TELEPHONE:	800–552–4723
WEB SITE:	www.florida529plans.com

Enrollment: The enrollment period usually runs from mid-October through January of the following year. Applications are accepted between enrollment periods but at prices to be set in the next enrollment period. The beneficiary or the beneficiary's parent must be a Florida resident at the time of enrollment.

Time/age restrictions: The beneficiary must be under 21 years old and below the 12th grade at the time of enrollment. Contract benefits must generally be used within 10 years from the expected date of college enrollment.

Contract benefits: Available plan packages covering registration, local fees and tuition differential (if applicable) include the 4-Year Florida University Plan, the 4-Year Florida College Plan, the 2-Year Florida College Plan, and a 2+2 Florida Plan combining Florida college and university attendance. Optional contracts for payment of dormitory housing are also available to those purchasing a university plan or 2+2 plan. A beneficiary attending a private or out-of-state institution receives the value of benefits that would be paid if attending a Florida public institution.

Contract prices: For the 2012-13 enrollment period, the price of a prepayment contract (not including dormitory) ranged from as little as $7,079 for a two-year Florida college contract for an 11th grader to as much as $53,729 for a four-year university plan for a newborn. Monthly payment plans are available.

Enrollment or application fee: $50 (or $80 for both Florida 529 plans).

Statutory state backing: Florida backs program obligations with its full faith and credit. In the event the program is terminated, all participants within five years of college enrollment will receive full promised benefits while others will receive a refund of payments made plus interest.

Added feature: A qualified beneficiary is classified a resident for tuition purposes regardless of actual home of record.

GEORGIA

Georgia's Path2College 529 Plan is a direct-sold 529 savings program is managed by TIAA-CREF Tuition Financing, Inc and offers two age-based options, four static options, and a guaranteed option.

STATE AGENCY: Georgia Higher Education Savings Plan

State income tax treatment: Contributions to Georgia's 529 plan of up to $2,000 per beneficiary per year (any filing status) are deductible in computing Georgia taxable income. Rollovers from another 529 plan are not eligible for the deduction. The contribution deadline is April 15 of the following year. Qualified distributions from Georgia and non-Georgia 529 plans are excluded from Georgia taxable income. Under the Georgia recapture rules, the principal portion of rollovers and nonqualified distributions from Georgia's 529 plan must be included in Georgia taxable income to the extent of prior Georgia tax deductions.

Maximum contribution limit: A contribution will not be accepted if it would cause the total of all Georgia 529 account balances for the same beneficiary to exceed $235,000.

Other considerations:

- Participation in the Georgia 529 plan does not affect the beneficiary's eligibility for financial aid programs administered by the state of Georgia.

Path2College 529 Plan

529 PROGRAM TYPE: Savings
PROGRAM MANAGER: TIAA-CREF Tuition Financing, Inc.
DISTRIBUTOR: TIAA-CREF Individual & Institutional Services, LLC
TELEPHONE: 877–424–4377
WEB SITE: www.gacollegesavings.com

Enrollment: Enroll directly. This program is not sold through financial advisors. There are no state residency requirements.

Investment options:

Option type	# of options	Underlying investments	Expense ratio[1]
Age- or enrollment-based	2 tracks		0.34%–0.41%
Static multi-fund	2	TIAA-CREF institutional mutual funds	0.37%–0.40%
Individual fund	2		0.28%–0.34%
Principal protection	1	Funding agreement with TIAA-CREF Life Insurance Company	0.00%

[1] 0.21% plan fee plus underlying fund expenses.

Minimum contributions: $25, or $15 per pay period via payroll deduction.

Account maintenance fee: None

HAWAII

The Aloha State offers a 529 savings program managed by Upromise Investments, featuring Vanguard funds in its age-based and static investment options.

STATE AGENCY: Hawaii Department of Budget and Finance

State income tax treatment: Contributions are not deductible on Hawaii income tax returns. Qualified distributions from Hawaii and non-Hawaii 529 plans are excluded from Hawaii taxable income.

Maximum contribution limit: A contribution will not be accepted if it would cause the total of all Hawaii 529 account balances for the same beneficiary to exceed $305,000.

Other considerations:

- Accounts can be linked to the Upromise Rewards Service.

Hawaii's College Savings Program

529 PROGRAM TYPE:	Savings
PROGRAM MANAGER:	Upromise Investments, Inc.
DISTRIBUTOR:	Upromise Investments, Inc.
TELEPHONE:	866–529–3343
WEB SITE:	www.hi529.com

Enrollment: Enroll directly. This program is not sold through financial advisors. There are no state residency requirements.

Investment options:

Option type	# of options	Underlying investments	Expense ratio
Age- or enrollment-based	1 track		
Static multi-fund	4	Vanguard mutual funds	0.75%[1]
Individual fund	2		

[1] 0.75% plan fee includes underlying fund expenses.

Minimum contributions: $15

Account maintenance fee: $20 annually.

IDAHO

Idaho offers a 529 savings program managed by Upromise Investments, featuring Vanguard funds in its age-based and static investment options.An FDIC-insured Savings Portfolio is also available and managed by Sallie Mae Bank.

STATE AGENCY: Idaho College Savings Program Board

State income tax treatment: Contributions to the Idaho College Savings Program of up to $4,000 per year by an individual filer, and up to $8,000 per year by a married couple filing jointly, are deductible in computing Idaho taxable income. Rollovers from another 529 plan are not eligible for the deduction. The contribution deadline is December 31. Qualified distributions from Idaho and non-Idaho 529 plans are excluded from Idaho taxable income. Under the Idaho recapture rules, the entire amount of a nonqualified distribution to an Idaho taxpayer must be included in Idaho taxable income, and outbound rollovers must be included in Idaho taxable income to the extent of contributions made during the 12 months preceding the date of the rollover.

Maximum contribution limit: A contribution will not be accepted if it would cause the total of all Idaho 529 account balances for the same beneficiary to exceed $350,000.

Other considerations:

- Under Idaho law, any rights accruing on account of money paid into the Idaho 529 plan are exempt from execution, attachment, garnishment, seizure, or other levy by or under any legal process, with exceptions for certain child support claims and other court orders.
- Accounts can be linked to the Upromise Rewards Service.

Idaho College Savings Program (IDeal)

529 PROGRAM TYPE:	Savings
PROGRAM MANAGER:	Upromise Investments, Inc.
DISTRIBUTOR:	Upromise Investments, Inc.
TELEPHONE:	866–433–2533
WEB SITE:	www.idsaves.org

Enrollment: Enroll directly. This program is not sold through financial advisors. There are no state residency requirements.

Investment options:

Option type	# of options	Underlying investments	Expense ratio
Age- or enrollment-based	3 tracks		
Static multi-fund	5	Vanguard mutual funds	0.75%[1]
Money market	1		
FDIC-insured	1	Sallie Mae Bank	0.34%

[1] 0.75% plan fee includes underlying fund expenses.

Minimum contributions: $25, or $15 per pay period via payroll deduction. Through the free Ugift service, friends and family are invited to make contributions of at least $25 each directly to a child's account.

Account maintenance fee: $20 annually, waived for Idaho residents.

ILLINOIS

Illinois offers two 529 savings programs and a prepaid tuition program. The Bright Start College Savings Program, managed by OFI Private Investments Inc., comes in a direct-sold version and an advisor-sold version. (The direct-sold Bright Start program has more investment options.) The Bright Directions College Savings Program is an advisor-sold 529 savings program managed by Union Bank & Trust Company, offering a wide and diverse selection of fund families including funds managed by female- and minority-owned firms. CollegeIllinois!, the state's prepaid tuition program, is available only to Illinois residents.

STATE AGENCY: Illinois State Treasurer for the savings programs; Illinois Student Assistance Commission for the prepaid tuition program

State income tax treatment: Contributions to Illinois 529 plans of up to $10,000 per year by an individual filer, and up to $20,000 per year by a married couple filing jointly, are deductible in computing Illinois taxable income. The principal portion of a rollover from another 529 plan is eligible for the deduction; however, the earnings portion is not. The contribution deadline is December 31. Qualified distributions from an Illinois 529 plan are excluded from Illinois taxable income. Qualified distributions from a non-Illinois 529 plan are also excluded, provided the plan provides adequate disclosures regarding the ability of Illinois residents to receive a tax deduction with an Illinois 529 plan only. Nonqualified distributions and rollovers to a non-Illinois 529 plan are subject to recapture of prior Illinois tax deductions. Employers may claim a credit against Illinois tax for 25 percent of matching contributions made to an employee's account in an Illinois 529 plan, with a maximum annual credit of $500 per employee (unused credits may be carried forward for 5 years).

Maximum contribution limit: A contribution will not be accepted if it would cause the total of all Illinois 529 account balances for the same beneficiary to exceed $350,000.

Other considerations:

- Except for non-exempt transfers, accounts in an Illinois 529 savings program are exempt from the claims of creditors of the account owner, contributor, and beneficiary. Non-exempt transfers include certain fraudulent conveyances as well as contributions made during the 365 day period prior to filing for bankruptcy that in the aggregate exceed the annual gift tax exclusion amount (currently $14,000) and contributions made during the 730 to 366 day period prior to filing for bankruptcy that in the aggregate exceed the annual gift tax exclusion amount. Contracts with the College Illinois! prepaid tuition program appear to be fully exempt under a separate provision that lacks any language regarding non-exempt transfers.

Bright Start College Savings Program—Direct-sold Plan

529 PROGRAM TYPE:	Savings
PROGRAM MANAGER:	OFI Private Investments Inc., an affiliate of OppenheimerFunds
DISTRIBUTOR:	OppenheimerFunds Distributor, Inc.
TELEPHONE:	877–432–7444
WEB SITE:	www.brightstartsavings.com

Enrollment: Enroll directly. This program is not sold through financial advisors. There are no state residency requirements.

Investment options:

Option type	# of options	Underlying investments	Expense ratio
Age- or enrollment-based - blended	1 track	OppenheimerFunds, American Century and Vanguard	0.49%–0.67% [1]
Static asset allocation - blended	4		0.38%–0.69% [1]
Age- or enrollment-based - index	1 track	Vanguard index funds and Oppenheimer Money Market	0.18%–0.21% [2]
Static asset allocation - index	3		0.18%–0.21% [2]
Money Market	1	Oppenheimer Institutional Money Market Fund	0.32%

[1] 0.18% plan fees plus underlying fund expenses.
[2] 0.14% plan fees plus underlying fund expenses.

Minimum contributions: The minimum initial contribution is $25, and the minimum subsequent contribution is $15. The minimum is waived under employer-sponsored arrangements.

Account maintenance fee: None for the Blended Portfolios; $10 annually per portfolio for the Index Portfolios.

Bright Start College Savings Program—Advisor-sold Plan

529 PROGRAM TYPE:	Savings
PROGRAM MANAGER:	OFI Private Investments Inc., an affiliate of OppenheimerFunds
DISTRIBUTOR:	OppenheimerFunds Distributor, Inc.
TELEPHONE:	877–432–7444
WEB SITE:	www.brightstartadvisor.com

Enrollment: Purchase through a financial advisor. There are no state residency requirements.

Investment options:

Option type	# of options	Underlying investments	Unit classes	Expense ratio [1]	Maximum sales charge	
					Initial	Contingent deferred
Age- or enrollment-based	1 track	OppenheimerFunds and American Century	A	0.76%–1.00%	3.50%	0.00%
			C	1.01%–1.25%	0.00%	0.50%
Static asset allocation	4		A	0.63%–0.99%	3.50%	0.00%
			C	0.88%–1.24%	0.00%	0.50%
Money market	1		-	0.32%	0.00%	0.00%

[1] 0.18% plan fees (0.15% for Money Market Portfolio) plus underlying fund expenses and distribution/servicing fees.

Minimum contributions: The minimum initial contribution is $25, and the minimum subsequent contribution is $15. The minimum is waived under employer-sponsored arrangements.

Account maintenance fee: None

Bright Directions College Savings Program

529 PROGRAM TYPE:	Savings
PROGRAM MANAGER:	Union Bank & Trust Company
DISTRIBUTOR:	Northern Trust Securities, Inc.
TELEPHONE:	866–722–7283
WEB SITE:	www.brightdirections.com

Enrollment: Purchase through a financial advisor (unit classes A and C), through an employer (unit class E), or through a fee-based financial planner (unit class F). There are no state residency requirements.

Investment options:

Option type	# of options	Underlying investments	Unit classes	Expense ratio [1]	Maximum initial sales charge
Age- or enrollment-based	3 tracks		A	0.94%–1.16%	3.50%
			C	1.19%–1.41%	0.00%
			E	0.94%–1.16%	0.00%
			F	0.69%–0.91%	0.00%
Static multi-fund	7	Mutual funds from PIMCO, BlackRock, DFA, American Century, Delaware Funds, Artisan, Northern Funds, OppenheimerFunds, William Blair, ING, T. Rowe Price, Templeton, Eagle, MFS, and Dodge & Cox	A	0.94%–1.16%	3.50%
			C	1.19%–1.41%	0.00%
			E	0.94%–1.16%	0.00%
			F	0.69%–0.91%	0.00%
Individual fund	29		A	0.47%–2.12%	3.50% [2]
			C	0.47%–2.37%	0.00%
			E	0.47%–2.12%	0.00%
			F	0.47%–1.87%	0.00%
Individual fund; female- and minority-owned managers	4	Mutual funds from Ariel Investments, John Hancock, Sit Mutual Funds, and Touchstone	A	1.15%–1.82%	3.50%
			C	1.40%–2.07%	0.00%
			E	1.15%–2.82%	0.00%
			F	0.90%–1.57%	0.00%
Individual fund: ETF	15	Exchange traded funds from Vanguard	F	0.45%–0.70%	0.00%

[1] 0.40% plan fees (0.35% for ETF options) plus underlying fund expenses and distribution/servicing fees.
[2] BlackRock Cash Funds, PIMCO Short Term Bond, and PIMCO Low Duration portfolios do not have a Class A sales charge.

Minimum contributions: None

Account maintenance fee: $10 initial set-up fee and $3 per quarter maintenance fee.

- Added feature: The Bright Directions 529 Rewards Visa Card contributes 1.529% of qualifying purchases to your account.

College Illinois! 529 Prepaid Tuition Program

529 PROGRAM TYPE: Prepaid
TELEPHONE: 877–877–3724
WEB SITE: www.529prepaidtuition.org

Enrollment: The 2012-2013 enrollment period began on October 1 and runs through April 30, 2013. The account owner or beneficiary must be an Illinois resident for at least 12 months prior to application.

Time/age restrictions: The contract must be purchased at least three years before benefits are used to pay for tuition and fees. The beneficiary must begin using contract benefits within 10 years of the projected enrollment date and then has 10 years to use all the benefits.

Contract benefits: The program pays up to nine semesters of in-state university level tuition and mandatory fees, up to four semesters of in-district community college level tuition and mandatory fees, or a combination of four university semesters and four community college semesters at an Illinois public institution. The University+ plan includes all Illinois public universities including the University of Illinois at Urbana-Champaign (UIUC) while the University plan includes all Illinois public universities except UIUC. A beneficiary attending a private or out-of-state institution receives benefits equal to the average mean-weighted credit hour value of Illinois public in-state costs.

Contract prices: For enrollment between January 1, 2013 and April 30, 2013, prices range from as little as $2,034 for a one-semester community college contract for a child in kindergarten or below, to as much as $113,231 for a nine-semester University+ contract for a child in the ninth grade or higher. Extended payment plans are available for children enrolling before the ninth grade.

Enrollment or application fee: None.

Statutory state backing: While the credit and taxing power of the State of Illinois is not pledged to directly make payments under a contract, under Illinois law, the Governor or the State of Illinois is required to request funding from the Illinois legislature sufficient to pay all program benefits during any year in which there is a current funding shortfall.

INDIANA

Upromise Investments manages two of the Hoosier State's three 529 savings programs. The direct-sold CollegeChoice plan offers an age-based option using mostly Vanguard funds along with 7 individual-fund options from various fund families. The advisor-sold CollegeChoice plan uses iShares ETFs in its year-of-enrollment option and six investment managers in its 10 individual-fund options. Both plans also offer a FDIC-insured savings account portfolio. The newest Indiana 529 plan is the CollegeChoice CD 529 Savings Plan, which opened in April 2011 and offers FDIC-insured savings options from College Savings Bank.

STATE AGENCY: Indiana Education Savings Authority (IESA)

State income tax treatment: A 20% tax credit on up to $5,000 per year in contributions to an Indiana 529 plan can be claimed against Indiana personal income tax (maximum yearly credit is $1,000 per tax return). Rollover contributions and contributions generated through a rewards program are not eligible for the credit. The contribution deadline is December 31. Qualified distributions from Indiana and non-Indiana 529 plans are excluded from Indiana taxable income.

Maximum contribution limit: A contribution will not be accepted if it would cause the total of all Indiana 529 account balances for the same beneficiary to exceed $298,770.

Other considerations:

- Participation in the Indiana 529 plan does not affect the beneficiary's eligibility for financial aid programs administered by the state of Indiana.
- Accounts in the Upromise-managed plans can be linked to the Upromise Rewards Service.

CollegeChoice 529 Direct Savings Plan

529 PROGRAM TYPE: Savings
PROGRAM MANAGER: Upromise Investments, Inc.
DISTRIBUTOR: Upromise Investments, Inc.
TELEPHONE: 866–485–9415
WEB SITE: www.collegechoicedirect.com

Enrollment: Enroll directly. This program is not sold through financial advisors. There are no state residency requirements.

Investment options:

Option type	# of options	Underlying investments	Expense ratio
Age- or enrollment-based	1 track	Mutual funds from Vanguard and Loomis Sayles	0.50%–0.57% [1]
Individual fund	7	Mutual funds from Vanguard, Dodge & Cox, Scout, and Western Asset	0.29%–0.91% [2]
FDIC-insured	1	Sallie Mae High-Yield Savings Account	0.27%

[1] 0.42% plan fee plus underlying fund expenses.
[2] 0.27% plan fee plus underlying fund expenses.

Minimum contributions: $25. Through the free Ugift service, friends and family are invited to make contributions of at least $25 each directly to a child's account.

Account maintenance fee: $20 annually. The fee is waived for Indiana residents or beneficiaries and for account balances of more than $25,000.

CollegeChoice Advisor 529 Savings Plan

529 PROGRAM TYPE:	Savings
PROGRAM MANAGER:	Upromise Investments, Inc.
DISTRIBUTOR:	Upromise Investments, Inc.
TELEPHONE:	866–485–9413
WEB SITE:	www.collegechoiceadvisor529.com

Enrollment: Purchase through a financial advisor. There are no state residency requirements.

Investment options:

Option type	# of options	Underlying investments	Unit classes	Expense ratio [1]	Maximum sales charge	
					Initial	Contingent deferred
Age- or enrollment-based	1 track	iShares ETFs	A	0.83%–0.89%	3.75%–5.25%	0.00%
			C	1.58%–1.64%	0.00%	1.00%
Individual fund	10	Mutual funds from Artio Global Management, BlackRock, iShares, Columbia, PIMCO, and T. Rowe Price	A	0.77%–1.72%	3.75%–5.25%	0.00%
			C	1.52%–2.47%	0.00%	1.00%
FDIC-insured	1	Sallie Mae High-Yield Savings Account	-	0.34%	0.00%	0.00%

[1] 0.44% plan fees (0.34% for Savings Portfolio) plus underlying fund expenses and distribution/servicing fees.

Minimum contributions: $25. Through the free Ugift service, friends and family are invited to make contributions of at least $25 each directly to a child's account.

Account maintenance fee: $20 annually. The fee is waived for Indiana residents or beneficiaries and for account balances of more than $25,000.

CollegeChoice CD 529 Savings Plan

529 PROGRAM TYPE:	Savings
PROGRAM MANAGER:	College Savings Bank
DISTRIBUTOR:	College Savings Bank
TELEPHONE:	888–913–2885
WEB SITE:	www.collegechoicecd.com

Enrollment: Enroll directly or through approved Indiana banks and financial advisors. There are no state residency requirements.

Investment options: Four types of FDIC-insured options are available: (1) the CollegeSure® CD is a variable rate certificate of deposit from College Savings Bank, with a maturity ranging from 1 to 22 years, that is credited with interest each year based on the previous year's college inflation rate, as measured by the change in the College Board's Independent College 500® Index (IC 500®) less an issue margin, and is subject to a maximum interest rate which is equal to the first year's interest rate plus an interest rate cap (the issue margin and interest rate cap are determined on the contribution date); (2) the InvestorSure® CD is a five-year certificate of deposit that pays 70% of the average increase in the S&P 500 Index at maturity based on a formula and is guaranteed not to lose principal; (3) Fixed Rate CDs are available in 1- and 3-year maturities. (4) The Honors™ Savings Account is a high yielding, variable rate savings account available exclusively online.

Minimum contributions:

CollegeSure® CD: With lump-sum contributions, the minimum initial contribution is $250. With the automatic investment plan, the minimum contribution level is $25 per month via electronic funds transfer, or $25 per payroll via payroll deduction. Deposits under $250 are held in an interest bearing savings account, and each time the balance reaches $250, a CD purchase is made.

InvestorSure® CD: With lump-sum contributions, the minimum initial contribution is $250. With the automatic investment plan, the minimum contribution level is $25 per month via electronic funds transfer, or $25 per payroll via payroll deduction. Deposits under $250 are held in an interest bearing savings account, and each time the balance reaches $250, a CD purchase is made on the next CD issue date.

Fixed-rate CD: With lump-sum contributions, the minimum initial contribution is $250. With the automatic investment plan, the minimum contribution level is $25 per month via electronic funds transfer, or $25 per pay period via payroll deduction. Deposits under $250 are held in an interest bearing savings account, and each time the balance reaches $250, a CD purchase is made.

Honors™ Savings Account: The minimum contribution is $250 and must be contributed by electronic check through the state 529 program website or the College Savings Bank website.

Account maintenance fee: No asset-based fees. Service-based and other fees may apply.

IOWA

The Iowa state treasurer's office has teamed with Upromise Investments in offering its direct-sold 529 savings program which uses The Vanguard Group as investment manager and features age-based and static portfolios using Vanguard funds. The advisor-sold plan in Iowa is managed by ING Group and features age-based, static allocation and single fund options using multiple investment managers.

STATE AGENCY: State Treasurer of Iowa

State income tax treatment: Contributions to an Iowa 529 plan of up to $3,045 (in 2013) per beneficiary by an individual filer, and up to $6,090 per beneficiary by married taxpayers filing jointly who each make their own contributions, are deductible in computing Iowa taxable income. The deduction limit is increased annually for inflation. Contributions must be from the account owner to be eligible for the deduction. The contribution deadline is December 31. Qualified distributions from Iowa and non-Iowa 529 plans are excluded from Iowa taxable income. Under the Iowa recapture rule, the principal portion of rollovers and nonqualified distributions from an Iowa 529 plan must be included in Iowa taxable income to the extent of prior Iowa tax deductions.

Maximum contribution limit: A contribution will not be accepted if it would cause the total of all Iowa 529 account balances for the same beneficiary to exceed $320,000.

Other considerations:

- Participation in an Iowa 529 plan does not affect the beneficiary's eligibility for financial aid programs administered by the state of Iowa.

College Savings Iowa

529 PROGRAM TYPE:	Savings
PROGRAM MANAGERS:	State Treasurer of Iowa, Upromise Investments, Inc., and The Vanguard Group, Inc.
DISTRIBUTORS:	State Treasurer of Iowa and Vanguard Marketing Corporation
TELEPHONE:	888–672–9116
WEB SITE:	www.collegesavingsiowa.com

Enrollment: Enroll directly. This program is not sold through financial advisors. There are no state residency requirements.

Investment options:

Option type	# of options	Underlying investments	Expense ratio
Age- or enrollment-based	4 tracks		
Static multi-fund	6	Vanguard mutual funds	0.28%[1]
Individual fund	4		

[1] 0.28% plan fee includes underlying fund expenses.

Minimum contributions: $25, or $15 per pay period via payroll deduction. Through the free Ugift service, friends and family are invited to make contributions of at least $25 each directly to a child's account.

Account maintenance fee: None

Added feature: Accounts can be linked to the Upromise Rewards Service.

IAdvisor 529 Plan

529 PROGRAM TYPE:	Savings
PROGRAM MANAGERS:	ING Investment Management, LLC
DISTRIBUTORS:	ING Investments Distributor, LLC
TELEPHONE:	1-800-774-5127
WEB SITE:	www.529plans.inginvestment.com/Iowa

Enrollment: Purchase through a financial advisor. There are no state residency requirements.

Investment options:

Option type	# of options	Underlying investments	Unit classes	Expense ratio [1]	Maximum sales charge	
					Initial	Contingent deferred
Age-based	1 track	Mutual funds from ING, including funds subadvised by BlackRock, Clarion, Delaware, JPMorgan, PIMCO, RBC, Thornburg, and Wellington	A	1.25%–1.51%	4.75%	0.00%
Static multi-fund	5		C	2.00%–2.26%	0.00%	1.00%
Individual fund	12		A	0.99%–1.80%	4.75%[2]	0.00%
			C	0.99%–2.55%	0.00%	1%[2]

[1] 0.50% plan fees (0.40% for the Money Market portfolio) plus underlying fund expenses and distribution/servicing fees.
[2] None for the ING Money Market portfolio

Minimum contributions: With lump-sum contributions, the minimum and subsequent contribution is $250 per investment option. With the automatic investment plan, the minimum contribution level is $50 per month, or $25 per pay period with payroll direct deposit.

Account maintenance fee: $25 annually, waived for balances of $25,000 or more, or for accounts using the automatic investment plan or payroll direct deposit plan depositing $100 per month per option for 12 consecutive months.

KANSAS

Kansas' three 529 savings programs use American Century Investments as program manager. The direct-sold Learning Quest program is available nationally and features American Century and Vanguard mutual funds. Learning Quest Advisor is sold through financial advisors and utilizes multiple fund families in its age-based and asset-allocation portfolios while also offering a menu of 12 American Century individual-fund options. The Schwab 529 College Savings plan is also a multi-manager 529 plan, but is sold through discount broker Charles Schwab & Co.

STATE AGENCY: Kansas State Treasurer

State income tax treatment: Contributions to Kansas and non-Kansas state-sponsored 529 plans of up to $3,000 per beneficiary per year by an individual filer, and up to $6,000 per beneficiary per year by a married couple filing jointly, are deductible in computing Kansas taxable income. Rollovers from another 529 plan are not eligible for the deduction. The contribution deadline is December 31. Qualified distributions from Kansas and non-Kansas 529 plans are excluded from Kansas taxable income. Under the Kansas recapture rules, the principal portion of nonqualified distributions from a 529 plan must be included in Kansas taxable income to the extent of prior Kansas tax deductions. Rollovers to another 529 plan are not subject to recapture.

Maximum contribution limit: A contribution will not be accepted if it would cause the total of all Kansas 529 account balances for the same beneficiary to exceed $325,000.

Other considerations:

- Under Kansas law, an account in a Kansas 529 plan owned by a Kansas resident for a beneficiary who is a lineal descendant is exempt from creditor claims. The protection is limited to $5,000 for amounts contributed between one and two years prior to the date of filing of a bankruptcy petition or execution of judgment for such claims against the account owner, and does not apply at all to amounts contributed within one year of the date of filing or execution.
- Accounts in a Kansas 529 plan can be linked to the Upromise Rewards Service.

Learning Quest 529 Education Savings Program

529 PROGRAM TYPE:	Savings
PROGRAM MANAGER:	American Century Investment Management, Inc.
DISTRIBUTOR:	American Century Investment Services, Inc.
TELEPHONE:	800–579–2203
WEB SITE:	www.learningquest.com

Enrollment: Enroll directly. There are no state residency requirements.

Investment options:

Option type	# of options	Underlying investments	Expense ratio
Age- or enrollment-based, index	1 track	Vanguard index funds	.50% [1]
Age- or enrollment-based	3 tracks	Mutual funds from American Century and Vanguard	0.43%–0.89% [2]
Static multi-fund	8		0.25%–0.94% [2]
Individual fund	4		0.24%–0.28% [2]
Tobacco-free	2	LIVESTRONG™ 2025 and LIVESTRONG™ 2015 Portfolios	0.98%–1.03% [2]

[1] Plan fee includes underlying fund expenses.
[2] 0.20% plan fees (none for Money Market option) plus the expenses of the underlying mutual funds.

Minimum contributions: $25. Through the free Ugift service, friends and family are invited to make contributions of at least $25 each directly to a child's account.

Account maintenance fee: None

Added feature: Kansas offers a dollar-for-dollar matching contribution of up to $600 per year to Kansas residents with incomes of less than 200% of the federal poverty level participating in this plan.

Learning Quest Advisor

529 PROGRAM TYPE:	Savings
PROGRAM MANAGER:	American Century Investment Management, Inc.
DISTRIBUTOR:	American Century Investment Services, Inc.
TELEPHONE:	877-882-6236
WEB SITE:	www.learningquest.com

Enrollment: Purchase through a financial advisor. There are no state residency requirements.

Investment options:

Option type	# of options	Underlying investments	Unit classes	Expense ratio [1]	Maximum sales charge	
					Initial	Contingent deferred
Age- or enrollment-based	3 tracks	Mutual funds from American Century, American Beacon, Columbia, OppenheimerFunds, and Principal	A	0.85%–1.46%	4.50%–5.75%	0.00%
			C	1.60%–2.21%	0.00%	1.00%
Static multi-fund	7		A	0.85%–1.51%	4.50%–5.75%	0.00%
			C	1.60%–2.26%	0.00%	1.00%
Individual fund	12	Mutual funds from American Century Investments	A	0.50%–1.85%	4.50%–5.75%	0.00%
			C	1.00%–2.60%	0.00%	1.00% [2]

[1] 0.20% plan fees (none for the Money Market Portfolio option) plus underlying fund expenses and distribution/servicing fees.
[2] None for the Money Market Portfolio.

Minimum contributions: $25. Through the free Ugift service, friends and family are invited to make contributions of at least $25 each directly to a child's account.

Account maintenance fee: None

Added feature: Kansas offers a dollar-for-dollar matching contribution of up to $600 per year to Kansas residents with incomes of less than 200% of the federal poverty level participating in this plan.

Schwab 529 College Savings Plan

529 PROGRAM TYPE:	Savings
PROGRAM MANAGER:	American Century Investment Management, Inc.
DISTRIBUTOR:	Charles Schwab & Co., Inc.
TELEPHONE:	888–903–3863
WEB SITE:	www.schwab.com/529

Enrollment: Purchase through Charles Schwab & Co., Inc. or through independent advisors associated with Schwab.

Investment options:

Option type	# of options	Underlying investments	Expense ratio [1]
Age- or enrollment-based	4 tracks	Mutual funds from American Century, Schwab, Laudus, PIMCO, Transamerica, American Beacon, Baron, and Metropolitan West	0.65%–1.41%
Static multi-fund	6		
Money market	1	Schwab Value Advantage Money Fund	0.41%

[1] 0.20% plan fees plus underlying fund expenses.

Minimum contributions: $25. Through the free Ugift service, friends and family are invited to make contributions of at least $25 each directly to a child's account.

Account maintenance fee: None

KENTUCKY

The Bluegrass State offers a 529 savings program (KESPT) managed by TIAA-CREF Tuition Financing, Inc. that features an age-based option, four static options, and a guaranteed option. Kentucky's 529 prepaid program (KAPT) was closed to new enrollments at the end of 2004.

STATE AGENCY: Kentucky Higher Education Assistance Authority

State income tax treatment: Contributions to a 529 plan are not deductible on Kentucky income tax returns. Qualified distributions from Kentucky and non-Kentucky 529 plans are excluded from Kentucky taxable income. Kentucky law imposes a 1% penalty on the earnings portion of a nonqualified withdrawal, but the penalty is currently not being enforced.

Maximum contribution limit: A contribution will not be accepted if it would cause the total of all Kentucky 529 account balances for the same beneficiary to exceed $235,000.

Other considerations:

- Under Kentucky law, the right to benefits in a Kentucky 529 plan is not subject to attachment, garnishment, or seizure by creditors of account owner or the beneficiary.
- Participation in a Kentucky 529 plan does not affect the beneficiary's eligibility for financial aid programs administered by Kentucky.

Kentucky Education Savings Plan Trust

529 PROGRAM TYPE: Savings
PROGRAM MANAGER: TIAA-CREF Tuition Financing, Inc.
DISTRIBUTOR: TIAA-CREF Individual & Institutional Services, LLC
TELEPHONE: 877–598–7878
WEB SITE: www.kysaves.com

Enrollment: Enroll directly. This program is not sold through financial advisors. There are no state residency requirements.

Investment options:

Option type	# of options	Underlying investments	Expense ratio
Age- or enrollment-based	1 track	TIAA-CREF institutional mutual funds	0.65% [1]
Static multi-fund	4		0.56%–0.91% [2]
Principal protection	1	Funding agreement with TIAA-CREF Life Insurance Company	0.00%

[1] 0.65% plan fee includes underlying fund expenses.
[2] 0.38% - 47% plan fee plus underlying fund expenses.

Minimum contributions: $25, or $15 per pay period via payroll deduction.

Account maintenance fee: None

Added feature: Beneficiaries with eight years of program participation and $2,400 in total contributions who move out-of-state remain eligible for resident tuition rates at Kentucky public institutions.

Kentucky's Affordable Prepaid Tuition (KAPT)

529 PROGRAM TYPE: Prepaid
TELEPHONE: 888–919–5278
WEB SITE: www.getkapt.com

Enrollment: This program was closed to new enrollment after its 2004 enrollment period and the decision to reopen is reviewed annually. The beneficiary must be a Kentucky resident at the time of program enrollment or have an intention to attend a Kentucky institution.

Contract benefits: The program has three tuition plans. The Value Plan covers Kentucky's public community and technical colleges. The Standard Plan covers the highest-cost Kentucky public university. The Premium Plan provides benefits based on the average cost of Kentucky's private institutions that grow in value at the same rate as tuition increases at the University of Kentucky. A beneficiary attending a private or out-of-state institution receives the contract payout value, regardless of institution type.

Statutory state backing: 75% of the state abandoned property fund is available to cover any unfunded liability.

LOUISIANA

Louisiana's 529 savings program is subsidized by the state, resulting in no costs to the participant above the underlying fund expenses. However, only those meeting Louisiana residency requirements may participate in this program. Vanguard mutual funds and the State Treasurer's fixed income fund are utilized in the age-based and static portfolio options available through this program.

STATE AGENCY: Louisiana Tuition Trust Authority (LATTA)

State income tax treatment: Contributions to the START Saving Program of up to $2,400 per account per year by an individual filer, and up to $4,800 per beneficiary per year by a married couple filing jointly, are deductible in computing Louisiana taxable income. The contribution deadline is December 31 for contributions completed online, or postmarked if mailed. Any unused cap amount with an active account may be carried over to increase the maximum deduction amount in subsequent tax years. An account opened for an eligible needy, non-related beneficiary can produce a double deduction of as much as $4,800 per year. Qualified distributions from Louisiana and non-Louisiana 529 plans are excluded from Louisiana taxable income. Under the Louisiana recapture rules, the principal portion of nonqualified distributions from the Louisiana 529 plan are included in Louisiana taxable income to the extent of prior Louisiana tax deductions. Rollovers to another 529 plan are not subject to recapture.

Maximum contribution limit: A contribution will not be accepted if it would cause the total of all Louisiana 529 account balances for the same beneficiary to exceed $289,900.

Other considerations:

- Louisiana provides a matching contribution, called an "earnings enhancement," equal to 2% to 14% (depending on income) of a Louisiana participant's contributions. The matching funds may only be used for qualifying expenses.
- Under Louisiana law, the right of a beneficiary to the assets of a Louisiana 529 account is not subject to collation, execution, garnishment, attachment, the operation of bankruptcy or insolvency laws or other process of law.
- Account ownership may not be transferred prior to the owner's death or incapacity.

START Saving Program

529 PROGRAM TYPE:	Savings
PROGRAM MANAGER:	Louisiana State Treasurer
DISTRIBUTOR:	Louisiana State Treasurer
TELEPHONE:	800–259–5626
WEB SITE:	www.startsaving.la.gov

Enrollment: Enroll directly. This program is not sold through financial advisors. The account owner or beneficiary must be a Louisiana resident at the time of enrollment.

Investment options:

Option type	# of options	Underlying investments	Expense ratio [1]
Age- or enrollment-based	3 tracks	Vanguard mutual funds and Louisiana State Treasurer's Fund	0.00%–0.17%
Individual fund	6	Vanguard mutual funds	0.10%–0.47%
Principal protection [2]	1	Louisiana State Treasurer's Fund	0.00%

[1] No plan fees. Underlying fund expenses only.
[2] State of Louisiana provides guarantee of principal.

Minimum contributions: $10

Account maintenance fee: None

MAINE

The NextGen 529 savings program is managed by Merrill Lynch for the state of Maine. A direct-sold version called the Client Direct Series offers 10 investment options, and an advisor-sold version called the Client Select Series has 31 investment options. Each series uses a selection of fund families.

STATE AGENCY: Finance Authority of Maine (FAME) with investment oversight provided by the Maine State Treasurer

State income tax treatment: Contributions to Maine and non-Maine 529 plans of up to $250 per beneficiary per year are deductible in computing Maine taxable income for taxpayers with federal adjusted gross income of $100,000 or less (single or married filing separate) or $200,000 or less (joint or head of household). The contribution deadline is December 31. Qualified distributions from Maine and non-Maine 529 plans are excluded from Maine taxable income. Maine has no recapture provisions relating to nonqualified distributions or rollovers.

Maximum contribution limit: A contribution will not be accepted if it would cause the total of all Maine 529 account balances for the same beneficiary to exceed $380,000.

Other considerations:

- Accounts naming either a Maine resident participant or beneficiary may be eligible for a matching grant upon account opening, or for matching grants on subsequent contributions, or for a matching grant for choosing an automated funding option.

Contact the Finance Authority of Maine for current matching grant details and terms and conditions.

- The Harold Alfond College Challenge will provide $500 for any Maine resident baby to open a NextGen account before their first birthday.
- Under Maine law, accounts in NextGen are not subject to levy, execution, judgment or other operation of law, garnishment or other judicial enforcement, and accounts are not an asset or property of either the account owner or beneficiary for purposes of Maine insolvency laws.

NextGen College Investing Plan—Client Direct Series

529 PROGRAM TYPE:	Savings
PROGRAM MANAGER:	Merrill Lynch, Pierce, Fenner & Smith Incorporated
DISTRIBUTOR:	Merrill Lynch, Pierce, Fenner & Smith Incorporated
TELEPHONE:	877–463–9843
WEB SITE:	www.nextgenplan.com

Enrollment: Enroll directly. There are no state residency requirements. This program is not sold through financial advisors.

Investment options:

Option type	# of options	Underlying investments	Expense ratio
Age- or enrollment-based	1 track	BlackRock mutual funds	0.53%–0.91% [1]
Age- or enrollment-based	1 track	iShares ETFs	0.41%–0.48% [2]
Static multi-fund	5	BlackRock, Franklin Templeton, iShares, or MFS	0.48%–0.81% [3]
Individual fund	1	BlackRock S&P 500 Index Fund	0.37% [4]
Principal protection	1	Funding agreement with Transamerica Life Insurance Company	0.20%
FDIC-insured	1	Bank of America deposit account	0.00%

[1] 0.10% plan fees plus underlying fund expenses.
[2] 0.25% plan fees plus underlying fund expenses.
[3] 0.10%–0.25% plan fees plus underlying fund expenses.
[4] 0.07% plan fees plus underlying fund expenses.

Minimum contributions: With lump-sum contributions, the minimum initial contribution is $250 ($25 per portfolio), and the minimum subsequent contribution is $50 ($25 per portfolio). With the automatic investment plan, no initial contribution is required but the minimum ongoing contribution level is $50 per month.

Account maintenance fee: None

NextGen College Investing Plan—Client Select Series

529 PROGRAM TYPE:	Savings
PROGRAM MANAGER:	Merrill Lynch, Pierce, Fenner & Smith Incorporated
DISTRIBUTOR:	Merrill Lynch, Pierce, Fenner & Smith Incorporated
TELEPHONE:	877–463–9843
WEB SITE:	www.nextgenplan.com

Enrollment: Purchase through a Merrill Lynch Financial Advisor or other approved Maine distribution agent. There are no state residency requirements.

Investment options:

Option type	# of options	Underlying investments	Unit classes	Expense ratio [1]	Initial	Contingent deferred
Age- or enrollment-based	1 track	Franklin Templeton mutual funds	A	0.81%–1.24%	5.25%	0.00%
			C	1.56%–1.99%	0.00%	1.00%
Age- or enrollment-based	1 track	MFS mutual funds	A	0.82%–1.18%	5.25%	0.00%
			C	1.57%–1.93%	0.00%	1.00%
Age- or enrollment-based	1 track	BlackRock mutual funds	A	0.64%–1.22%	5.25%	0.00%
			C	1.39%–1.97%	0.00%	1.00%
Age- or enrollment-based	1 track	Allianz mutual funds	A	0.83%–1.25%	5.25%	0.00%
			C	1.58%–2.00%	0.00%	1.00%
Static multi-fund and individual-fund	25	Allianz, BlackRock, Eaton Vance, Franklin Templeton, MainStay, MFS, PIMCO, and Thornburg	A	0.94%–1.38%	4.50%–5.25%	0.00%
			C	1.69%–2.13%	0.00%	1.00%
Principal protection	1	Funding agreement with Transamerica Life Insurance Company	A/C	0.46%	0.00%	0.25%
FDIC-insured	1	Bank of America deposit account	A/C	0.000%	0.00%	0.00%

[1] Plan administration and servicing fees plus underlying fund expenses.

Minimum contributions: With lump-sum contributions, the minimum initial contribution is $250 ($25 per portfolio), and the minimum subsequent contribution is $50 ($25 per portfolio). With the automatic investment plan, no initial contribution is required but the minimum ongoing contribution level is $50 per month.

Account maintenance fee: $50 annually. The fee is waived for Maine residents, for account balances of $20,000 or greater, and for accounts receiving at least $2,500 in contributions during the year. The fee is reduced to $25 if an employer has arranged for an employee payroll direct deposit relationship with the program manager.

MARYLAND

Maryland offers a direct-sold 529 savings program and a prepaid tuition program. The savings program is managed by T. Rowe Price and offers age-based and static options using T. Rowe Price mutual funds. Enrollment in the prepaid tuition program is open to account holders or beneficiaries who are residents of Maryland or the District of Columbia at the time of enrollment.

STATE AGENCY: College Savings Plans of Maryland

State income tax treatment: Contributions to the Maryland College Investment Plan of up to $2,500 per beneficiary per year by an individual filer, and up to $5,000 per beneficiary per year for married taxpayers who each make contributions to their own accounts, are deductible in computing Maryland taxable income. Contributions in excess of annual limits may be carried over and taken as deductions for up to 10 years. Contributions to the Maryland Prepaid College Trust of up to $2,500 per account are deductible in computing Maryland taxable income, and excess contributions may be carried over for an unlimited number of years until fully deducted. Under either program, contributions must be from the account owner to be eligible for the deduction. The contribution deadline is December 31. Qualified distributions from Maryland and non-Maryland 529 plans are excluded from Maryland taxable income. Under the Maryland recapture rules, the principal portion of nonqualified distributions from a Maryland 529 plan must be included in Maryland taxable income to the extent of prior Maryland tax deductions. Rollovers to another 529 plan are not subject to recapture.

Maximum contribution limit: A contribution will not be accepted if it would cause the total of all Maryland 529 account balances for the same beneficiary to exceed $320,000.

Maryland College Investment Plan

529 PROGRAM TYPE: Savings
PROGRAM MANAGER: T. Rowe Price Associates, Inc.
DISTRIBUTOR: T. Rowe Price Associates, Inc.
TELEPHONE: 888–463–4723
WEB SITE: www.collegesavingsmd.org

Enrollment: Enroll directly. This program is not sold through financial advisors. There are no state residency requirements.

Investment options:

Option type	# of options	Underlying investments	Expense ratio [1]
Age- or enrollment-based	1 track		0.66%–0.86%
Static multi-fund	2	T. Rowe Price mutual funds	0.85%–0.87%
Individual fund	4		0.14%–0.89%

[1] 0.20% plan fees plus underlying fund expenses. The Money Market Portfolio may waive fees to maintain a 0.00% yield.

Minimum contributions: With lump-sum contributions, the minimum initial contribution is $250, and the minimum subsequent contribution is $25. With the automatic investment plan, the minimum contribution level is $25 per month.

Account maintenance fee: $20 annually ($10 effective July 2013). The fee is waived for account balances of $25,000 or greater and for accounts in the automatic investment plan.

Maryland Prepaid College Trust

529 PROGRAM TYPE: Prepaid
TELEPHONE: 888–463–4723
WEB SITE: www.collegesavingsmd.org

Enrollment: The 2012-2013 enrollment period began on December 1 and runs through April 8, 2013. Newborn infants can be enrolled anytime until their first birthday at prices in effect at the time of enrollment. Additional semesters or years for the same account holder/beneficiary may also be purchased at any time. The account holder or beneficiary must be a Maryland or District of Columbia resident at the time of program enrollment.

Time/age restrictions: Beneficiaries must be in the 12th grade or below at the time of program enrollment and must be enrolled for at least 3 years before they are eligible to receive tuition benefits.

Contract benefits: Available contract options consist of one semester to five years of tuition and mandatory fees at a Maryland public 4-year university, one or two years at a Maryland community college, and a community/university combination (2 years of each). A beneficiary attending a private or out-of-state institution receives up to the weighted average tuition and mandatory fees of the Maryland public colleges in the tuition plan purchased or the beneficiary's actual tuition and mandatory fees, whichever is less. A minimum benefit provision also applies.

Contract prices: For the 2012-2013 enrollment period, prices ranged from as little as $4,283 for a one-year community college contract for a newborn to as much as $53,901 for a five-year university contract for a child in the ninth grade or higher. Extended payment plans are available.

Enrollment or application fee: $75 for paper application or $50 for online application, reduced to $20 if the same account holder and beneficiary have an account in the Maryland College Investment Plan.

Statutory state backing: Maryland provides a legislative guarantee by which the governor is required to include in the state budget, and the legislature is required to consider, but not necessarily approve, an appropriation to cover any shortfall, with any such appropriations repayable within two years.

Added feature: Under Maryland law, the right to benefits from the Prepaid College Trust is not subject to attachment, garnishment, or seizure by creditors.

MASSACHUSETTS

The Bay State offers the U.Fund College Investing Plan, a direct-sold 529 savings program managed by Fidelity Investments using Fidelity mutual funds and non-Fidelity funds, and the U.Plan Prepaid Tuition Program offered by MEFA. The U.Plan is not a qualifying 529 plan but is nevertheless tax-free for federal and Massachusetts income tax purposes because participants are purchasing Massachusetts general obligation bonds. The bonds are redeemable to pay specified percentages of tuition and mandatory fees at 80 participating private and public Massachusetts colleges and universities, thereby keeping pace with tuition inflation at those institutions.

STATE AGENCY: Massachusetts Educational Financing Authority (MEFA)

State income tax treatment: Contributions to a 529 plan or the U.Plan are not deductible on Massachusetts income tax returns. Qualified distributions from the U.Fund and from non-Massachusetts 529 plans are excluded from Massachusetts taxable income. The U.Plan's general obligation bonds are tax-free in Massachusetts, but residents of states other than Massachusetts may owe state income tax on an investment in the U.Plan if their state law requires that bond interest on out-of-state bonds be included in state taxable income.

Maximum contribution limit: A contribution will not be accepted if it would cause the total of all Massachusetts 529 account balances for the same beneficiary to exceed $350,000.

Other considerations:

- Because the U.Plan is not a 529 plan, the gift and estate tax treatment does not follow the Section 529 rules. Furthermore, the federal 10 percent penalty on non-qualified distributions from a 529 plan does not apply to this program.
- Account ownership in the U.Fund may not be transferred prior to the owner's death or incapacity. Ownership in the U.Plan is transferable.

U.Fund College Investing Plan

529 PROGRAM TYPE:	Savings
PROGRAM MANAGER:	Fidelity Investments
DISTRIBUTOR:	Fidelity Brokerage Services, LLC
TELEPHONE:	800–544–2776
WEB SITE:	www.fidelity.com/ufund

Enrollment: Enroll directly. This program is not sold through financial advisors. There are no state residency requirements.

Investment options:

Option type	# of options	Underlying investments	Expense ratio [1]
Age-based (index)	1 track		0.31%–0.35%
Age-based (active)	1 track		0.67%–1.01%
Static multi-fund (index)	3	Fidelity Investments mutual funds	0.30%–0.35%
Static multi-fund (active)	3		0.56%–1.01%
Individual fund	5		0.25%–0.57%
Age-based (multi-firm)	1 track	Mutual funds from Fidelity Investments, Acadian, Artisan, Aston, BlackRock Causeway, Credit Suisse, Eaton Vance, Harbor, Invesco, JP Morgan, MFS, Nataxis, OppenheimerFunds, PIMCO, Royce, Western Asset, and William Blair	0.94%–1.40%
FDIC-insured	1	Wells Fargo Bank, N.A.	0.05%–0.50%

[1] 0.15% (index), 0.20% (active), or 0.35% (multi-fund) plan fees plus underlying fund expenses. Fees on Bank Deposit Portfolio are variable.

Minimum contributions: With lump-sum contributions, the minimum initial contribution is $50, and the minimum subsequent contribution is $25. With the automatic investment plan, the minimum contribution level is $15 per month or $45 per quarter.

Account maintenance fee: None

Added feature: Accounts can be linked to the Fidelity Investments 529 Rewards American Express Card.

U.Plan Prepaid Tuition Program

529 PROGRAM TYPE:	Prepaid
PROGRAM MANAGER:	Massachusetts Educational Financing Authority (MEFA)
TELEPHONE:	800–449–6332
WEB SITE:	www.mefa.org/uplan

Enrollment: The enrollment period is usually during May and June each year. There are no state residency requirements.

Time/age restrictions: A tuition certificate must be redeemed within 6 years after its maturity date.

Program benefits: Massachusetts general obligation bonds issued under this plan may be redeemed for a pre-determined percentage of tuition and mandatory fees at 80 participating public and private Massachusetts colleges and universities. When redeemed for other purposes, the bond owner will receive principal plus interest compounded annually at a rate equal to increases in the Consumer Price Index.

Minimum contributions: $300 per maturity year.

Maximum contributions: The cost of tuition and mandatory fees for four years at the highest cost participating Massachusetts institution.

Enrollment or application fee: None

Statutory state backing: Massachusetts backs the obligations under this program with its full faith and credit.

MICHIGAN

Michigan offers the Michigan Education Savings Program (MESP), a direct-sold 529 savings program managed by TIAA-CREF Tuition Financing, Inc; the MI 529 Advisor Plan (MAP) an advisor-sold plan managed by TIAA-CREF and distributed by Allianz Global Distributors LLC; and the Michigan Education Trust (MET), a 529 prepaid tuition program open to Michigan beneficiaries.

STATE AGENCIES:	Michigan Department of Treasury (MESP);
	MET Board of Directors (MET)

State income tax treatment: All contributions to MET are deductible in computing Michigan taxable income. Contributions to either of Michigan's two 529 savings programs (MESP and MAP) of up to $5,000 per year by an individual filer, and up to $10,000 per year by a married couple filing jointly, are deductible in computing Michigan taxable income. Contributions must be reduced by qualified distributions during the year in determining the amount that may be deducted. Rollover contributions are not eligible for the deduction, according to the Michigan Department of Treasury. The contribution deadline is December 31. Qualified distributions from Michigan and non-Michigan 529 plans are excluded from Michigan taxable income. Also excluded are distributions from a Michigan 529 plan attributable to the beneficiary's death, disability, scholarship, or attendance at one of the U.S. military academies. Under the Michigan recapture rules, the principal portion of nonqualified distributions must be included in Michigan taxable income to the extent of prior Michigan tax deductions. Rollovers to another 529 plan are not subject to recapture.

Maximum contribution limit: A contribution will not be accepted if it would cause the total of all Michigan 529 account balances for the same beneficiary to exceed $235,000.

Other considerations:

- Participation in a Michigan 529 plan does not affect the beneficiary's eligibility for financial aid programs administered by the state of Michigan.

Michigan Education Savings Program (MESP)

529 PROGRAM TYPE:	Savings
PROGRAM MANAGER:	TIAA-CREF Tuition Financing, Inc.
DISTRIBUTOR:	TIAA-CREF Individual & Institutional Services, LLC
TELEPHONE:	877–861–6377
WEB SITE:	www.MIsaves.com

Enrollment: Enroll directly. This program is not sold through financial advisors. There are no state residency requirements.

Investment options:

Option type	# of options	Underlying investments	Expense ratio[1]
Age- or enrollment-based	3 tracks		0.21%–0.28%
Static multi-fund	4	TIAA-CREF institutional mutual funds	0.21%–0.30%
Individual fund	1		0.20%
Principal protection	1	Funding agreement with TIAA-CREF Life Insurance Company	0.00%

[1] 0.13% plan fees (none for Principal Protection) plus underlying fund expenses.

Minimum contributions: $25 per investment option, or $15 per pay period via payroll deduction.

Account maintenance fee: None

MI 529 Advisor Plan

529 PROGRAM TYPE:	Savings
PROGRAM MANAGER:	TIAA-CREF Tuition Financing, Inc. and Allianz Global Investors Distributors LLC
DISTRIBUTOR:	Allianz Global Investors Distributors LLC
TELEPHONE:	866-529-8818
WEB SITE:	www.mi529advisor.com

Enrollment: Purchase through a financial advisor. There are no state residency requirements.

Investment options:

					Maximum sales charge	
Option type	# of options	Underlying investments	Unit classes	Expense ratio [1]	Initial	Contingent deferred
Age- or enrollment-based	1 track		A	1.29%–1.48%	4.50%	0.00%
			C	1.69%–1.88%	0.00%	0.65%
Static multi-fund	2	Mutual funds from Allianz, NFJ, PIMCO and TIAA-CREF	A	1.32%–1.48%	4.50%	0.00%
			C	1.72%–1.88%	0.00%	0.65%
Individual fund	12		A	0.83%–1.84%	4.50% [2]	0.00%
			C	0.83%–1.92%	0.00%	0.33% [2]

[1] 0.50% management fee plus underlying fund expenses and distribution/servicing fees.
[2] None for the Money Market Portfolio.

Minimum contributions: $25 per investment portfolio.

Account maintenance fee: None

Michigan Education Trust (MET)

529 PROGRAM TYPE:	Prepaid
TELEPHONE:	800–638–4543
WEB SITE:	www.SETwithMET.com

Enrollment: The 2013 enrollment period began on December 10, 2012 and runs through September 30, 2013. The beneficiary must be a Michigan resident at the time of program enrollment. The purchaser can live anywhere in the U.S. except Arizona, Illinois, New York, North Dakota, Ohio, or Vermont due to those states' securities laws.

Time/age restrictions: The age restriction for beneficiaries has been removed. Contract benefits must be used within 15 years after the beneficiary's projected college entrance date.

Contract benefits: The Full Benefits contract pays for one to ten semesters of tuition and mandatory fees at any Michigan public institution. The Limited Benefits contract pays for one to ten semesters of tuition and mandatory fees at Michigan public institutions limited to 105% of the weighted average tuition of all Michigan four-year universities. The Community College contract pays one to four semesters of in-district tuition and mandatory fees at any Michigan public community college. A beneficiary with a Full Benefits Contract attending an in-state private institution receives the Michigan weighted-average public tuition while a beneficiary attending an out-of-state institution receives the Michigan average public tuition.

Contract prices: For the 2013 enrollment period, prices range from as little as $1,549 (increasing to $1,572 in May 2013) for a one-semester community college contract to as much as $66,946 (increasing to $67,946 in May 2013) for a four-year full benefits contract. Extended payment plans are available.

Contract processing fee: $25 to $60, depending on the timing and mode of the contract submission.

Statutory state backing: None

MINNESOTA

Minnesota's 529 plan is managed by TIAA-CREF Tuition Financing, Inc. and offers an age-based option along with 5 static investment options.

STATE AGENCIES: Minnesota Office of Higher Education and the State Board of Investment

State income tax treatment: Contributions to a 529 plan are not deductible on Minnesota income tax returns. Qualified distributions from Minnesota and non-Minnesota 529 plans are excluded from Minnesota taxable income.

Maximum contribution limit: A contribution will not be accepted if it would cause the total of all Minnesota 529 account balances for the same beneficiary to exceed $235,000.

Minnesota College Savings Plan

529 PROGRAM TYPE: Savings
PROGRAM MANAGER: TIAA-CREF Tuition Financing, Inc.
DISTRIBUTOR: TIAA-CREF Individual & Institutional Services, LLC
TELEPHONE: 877–338–4646
WEB SITE: www.mnsaves.org

Enrollment: Enroll directly. There are no state residency requirements. This program is not sold through financial advisors.

Investment options:

Option type	# of options	Underlying investments	Expense ratio [1]
Age- or enrollment-based	1 track	TIAA-CREF institutional mutual funds	0.4625%
Static multi-fund	3		0.5025%–0.5625%
Money market	1		0.4925%
Principal protection	1	Funding agreement with TIAA-CREF Life Insurance Company	0.00%

[1] Expense ratio includes plan fees plus underlying fund expenses.

Minimum contributions: $25 per investment option, or $15 per investment option via payroll deduction.

Account maintenance fee: None

MISSISSIPPI

The Mississippi Affordable College Savings (MACS) Program is a direct-sold program managed by TIAA-CREF Tuition Financing, Inc. (TFI). The MACS Advisor program, an advisor-sold program also managed by TFI, was terminated in May 2013. Mississippi also offers a prepaid tuition program (MPACT). MPACT is open only to Mississippi residents.

STATE AGENCIES: College Savings Plans of Mississippi and Mississippi Treasury Department

State income tax treatment: All contributions to the MPACT prepaid tuition program, and contributions to the MACS savings programs of up to $10,000 ($20,000 for a married couple filing jointly), are deductible in computing Mississippi taxable income. The contribution deadline is April 15 of the following year. Qualified distributions from Mississippi and non-Mississippi 529 plans are excluded from Mississippi taxable income. Under the Mississippi recapture rules, the principal portion of nonqualified distributions from a Mississippi 529 plan must be included in Mississippi taxable income to the extent of prior Mississippi tax deductions. A rollover to another 529 plan is not subject to recapture.

Maximum contribution limit: A contribution will not be accepted if it would cause the total of all Mississippi 529 account balances for the same beneficiary to exceed $235,000.

Other considerations:

- Participation in a Mississippi 529 plan does not affect the beneficiary's eligibility for financial aid programs administered by the state of Mississippi.

Mississippi Affordable College Savings (MACS) Program

529 PROGRAM TYPE:	Savings
PROGRAM MANAGER:	TIAA-CREF Tuition Financing, Inc.
DISTRIBUTOR:	TIAA-CREF Individual & Institutional Services, LLC
TELEPHONE:	800–486–3670
WEB SITE:	www.ms529.com

Enrollment: Enroll directly. This program is not sold through financial advisors. There are no state residency requirements.

Investment options:

Option type	# of options	Underlying investments	Expense ratio
Age- or enrollment-based	1 track	TIAA-CREF institutional mutual funds	0.65%–0.72% [1]
Static multi-fund	2		0.69%–0.72% [1]
Principal protection	1	Funding agreement with TIAA-CREF Life Insurance Company	0.00%

[1] 0.50% plan fees plus underlying fund expenses.

Minimum contributions: $25 per investment option, or $15 per pay period via payroll deduction.

Account maintenance fee: None

Mississippi Prepaid Affordable College Tuition (MPACT) Program

529 PROGRAM TYPE:	Prepaid
TELEPHONE:	800–987–4450
WEB SITE:	www.collegesavingsmississippi.com

Enrollment: The enrollment period usually runs from September through December each year. The 2012 enrollment was deferred pending an actuarial audit. The account owner or beneficiary must be a Mississippi resident at the time of program enrollment.

Time/age restrictions: The beneficiary must be 18 years old or younger at the time of program enrollment. Contract benefits must be used within ten years of the beneficiary's projected college entrance date.

Contract benefits: The program offers a senior college (university) plan for one to five years of tuition and mandatory fees at a Mississippi public university, a community college plan for one or two years, and a combination plan. A beneficiary attending a private or out-of-state institution receives the weighted average tuition and mandatory fees at Mississippi public institutions, not to exceed the beneficiary's actual tuition and mandatory fees.

Contract prices: For the 2011 enrollment period, prices ranged from as little as $1,925 for a one-year junior/community college contract for a newborn to as much as $29,688 for a five-year university contract for a twelfth grader. Extended payment plans are available.

Enrollment or application fee: $60

Statutory state backing: Program obligations are backed by the full faith and credit of the state of Mississippi.

Added feature: A beneficiary is considered a resident for purposes of tuition regardless of the beneficiary's residence at college enrollment if the original purchaser was the parent, grandparent, or legal guardian of the beneficiary or the beneficiary was a resident of Mississippi at the time the MPACT contract was purchased.

MISSOURI

Missouri offers a direct-sold 529 savings program managed by Upromise Investments using mutual funds from Vanguard. Missouri also offers an advisor-sold 529 savings program managed by Upromise Investments featuring the use of mutual funds from several fund families, exchange traded funds (ETF), and an anti-terror portfolio option.

STATE AGENCY: Missouri Higher Education Savings Program Board

State income tax treatment: Contributions to a Missouri or non-Missouri 529 plan of up to $8,000 per year by an individual filer, and up to $16,000 per year by a married couple filing jointly, are deductible in computing Missouri taxable income. Contributions must be from the account owner to be eligible for the deduction. The contribution deadline is December 31. Rollover contributions from another 529 plan are not eligible for the deduction. Qualified distributions from Missouri and non-Missouri 529 plans are excluded from Missouri taxable income. Under the Missouri recapture rule, the principal portion of rollovers and nonqualified distributions from a 529 plan must be included in Missouri taxable income to the extent of prior Missouri tax deductions. A rollover that is a not a direct trustee-to-trustee rollover is considered a nonqualified distribution for Missouri tax purposes.

Maximum contribution limit: A contribution will not be accepted if it would cause the total of all Missouri 529 account balances for the same beneficiary to exceed $325,000.

Other considerations:

- Participation in a Missouri 529 plan does not affect the beneficiary's eligibility for financial aid programs administered by the state of Missouri.
- Accounts in a Missouri 529 plan can be linked to the Upromise Rewards Service.

MOST – Missouri's 529 College Savings Plan

529 PROGRAM TYPE:	Savings
PROGRAM MANAGER:	Upromise Investments, Inc.
DISTRIBUTOR:	Vanguard Marketing Corporation
TELEPHONE:	888–414–6678
WEB SITE:	www.missourimost.org

Enrollment: Enroll directly. This program is not sold through financial advisors. There are no state residency requirements.

Investment options:

Option type	# of options	Underlying investments	Expense ratio [1]
Age- or enrollment-based	3 tracks		0.29%–0.32%
Static multi-fund	6	Vanguard mutual funds	0.32%
Individual fund	8		0.29%–0.60%

[1] Includes plan fees plus underlying fund expenses.

Minimum contributions: $25, or $15 per pay period via payroll deduction. Through the free Ugift service, friends and family are invited to make contributions of at least $25 each directly to a child's account.

Account maintenance fee: $10 annually. The fee is waived for Missouri residents, for account balances of $10,000 or greater, and for account owners who elect to have electronic delivery of plan documents.

Added feature: A matching grant is available for eligible applicants who are Missouri residents and who have opened a plan account for a beneficiary 13 years old or younger who is also a Missouri resident. The matching rate is dollar for dollar up to a maximum of $500 per beneficiary with a lifetime maximum of $2,500 per beneficiary. The applicant must be an account owner who is a parent or legal guardian of the beneficiary and the account owner's household Missouri adjusted gross may not exceed $74,999. Applications for matching grants must be submitted each year between June 1 and June 30. A total of up to $500,000 in matching grants is available over a four year period beginning March 1, 2012. Each year's $125,000 allocation is awarded on a first come first serve basis, with any unused amounts added to the following year.

MOST—Missouri's 529 Advisor Plan

529 PROGRAM TYPE:	Savings
PROGRAM MANAGER:	Upromise Investments, Inc.
DISTRIBUTOR:	DWS Investments Distributors, Inc.
TELEPHONE:	800-617-5097
WEB SITE:	www.most529advisor.org

Enrollment: Purchase through financial advisor. There are no state residency requirements.

Investment options:

					Maximum sales charge	
Option type	**# of options**	**Underlying investments**	**Unit classes**	**Expense ratio [1]**	**Initial**	**Contingent deferred**
Static multi-fund	3	Portfolios of iShares exchange traded funds (ETF)	A	0.82%–0.85%	3.75%–5.50%	0.00%
			C	1.57%–1.60%	0.00%	1.00%
Anti-terror	1	Anti-terror portfolio managed by Scout Investment Advisors	A	1.45%	5.50%	0.00%
			C	2.20%	0.00%	1.00%
Individual fund	14	Mutual funds from American Century, American Funds, Columbia, DWS, PIMCO, Franklin Templeton, T. Rowe Price, and Van Kampen	A	0.75%–1.44%	3.75%–5.50%	0.00%
			C	1.50%–2.19%	0.00%	1.00%

[1] 0.30% plan fees plus underlying fund expenses and distribution/servicing fees.

Minimum contributions: With lump-sum contributions, the minimum initial contribution is $500. With the automatic investment plan, the minimum contribution level is $50 per month ($150 per quarter) via electronic funds transfer or $25 per payroll via payroll direct deposit. Through the free Ugift service, friends and family are invited to make contributions of at least $50 each directly to a child's account.

Account maintenance fee: $25 annually. The fee is waived for account balances of $25,000 or greater.

MONTANA

The Montana Family Education Savings Program includes two direct-sold 529 savings programs. One offers FDIC-insured bank products through College Savings Bank and the other offers age-based and static investment options using Vanguard funds.

STATE AGENCY: Montana Board of Regents of Higher Education

State income tax treatment: Contributions to a Montana 529 plan of up to $3,000 by an individual filer, and up to $6,000 per year by a married couple filing jointly, are deductible in computing Montana taxable income. The contributions must be from the account owner, the account owner's spouse, or the account owner's custodian/parent to be eligible for the deduction. The contribution deadline is December 31. Qualified distributions from Montana and non-Montana 529 plans are excluded from Montana taxable income, except that any distributions from a Montana 529 within the first three years of account ownership require that prior deductions be recaptured into income. The Montana recapture rules also require that the principal portion of a rollover or nonqualified distribution from a Montana 529 plan is subject to Montana tax at the highest Montana marginal rate to the extent of prior Montana tax deductions.

Maximum contribution limit: A contribution will not be accepted if it would cause the total of all Montana 529 account balances for the same beneficiary to exceed $374,000.

Montana Family Education Savings Program — Bank Plan

529 PROGRAM TYPE: Savings
PROGRAM MANAGER: College Savings Bank
DISTRIBUTOR: College Savings Bank
TELEPHONE: 800–888–2723
WEB SITE: http://montana.collegesavings.com

Enrollment: Enroll directly or through contracted partners including certain financial advisors and financial institutions within the state of Montana. There are no state residency requirements.

Investment options: Four types of FDIC-insured options are available: (1) the CollegeSure® CD is a variable rate certificate of deposit from College Savings Bank, with a maturity ranging from 1 to 22 years, that is credited with interest each year based on the previous year's college inflation rate, as measured by the change in the College Board's Independent College 500® Index (IC 500®) less an issue margin, and is subject to a maximum interest rate which is equal to the first year's interest rate plus an interest rate cap (the issue margin and interest rate cap are determined on the contribution date); (2) the InvestorSure® CD is a five-year certificate of deposit that pays 70% of the average increase in the S&P 500 Index at maturity based on a formula and is guaranteed not to lose principal; (3) Fixed Rate CDs are available in 1- and 3-year maturities, (4) the Honors™ Savings Account, a high-yielding, variable rate savings account available exclusively online.

Minimum contributions:

CollegeSure® CD: With lump-sum contributions, the minimum initial contribution is $250. With the automatic investment plan, the minimum contribution level is $25 per month via electronic funds transfer, or $25 per payroll via payroll deduction. Deposits under $250 are held in an interest bearing savings account, and each time the balance reaches $250, a CD purchase is made.

InvestorSure® CD: With lump-sum contributions, the minimum initial contribution is $250. With the automatic investment plan, the minimum contribution level is $25 per month via electronic funds transfer, or $25 per payroll via payroll deduction. Deposits under $250 are held in an interest bearing savings account, and each time the balance reaches $250, a CD purchase is made on the next CD issue date.

Fixed-rate CD: With lump-sum contributions, the minimum initial contribution is $250. With the automatic investment plan, the minimum contribution level is $25 per month via electronic funds transfer, or $25 per pay period via payroll deduction. Deposits under $250 are held in an interest bearing savings account, and each time the balance reaches $250, a CD purchase is made.

Honors™ Savings Account: The minimum contribution is $250 and must be contributed by electronic check through the state 529 program website or the College Savings Bank website.

Account maintenance fee: No asset-based fees. Service-based and other fees may apply.

Montana Family Education Savings Program — Investment Plan

529 PROGRAM TYPE:	Savings
PROGRAM MANAGER:	College Savings Bank and Upromise Investments, Inc.
DISTRIBUTOR:	Upromise Investments, inc.
TELEPHONE:	800–888-2723
WEB SITE:	www.montanasaves.com

Enrollment: Enroll directly. This program is not sold through financial advisors. There are no state residency requirements.

Investment options:

Option type	# of options	Underlying investments	Expense ratio [1]
Static asset allocation	3	Vanguard LifeStrategy funds	0.87%–0.89%
100% equity	2	Vanguard index funds	0.82%–0.88%

[1] 0.67%–0.77% plan fees plus underlying fund expenses.

Minimum contributions: $25, or $15 through payroll deduction. Through the free Ugift service, friends and family are invited to make contributions of at least $15 each directly to a child's account.

Account maintenance fee: $25 annually. The fee is waived for Montana residents, for accounts with greater than $25,000, and for accounts in the automatic contribution or payroll deduction plan.

Added feature: Accounts can be linked to the Upromise Rewards Service.

NEBRASKA

The Cornhusker State offers four 529 savings programs under its program manager, First National Bank of Omaha. The Nebraska Education Savings Trust (NEST) is available in a direct-sold version and an advisor-sold version and employs several fund families on its investment platform. The TD Ameritrade 529 College Savings Plan is similar to NEST, but is distributed through discount broker.TD Ameritrade. The State Farm College Savings Plan uses OFI Private Investments Inc. for administration and investment management services and is distributed exclusively through State Farm representatives.

STATE AGENCIES: Nebraska State Treasurer and Nebraska Investment Council

State income tax treatment: Contributions to a Nebraska 529 plan of up to $5,000 per year for single taxpayers and married taxpayers filing jointly, and up to $2,500 for married taxpayers filing separately, are deductible in computing Nebraska taxable income. Contributions must be from the account owner to be eligible for the deduction. The contribution deadline is December 31. Qualified distributions from Nebraska and non-Nebraska 529 plans are excluded from Nebraska taxable income. Under the Nebraska recapture rules, the principal portion of rollovers to another state's 529 plan and nonqualified distributions from a Nebraska 529 plan must be included in Nebraska taxable income to the extent of prior Nebraska tax deductions.

Maximum contribution limit: A contribution will not be accepted if it would cause the total of all Nebraska 529 account balances for the same beneficiary to exceed $360,000.

Other considerations:

- Under Nebraska law, an account in a Nebraska 529 plan is not susceptible to any levy, execution, judgment, or other operation of law, garnishment, or other judicial enforcement, and the account is not an asset or property of either the participant or the beneficiary for purposes of any state insolvency laws.
- Participation in a Nebraska 529 plan does not affect the beneficiary's eligibility for financial aid programs administered by the state of Nebraska.
- Accounts in NEST can be linked to the Upromise Rewards Service.

NEST Direct Plan

529 PROGRAM TYPE:	Savings
PROGRAM MANAGER:	First National Bank of Omaha
DISTRIBUTOR:	First National Bank of Omaha
TELEPHONE:	888–993–3746
WEB SITE:	www.nest529direct.com

Enrollment: Enroll directly. There are no state residency requirements.

Investment options:

Option type	# of options	Underlying investments	Expense ratio [1]
Age- or enrollment-based	4 tracks	ETFs from iShares and SSgA, and mutual funds from Tributary, Goldman Sachs, PIMCO, State Street, T. Rowe Price, and Vanguard	0.35%–0.53%
Static multi-fund	3		0.35%–0.53%
Individual fund	16		0.31%–1.26%
FDIC-insured	1	First National Bank of Omaha savings account	0.20%

[1] 0.29% plan fees (0.20% for Bank Savings option) plus underlying fund expenses.

Minimum contributions: The program has no minimum contribution.

Account maintenance fee: None

NEST Advisor Plan

529 PROGRAM TYPE:	Savings
PROGRAM MANAGER:	First National Bank of Omaha
DISTRIBUTOR:	First National Capital Markets, Inc.
TELEPHONE:	888-659-6378
WEB SITE:	www.nest529advisor.com

Enrollment: Purchase through a financial advisor. There are no state residency requirements.

Investment options:

Option type	# of options	Underlying investments	Unit classes	Expense ratio [1][2]	Maximum sales charge	
					Initial [2]	Contingent deferred [2]
Age- or enrollment-based	4 tracks	ETFs from iShares, Vanguard, SSgA, and mutual funds from Tributary, American Century, T. Rowe Price, Federated, State Street, Dreyfus, Goldman Sachs, and PIMCO	A	0.41%–0.84%	4.75%	0.00%
			C	0.41%–1.59%	0.00%	1.00%
Static multi-fund	3		A	0.65%–0.81%	4.75%	0.00%
			C	1.40%–1.56%	0.00%	1.00%
Individual fund	18		A	0.47%–1.51%	4.75%	0.00%
			C	0.47%–2.26%	0.00%	1.00%
FDIC-insured	1	First National Bank of Omaha savings account	A	0.20%	0.00%	0.00%
			C			

[1] 0.29% plan fees (0.20% for Bank Savings option) plus underlying fund expenses and distribution/servicing fees.
[2] The program manager has waived distribution fees and sales charges for the Goldman Sachs Prime Money Market, Bank Savings and Age Based 19+ Conservative investment options.

Minimum contributions: The program has no minimum contribution.

Account maintenance fee: None

TD Ameritrade 529 College Savings Plan

529 PROGRAM TYPE:	Savings
PROGRAM MANAGER:	First National Bank of Omaha
DISTRIBUTOR:	TD Ameritrade, Inc.
TELEPHONE:	877–408–4644
WEB SITE:	http://collegesavings.tdameritrade.com/index.asp

Enrollment: Purchase through TD Ameritrade. There are no state residency requirements.

Investment options:

Option type	# of options	Underlying investments	Expense ratio [1]
Age- or enrollment-based	4 tracks	ETFs from Vanguard, iShares, and SSgA, and mutual funds from American Century, Tributary, Goldman Sachs, PIMCO, State Street, T. Rowe Price, and Vanguard	0.54%–0.68%
Static multi-fund	3		0.54%–0.66%
Individual fund	17		0.50%–1.45%

[1] 0.29% management/administrative fees plus 0.19% distribution fee and underlying fund expenses.

Minimum contributions: The program has no minimum contribution.

Account maintenance fee: None

State Farm College Savings Plan

529 PROGRAM TYPE:	Savings
PROGRAM MANAGER:	First National Bank of Omaha and OFI Private Investments Inc.
DISTRIBUTOR:	OppenheimerFunds Distributor, Inc.
TELEPHONE:	800–321–7520
WEB SITE:	www.statefarm.com/mutual/acct_types/529.asp

Enrollment: Purchase through a State Farm VP Management Corp. Registered Representative. There are no state residency requirements.

Investment options:

					Maximum sales charge	
Option type	**# of options**	**Underlying investments**	**Unit classes**	**Expense ratio [1]**	**Initial**	**Contingent deferred**
Age- or enrollment-based	1 track	Mutual funds from OppenheimerFunds, Federated, and State Farm	A	0.86%–1.23%	5.50%	0.00%
Static multi-fund	3	Mutual funds from OppenheimerFunds and State Farm	A	1 14%–1.23%	5.50%	0.00%
Money market	1	Oppenheimer Institutional Money Market Fund	-	0.39%	0.00%	0.00%

[1] 0.22% plan fees plus underlying fund expenses and distribution/servicing fees.

Minimum contributions: With lump-sum contributions, the minimum initial contribution is $250, and the minimum subsequent contribution is $50 per portfolio. With the automatic investment plan, the minimum contribution level is $50 per portfolio.

Account maintenance fee: None

NEVADA

The Silver State offers five different 529 plans including a prepaid tuition plan, an advisor-sold savings program through Putnam Investments, and three direct-sold savings programs. The direct-sold plans include a plan featuring Vanguard mutual funds, another featuring USAA mutual funds, and the third featuring ETF Portfolios from SSgA. The prepaid tuition plan has a state residency requirement.

STATE AGENCIES:	Board of Trustees of the College Savings Plans of Nevada and the State Treasurer's Office

State income tax treatment: Nevada does not have a personal income tax.

Maximum contribution limit: A contribution will not be accepted if it would cause the total of all Nevada 529 account balances for the same beneficiary to exceed $370,000.

Other considerations:

- Nevada law provides that up to $500,000 of an account owner's assets in a Nevada 529 Plan may be protected from creditors, depending on when such assets were contributed to the account and whether they are eventually used to pay qualified higher education expenses.

The SSgA Upromise 529 Plan

529 PROGRAM TYPE:	Savings
PROGRAM MANAGERS:	Upromise Investments, Inc. and State Street Global Advisors (SSgA)
DISTRIBUTOR:	Upromise Investments, Inc.
TELEPHONE:	800-587-7305
WEB SITE:	www.ssga.upromise529.com (http://uii.s.upromise.com/content/home.html)

Enrollment: Enroll directly. This program is not sold through financial advisors. There are no state residency requirements.

Investment options:

Option type	# of options	Underlying investments	Expense ratio
Age- or enrollment-based	1 track		0.45%–0.55% [1]
Static multi-fund	3	ETFs and mutual funds from SSgA	0.45%–0.57% [1]
Individual fund	15		0.33%–0.89% [2]
FDIC-insured	1	Sallie Mae High-Yield Savings Account	0.29%

[1] 0.33% plan fees plus underlying fund expenses and distribution/servicing fees.
[2] 0.24% plan fees plus underlying fund expenses and distribution/servicing fees.

Minimum contributions: With lump-sum contributions, the minimum initial contribution is $250, and the minimum subsequent contribution is $50. With the automatic investment plan, the minimum contribution level is $50 per month (or $150 per quarter) via electronic funds transfer or $15 per pay period via payroll deduction or $25 Upromise Service contributions. Through the free Ugift service, friends and family are invited to make contributions of at least $15 each directly to a child's account.

Account maintenance fee: $20 annually. The fee is waived if either the account owner or beneficiary is a Nevada resident, or if the account owner is invested in the Savings Portfolio at the time the annual fee is assessed.

Added feature: Accounts can be linked to the Upromise Rewards Service.

Added feature: The Silver State Matching Grant Program will match 100% of up to $300 in contributions per beneficiary each year for Nevada residents with household adjusted gross incomes of $41,300 or less, and 50% of up to $600 in contributions for Nevada families with incomes of less than $75,000. The lifetime maximum match is $1,500. Applications are accepted each year from April 1 through July 31.

The Vanguard 529 Savings Plan

529 PROGRAM TYPE:	Savings
PROGRAM MANAGERS:	Upromise Investments, Inc
DISTRIBUTORS:	Vanguard Marketing Corporation
TELEPHONE:	866–734–4530
WEB SITE:	www.vanguard.com

Enrollment: Enroll directly. This program is not sold through financial advisors. There are no state residency requirements.

Investment options:

Option type	# of options	Underlying investments	Expense ratio
Age- or enrollment-based	3 tracks		0.25% [1]
Static multi-fund	5	Vanguard mutual funds	
Individual fund	14		0.25%–0.55% [2]

[1] 0.25% plan fee includes underlying fund expenses.
[2] Varying plan fees plus underlying fund expenses.

Minimum contributions: The minimum initial contribution is $3,000 ($50 through an employer automatic investment plan), and the minimum subsequent contribution is $50. Through the free Ugift service, friends and family are invited to make contributions of at least $50 each directly to a child's account.

Account maintenance fee: $20 annually. The fee is waived on account balances of $3,000 or greater.

Added feature: Accounts can be linked to the Upromise Rewards Service.

Putnam 529 for America

529 PROGRAM TYPE:	Savings
PROGRAM MANAGER:	Putnam Investment Management, LLC
DISTRIBUTOR:	Putnam Retail Management LP
TELEPHONE:	877-788-6265
WEB SITE:	www.Putnam529forAmerica.com

Enrollment: Purchase through a financial advisor. There are no state residency requirements.

Investment options:

Option type	# of options	Underlying investments	Unit classes [1]	Expense ratio [2]	Maximum sales charge	
					Initial	Contingent deferred
Age- or enrollment-based	3 tracks	Putnam-managed portfolios	A	0.93%–1.15%	5.75%	0.00%
			B	1.68%–1.90%	0.00%	5.00%
			C	1.68%–1.90%	0.00%	1.00%
Static asset allocation	3		A	1.09%–1.15%	4.00%–5.75%	0.00%
			B	1.84%–1.90%	0.00%	5.00%
			C	1.84%–1.90%	0.00%	1.00%
Static absolute return	4	Putnam Absolute Return Funds	A	1.17%–1.77%	1.00%–5.75%	0.00%
			B	1.37%–2.52%	0.00%	1.00%–5.00%
			C	1.92%–2.52%	0.00%	1.00%
Individual fund	10	Mutual funds from Putnam, Fidelity, MFS, State Street, Principal, and Federated	A	0.57%–1.77%	4.00%–5.75%	0.00%
			B	1.32%–2.52%	0.00%	5.00%
			C	1.32%–2.52%	0.00%	1.00%
Money market	1	Putnam Money Market Fund	A, B	0.90%	0.00%	0.00%
			C	1.15%	0.00%	0.00%

[1] B units automatically convert to A units at the end of the 8th year.
[2] 0.10% plan fees plus underlying fund expenses and distribution/servicing fees.

Minimum contributions: The minimum initial contribution is $25, which may be waived.

Account maintenance fee: $15 annually. The fee is waived for residents of Nevada, account balances of more than $25,000, and for accounts enrolled in the automatic contribution plan.

USAA 529 College Savings Plan

529 PROGRAM TYPE:	Savings
PROGRAM MANAGERS:	Upromise Investments, Inc.
DISTRIBUTOR:	USAA Investment Management Company (USAA)
TELEPHONE:	800-645-6834
WEB SITE:	www.usaa.com/529

Enrollment: Enroll through USAA. There are no state residency requirements.

Investment options:

Option type	# of options	Underlying investments	Expense ratio [1]
Age- or enrollment-based	1 track	USAA mutual funds	0.71%–1.05%
Static multi-fund	6		
Money market	1	USAA Money Market Fund	0.65%

[1] Plan fee includes underlying fund expenses.

Minimum contributions: With lump-sum contributions, the minimum initial contribution is $250, and the minimum subsequent contribution is $50. With the automatic investment plan, the minimum contribution level is $50 per month. Through the free Ugift service, friends and family are invited to make contributions of at least $15 each directly to a child's account.

Account maintenance fee: $15 annually, waived for Nevada residents. In addition, there is a $15 annual minimum balance fee for any account that is not in the monthly automatic investment plan and has a balance below $5,000.

Added feature: Accounts can be linked to the Upromise Rewards Service.

Added feature: The USAA Distinguished Valor Matching Grant Program for Nevada residents will match 100% of up to $1,500 (cumulative) in contributions for 1) an account owner on active military duty with adjusted gross income of less than $75,000 and with a beneficiary under the age of 13, or 2) the child or spouse of an account owner or account owner's spouse awarded a Purple Heart in either Operation Iraqi Freedom or Operation Enduring Freedom.

Nevada Prepaid Tuition Plan

529 PROGRAM TYPE: Prepaid
TELEPHONE: 888–477–2667
WEB SITE: www.nvprepaid.gov

Enrollment: The enrollment period usually runs from December through the following February and is extended through June for newborns. The account owner or beneficiary must be a Nevada resident, or the account owner must be an alumnus of a Nevada college or university, at the time of enrollment.

Time/age restrictions: The beneficiary must be in the 9th grade or below and 18 years old or younger at the time the contract is purchased. The beneficiary has up to six years from high school graduation to use benefits, with extensions granted for military service.

Contract benefits: The program offers a four-year university plan, two-year university plan, one-year university plan, two-year community college plan, and a combination plan for Nevada's public institutions. A beneficiary attending a private or out-of-state institution receives the weighted average tuition at Nevada public institutions, not to exceed the beneficiary's actual tuition.

Contract prices: For the 2012-13 enrollment period, lump sum prices ranged from as little as $4,300 for a two-year community college contract for a newborn to as much as $22,870 for a four-year university contract for a ninth grader. Extended payment plans are available.

Enrollment or application fee: $100

Statutory state backing: None

NEW HAMPSHIRE

Fidelity Investments manages two 529 savings programs for the Granite State. One is direct-sold (UNIQUE) and the other is advisor-sold (Fidelity Advisor 529). Both programs feature Fidelity Investments mutual funds.

STATE AGENCY: New Hampshire State Treasurer

State income tax treatment: New Hampshire does not have a personal income tax. Qualified distributions from New Hampshire and non-New Hampshire 529 plans are excluded from New Hampshire's tax on interest and dividends.

Maximum contribution limit: A contribution will not be accepted if it would cause the total of all New Hampshire 529 account balances for the same beneficiary to exceed $350,000.

Other considerations:

- Accounts in a New Hampshire 529 plan can be linked to the Fidelity Investments 529 Rewards American Express Card.
- Account ownership may not be transferred prior to the owner's death or incapacity.

UNIQUE College Investing Plan

529 PROGRAM TYPE:	Savings
PROGRAM MANAGER:	Fidelity Investments
DISTRIBUTOR:	Fidelity Brokerage Services, LLC
TELEPHONE:	800–544–1914
WEB SITE:	www.fidelity.com/unique

Enrollment: Enroll directly. This program is not sold through financial advisors. There are no state residency requirements.

Investment options:

Option type	# of options	Underlying investments	Expense ratio [1]
Age-based (index)	1 track		0.31%–0.35%
Age-based (active)	1 track		0.67%–1.01%
Static multi-fund (index)	3	Fidelity Investments mutual funds	0.30%–0.35%
Static multi-fund (active)	3		0.56%–1.01%
Individual fund	5		0.25%–0.57%
Age-based (multi-firm)	1 track	Mutual funds from Fidelity Investments, Acadian, Artisan, Aston, BlackRock Causeway, Credit Suisse, Eaton Vance, Harbor, Invesco, JP Morgan, MFS, Nataxis, OppenheimerFunds, PIMCO, Royce, Western Asset, and William Blair	0.94%–1.40%
FDIC-insured	1	Wells Fargo Bank, N.A.	0.05%–0.50%

[1] 0.15% (index), 0.20% (active), or 0.35% (multi-firm) plan fees plus underlying fund expenses. Fees on Bank Deposit Portfolio are variable.

Minimum contributions: With lump-sum contributions, the minimum initial contribution is $50, and the minimum subsequent contribution is $25. With the automatic investment plan, the minimum contribution level is $15 per month or $45 per quarter.

Account maintenance fee: None

Fidelity Advisor 529 Plan

529 PROGRAM TYPE:	Savings
PROGRAM MANAGER:	Fidelity Investments
DISTRIBUTOR:	Fidelity Investments Institutional Services Company, Inc.
TELEPHONE:	800–522–7297
WEB SITE:	www.advisor.fidelity.com

Enrollment: Purchase through a financial advisor (unit classes A or C) or through your employer (unit class P). There are no state residency requirements.

Investment options:

Option type	# of options	Underlying investments	Unit classes	Expense ratio [1]	Maximum sales charge	
					Initial	Contingent deferred
Age- or enrollment-based	1 track	Fidelity Advisor mutual funds and Fidelity Cash Reserves	A	0.96%–1.34%	5.75%	0.00%
			C	1.71%–2.09%	0.00%	1.00%
			P	1.46%–1.84%	0.00%	0.00%
Static multi-fund	2		A	1.27%–1.35%	5.75%	0.00%
			C	2.02%–2.10%	0.00%	1.00%
			P	1.77%–1.85%	0.00%	0.00%
Individual fund	13		A	0.82%–1.49%	3.75%–5.75% [2]	0.00%
			C	1.57%–2.24%	0.00%	1.00%
			P	1.32%–1.99%	0.00%	0.00%

[1] 0.20% plan fees plus underlying fund expenses and distribution/servicing fees.
[2] None for the Money Market Portfolio.

Minimum contributions: With lump-sum contributions, the minimum initial contribution is $1,000, with no minimum for subsequent investments. With the automatic investment plan, the minimum contribution level is $50 per month or $150 per quarter.

Account maintenance fee: $20 annually. The fee is waived for account balances of $25,000 or greater and for accounts in the automatic investment plan.

NEW JERSEY

The Garden State offers two 529 savings program managed by Franklin Templeton Investments, one that is direct-sold and available only to New Jersey residents (NJBEST), and another that is sold nationwide through financial advisors (Franklin Templeton 529).

STATE AGENCY: New Jersey Higher Education Student Assistance Authority (HESAA)

State income tax treatment: Contributions to a 529 plan are not deductible on New Jersey income tax returns. Qualified distributions from New Jersey and non-New Jersey 529 plans are excluded from New Jersey taxable income.

Maximum contribution limit: A contribution will not be accepted if it would cause the total of all New Jersey 529 account balances for the same beneficiary to exceed $305,000.

Other considerations:

- New Jersey beneficiaries in a New Jersey 529 plan are eligible for a one-time scholarship of up to $1,500 for their first semester at any New Jersey college or university, subject to minimum participation and contribution requirements.
- Under New Jersey law, moneys paid into or out of a New Jersey 529 account by or on behalf of a contributor or designated beneficiary for the purposes of financing the cost of qualified higher education expenses are exempt from all claims of creditors of the contributor or the designated beneficiary.
- Under New Jersey regulations, the account value is excluded in determining the beneficiary's eligibility for need-based financial aid programs administered by the state of New Jersey.

NJBEST 529 College Savings Plan

529 PROGRAM TYPE:	Savings
PROGRAM MANAGER:	Franklin Templeton Distributors, Inc.
DISTRIBUTOR:	Franklin Templeton Distributors, Inc.
TELEPHONE:	877–465–2378
WEB SITE:	www.njbest.com

Enrollment: Enroll directly. This program is not sold through financial advisors. The contributor or the beneficiary must be a New Jersey resident at the time of program enrollment.

Investment options:

Option type	# of options	Underlying investments	Expense ratio [1]
Age- or enrollment-based'	3 tracks	Franklin Templeton mutual funds	0.32%–1.05%
Static multi-fund	4		0.73%–1.05%
S&P 500 Index	1	JPMorgan Equity Index Fund	0.40%
Stable value	1	Wrapper agreements with financial institutions	0.55%

[1] 0.20% plan fees plus underlying fund expenses.

Minimum contributions: $25 per investment option

Account maintenance fee: None

Franklin Templeton 529 College Savings Plan

529 PROGRAM TYPE:	Savings
PROGRAM MANAGER:	Franklin Templeton Distributors, Inc.
DISTRIBUTOR:	Franklin Templeton Distributors, Inc.
TELEPHONE:	866–362–1597
WEB SITE:	www.franklintempleton.com

Enrollment: Purchase through a financial advisor. There are no state residency requirements.

Investment options:

Option type	# of options	Underlying investments	Unit classes (1)	Expense ratio (2)	Maximum sales charge	
					Initial	Contingent deferred
Age- or enrollment-based	3 tracks	Franklin Templeton mutual funds	A	0.77%–1.50%	5.75%	0.00%
			B	1.52%–2.25%	0.00%	4.00%
			C	1.52%–2.25%	0.00%	1.00%
Static multi-fund	5		A	1.18%–1.50%	4.25%–5.75%	0.00%
			B	1.93%–2.25%	0.00%	4.00%
			C	1.93%–2.25%	0.00%	1.00%
Individual fund	6	Franklin Templeton and JP Morgan mutual funds	A	0.85%–1.51%	4.25%–5.75%	0.00%
			B	1.60%–2.26%	0.00%	4.00%
			C	1.60%–2.26%	0.00%	1.00%
Stable value	1	Wrapper agreements with financial institutions	A	0.68%	4.25%	0.00%
			B	0.85%	0.00%	4.00%
			C	0.85%	0.00%	1.00%

(1) B units automatically convert to A units at the end of the 8th year.
(2) 0.40% plan fees (0.33%–0.40% for Stable Value) plus underlying fund expenses and distribution/servicing fees.

Minimum contributions: With lump-sum contributions, the minimum initial contribution is $250 per investment option, and the minimum subsequent contribution is $50. With the automatic investment plan, the minimum contribution level is $50 per month.

Account maintenance fee: None

NEW MEXICO

OFI Private Investments Inc. manages New Mexico's direct-sold and advisor-sold 529 savings programs. Both programs use OppenheimerFunds along with mutual funds from several other fund families. New Mexico's prepaid tuition plan was terminated in 2004.

STATE AGENCY: Education Trust Board of New Mexico

State income tax treatment: All contributions made to a New Mexico 529 plan during the year, including rollover contributions, are deductible in computing New Mexico taxable income. Qualified distributions from New Mexico and non-New Mexico 529 plans are excluded from New Mexico taxable income. Under the New Mexico recapture rules, the principal portion of rollovers and nonqualified distributions from a New Mexico 529 plan must be included in New Mexico taxable income to the extent of prior New Mexico tax deductions.

Maximum contribution limit: A contribution will not be accepted if it would cause the total of all New Mexico 529 account balances for the same beneficiary to exceed $294,000.

Other considerations:

- Participation in a New Mexico 529 plan does not affect the beneficiary's eligibility for financial aid programs administered by the state of New Mexico.

The Education Plan's College Savings Program

529 PROGRAM TYPE:	Savings
PROGRAM MANAGER:	OFI Private Investments Inc., an affliate of OppenheimerFunds, Inc.
DISTRIBUTOR:	OppenheimerFunds Distributor, Inc.
TELEPHONE:	877–337–5268
WEB SITE:	www.theeducationplan.com

Enrollment: Enroll directly. This program is not sold through financial advisors. There are no state residency requirements.

Investment options:

Option type	# of options	Underlying investments	Expense ratio
Age- or enrollment-based, blended	1 track	Mutual funds from OppenheimerFunds, Vanguard, Thornburg, TIAA-CREF, and Dreyfus	0.58%–0.77% [1]
Static multi-fund	6		
Age- or enrollment-based, index	1 track	Mutual funds from OppenheimerFunds, Dreyfus, TIAA-CREF, and Vanguard	0.29%–0.38% [2]
Static multi-fund, index	6		
Money market	1	Oppenheimer Institutional Money Market Fund	0.37% [1]

[1] 0.20% plan fees plus underlying fund expenses.
[2] 0.15% plan fees plus underlying fund expenses.

Minimum contributions: With lump-sum contributions, the minimum initial contribution is $250, and the minimum subsequent contribution is $25. With the automatic investment plan, the minimum contribution level is $25 per month or $75 per quarter.

Account maintenance fee: $25 annually. The fee is waived for New Mexico residents, for account balances of $10,000 or greater, for accounts in the automatic investment plan, and for accounts with all assets invested in the index options.

Scholar'sEdge

529 PROGRAM TYPE:	Savings
PROGRAM MANAGER:	OFI Private Investments Inc., an affliate of OppenheimerFunds, Inc.
DISTRIBUTOR:	OppenheimerFunds Distributor, Inc.
TELEPHONE:	866–529–7283
WEB SITE:	www.scholarsedge529.com

Enrollment: Purchase through a financial advisor. There are no state residency requirements.

Investment options:

Option type	# of options	Underlying investments	Unit classes [1]	Expense ratio [2]	Maximum sales charge Initial	Maximum sales charge Contingent deferred
Age- or enrollment-based	1 track	Mutual funds from OppenheimerFunds, Mainstay, Thornburg, and American Century	A	0.99%–1.18%	4.75%	0.00%
			B	1.74%–1.93%	0.00%	5.00%
			C	1.74%–1.93%	0.00%	1.00%
Static multi-fund	6		A	0.99%–1.18%	4.75%	0.00%
			B	1.74%–1.93%	0.00%	5.00%
			C	1.74%–1.93%	0.00%	1.00%
Individual fund	7		A	1.03%–1.34%	4.75%	0.00%
			B	1.78%–2.09%	0.00%	5.00%
			C	1.78%–2.09%	0.00%	1.00%
Principal protection	1	New York Life Insurance Funding Agreement	A	0.46%	4.75%	0.00%
			B	1.21%	0.00%	0.00%
			C	1.21%	0.00%	1.00%
Money market	1	Oppenheimer Institutional Money Market Fund	A	0.37%	0.00%	0.00%
			B			
			C			

[1] B units automatically convert to A units at the end of the 6th year.
[2] 0.20% plan fees plus underlying fund expenses and distribution/servicing fees.

Minimum contributions: With lump-sum contributions, the minimum initial contribution is $250, and the minimum subsequent contribution is $25. With the automatic investment plan, the minimum contribution level is $25 or $75 per quarter.

Account maintenance fee: $25 annually. The fee is waived for New Mexico residents, for account balances of $25,000 or greater, and for accounts in the automatic investment plan.

NEW YORK

The Empire State offers two 529 savings programs, a direct-sold program featuring Vanguard mutual funds, and an advisor-sold plan distributed by JPMorgan and featuring funds from JPMorgan and SSgA. Both are managed by Upromise Investments.

STATE AGENCIES: Office of the State Comptroller and the New York State Higher Education Services Corporation

State income tax treatment: Contributions to a New York 529 plan of up to $5,000 by an individual filer, and up to $10,000 per year by a married couple filing jointly, are deductible in computing New York taxable income. Contributions must be from the account owner, or if filing jointly, from the account owner's spouse, to be eligible for the deduction. The contribution deadline is December 31. Qualified distributions from New York and non-New York 529 plans are excluded from New York taxable income. Rollovers to another 529 plan and non-trustee-to-trustee rollovers to another New York 529 account, although tax-free for federal purposes, are considered nonqualified distributions for New York income tax purposes. Under the New York recapture rule, the principal portion of rollovers and nonqualified distributions from a New York 529 plan must be included in New York taxable income to the extent of prior New York tax deductions.

Maximum contribution limit: A contribution will not be accepted if it would cause the total of all New York 529 account balances for the same beneficiary to exceed $375,000.

Other considerations:

- Under New York law, assets in a New York 529 account are exempt from application to satisfy a money judgment against an account owner/designated beneficiary who is a minor. Protection for an account owner who is not a minor is limited to $10,000 on an aggregate basis.
- Participation in a New York 529 plan does not affect the beneficiary's eligibility for financial aid programs administered by the state of New York.
- Accounts in a New York 529 plan can be linked to the Upromise Rewards Service.

New York's 529 College Savings Program—Direct Plan

529 PROGRAM TYPE:	Savings
PROGRAM MANAGER:	Upromise Investments, Inc.
DISTRIBUTOR:	Vanguard Marketing Corporation
TELEPHONE:	877–697–2837/877-NYSAVES
WEB SITE:	www.nysaves.org

Enrollment: Enroll directly. This program is not sold through financial advisors. There are no state residency requirements.

Investment options:

Option type	# of options	Underlying investments	Expense ratio [1]
Age- or enrollment-based	3 tracks		
Static multi-fund	4	Vanguard mutual funds	0.17%
Individual fund	9		

[1] 0.17% plan fee includes underlying fund expenses.

Minimum contributions: $25, or $15 per payroll via payroll deduction.

Account maintenance fee: None

New York's 529 Advisor–Guided College Savings Program

529 PROGRAM TYPE:	Savings
PROGRAM MANAGERS:	Upromise Investments, Inc.
DISTRIBUTOR:	JPMorgan Distribution Services, Inc.
TELEPHONE:	800–774–2108
WEB SITE:	www.ny529advisor.com

Enrollment: Purchase through a financial advisor. There are no state residency requirements.

Investment options:

					Maximum sales charge	
Option type	# of options	Underlying investments	Unit classes	Expense ratio [1]	Initial	Contingent deferred
Age- or enrollment-based	1 track		A	0.91%–1.22%	4.50%–5.25%	0.00%
			C	1.66%–1.97%	0.00%	1.00%
			Advisor	0.66%–0.97%	0.00%	0.00%
Static multi-fund	7	Mutual funds from J.P. Morgan and ETFs from SSgA	A	0.91%–1.22%	4.50%–5.25%	0.00%
			C	1.66%–1.97%	0.00%	1.00%
			Advisor	0.66%–0.97%	0.00%	0.00%
Individual fund	16		A	0.75%–1.54%	3.75% -5.25%	0.00%
			C	1.50%–2.29%	0.00%	1.00%
			Advisor	0.50%–1.29%	0.00%	1.00%

[1] includes 0.30% plan fees plus underlying fund expenses and distribution/servicing fees.

Minimum contributions: The minimum initial contribution is $1,000 per account (None for Advisor Class). The minimum subsequent contribution is $25 per account.

Account maintenance fee: $25 annually. The fee is waived for account balances greater than $25,000.

NORTH CAROLINA

North Carolina has simplified its 529 investment menu in recent years and now offers age-based and static portfolios using Vanguard funds, a fixed-income option managed by the state treasurer, and a federally-insured deposit account with the State Employees' Credit Union.

STATE AGENCY:　North Carolina State Education Assistance Authority

State income tax treatment: Contributions to North Carolina's 529 plan, including rollover contributions, of up to $2,500 per year by an individual filer, and up to $5,000 per year by a married couple filing jointly, are deductible in computing North Carolina taxable income. The contribution deadline is December 31. Qualified distributions from North Carolina 529 plans are excluded from North Carolina taxable income. Under the North Carolina recapture rules, the principal portion of rollovers and nonqualified distributions from the North Carolina 529 plan must be included in North Carolina taxable income to the extent of prior North Carolina tax deductions. Nonqualified distributions for this purpose do not include distributions made on account of the beneficiary's death or disability.

Maximum contribution limit: A contribution will not be accepted if it would cause the total of all North Carolina 529 account balances for the same beneficiary to exceed $400,000.

National College Savings Program

529 PROGRAM TYPE:　Savings
PROGRAM MANAGER:　College Foundation, Inc.
DISTRIBUTOR:　College Foundation, Inc.
TELEPHONE:　800–600–3453
WEB SITE:　www.CFNC.org/NC529

Enrollment: Enroll directly. This program is not sold through financial advisors. There are no state residency requirements.

Investment options:

Option type	# of options	Underlying investments	Expense ratio [1]
Age- or enrollment-based	3 tracks		0.36%–0.41%
Static multi-fund	5	Vanguard mutual funds	0.36%–0.39%
Individual fund	4		0.34%–0.42%
Fixed income	1	NC State Treasurer Fund	0.25%–0.30%
Credit union deposit	1	State Employees' Credit Union deposit account	0.25%

[1] 0.25% plan fees plus underlying fund expenses.

Minimum contributions: $25

Account maintenance fee: A $1.50/month ($18/year) fee is assessed per Account for paper delivery of statements and confirmations. This fee is waived if the Participant elects to receive electronic delivery.

NORTH DAKOTA

Upromise Investments is program manager for North Dakota's 529 savings program, which offers 9 investment options featuring Vanguard funds.

STATE AGENCY: Bank of North Dakota

State income tax treatment: Contributions to College SAVE of up to $5,000 per year by an individual filer, and up to $10,000 per year by a married couple filing jointly, are deductible in computing North Dakota taxable income. The contribution deadline is December 31. Qualified distributions from North Dakota and non-North Dakota 529 plans are excluded from North Dakota taxable income. North Dakota tax law does not contain any deduction recapture provisions for nonqualified distributions.

Maximum contribution limit: A contribution will not be accepted if it would cause the total of all North Dakota 529 account balances for the same beneficiary to exceed $269,000.

Other considerations:

- Under North Dakota law, the interests of the participant and designated beneficiary in the North Dakota 529 plan are not subject to attachment or alienation by third-party creditors.
- The program provides a one-time match of contributions of up to $500 for North Dakota residents where the beneficiary is 15 years old or younger and family income is below $60,000 (single) or $100,000 (joint). For participants with incomes below $30,000 (single) or $60,000 (joint), the match is available for an additional two years.
- An additional matching program, Children FIRST, provides a North Dakota resident newborn (12 months old or younger) with an initial $100 contribution for participants who opt into the program. Children FIRST participants have until their child turns 4 years old to match the $100 contribution and retain the state-sponsored donation. This match can be combined with the $500 match described above.
- Accounts may be linked to the Upromise Rewards service.

College SAVE

529 PROGRAM TYPE:	Savings
PROGRAM MANAGER:	Upromise Investments, Inc.
DISTRIBUTOR:	Bank of North Dakota
TELEPHONE:	866–728–3529
WEB SITE:	www.collegesave4u.com

Enrollment: Enroll directly or through an approved financial advisor. There are no state residency requirements.

Investment options:

Option type	# of options	Underlying investments	Expense ratio [1]
Age- or enrollment-based	3 tracks	Vanguard mutual funds	0.85%
Static multi-fund	5		
Money market	1	Vanguard Prime Money Market Fund	

[1] 0.85% plan fee includes underlying fund expenses.

Minimum contributions: $25. Through the free Ugift service, friends and family are invited to make contributions of at least $25 each directly to a child's account.

Account maintenance fee: $20 annually. The fee is waived for North Dakota residents.

OHIO

The Buckeye State's direct-sold Ohio CollegeAdvantage 529 Savings Plan is available to residents of any state and offers certificates of deposits and savings accounts from Fifth Third Bank in addition to a menu of options using mutual funds from Vanguard, PIMCO, OppenheimerFunds, and GE Asset Management. Ohio's advisor-sold 529 savings program (BlackRock CollegeAdvantage) features BlackRock funds and iShares ETFs in its age-based and asset-allocation options along with individual-fund options from iShares and a variety of mutual fund families. Ohio also has a prepaid tuition/guaranteed savings plan (Guaranteed Savings Fund) that was closed to new enrollments in 2003 and will remain closed until further action is taken by Ohio's state agency.

STATE AGENCY: Ohio Tuition Trust Authority (OTTA)

State income tax treatment: Contributions to an Ohio 529 plan, including rollover contributions, of up to $2,000 per beneficiary are deductible in computing Ohio taxable income. The contribution deadline is December 31. Contributions in excess of annual limits may be carried over and taken as deductions for an unlimited number of years. Qualified distributions from Ohio and non-Ohio 529 plans are excluded from Ohio taxable income. Under the Ohio recapture rule, the principal portion of nonqualified distributions from an Ohio 529 plan must be included in Ohio taxable income to the extent of prior Ohio tax deductions. Nonqualified distributions for this purpose do not include withdrawals made as the result of the beneficiary's death or disability, or distributions made on account of the beneficiary's receipt of a scholarship. Distributions subsequently rolled over to another 529 plan are subject to Ohio tax recapture.

Maximum contribution limit: A contribution will not be accepted if it would cause the total of all Ohio 529 account balances for the same beneficiary to exceed $377,000.

Other considerations:

- Under Ohio law, an account in an Ohio 529 plan shall not be subject to execution, garnishment, attachment, the operation of bankruptcy or the insolvency laws, or other process of law.

Ohio CollegeAdvantage 529 Savings Plan

529 PROGRAM TYPE:	Savings
PROGRAM MANAGER:	Ohio Tuition Trust Authority
DISTRIBUTOR:	Ohio Tuition Trust Authority
TELEPHONE:	800–233–6734
WEB SITE:	www.collegeadvantage.com

Enrollment: Enroll directly. This program is not sold through financial advisors. There are no state residency requirements.

Investment options:

Option type	# of options	Underlying investments	Expense ratio
Age- or enrollment-based	3 tracks		0.21%–0.27% [1]
Static multi-fund	5	Vanguard mutual funds	0.21%–0.25% [1]
Individual fund	8		0.15%–0.48% [1]
Age- or enrollment-based	1 track	Mutual funds from Vanguard, PIMCO, OppenheimerFunds, and GE Asset Management	0.38%–0.48% [2]
Individual fund	4		0.61%–0.98% [2]
FDIC-insured	2	Fifth Third Bank CDs and savings accounts	0.00%

[1] 0.18% plan fees (0.13% for Vanguard 500 Index Option) plus underlying fund expenses.
[2] 0.15%–0.16% plan fees plus underlying fund expenses.

Minimum contributions: $25 ($500 for the Fifth Third CD Option)

Account maintenance fee: None

BlackRock CollegeAdvantage 529 Plan

529 PROGRAM TYPE:	Savings
PROGRAM MANAGER:	BlackRock Advisors
DISTRIBUTOR:	BlackRock Investments
TELEPHONE:	800–529–8582
WEB SITE:	www.BlackRock.com/CollegeAdvantage

Enrollment: Purchase through a financial advisor. There are no state residency requirements.

Investment options:

Option type	# of options	Underlying investments	Unit classes	Expense ratio [1]	Maximum sales charge	
					Initial	Contingent deferred
Age- or enrollment-based	3 tracks	BlackRock mutual funds and iShares ETFs	A	1.07%–1.30%	5.75%	0.00%
			C	1.81%–2.05%	0.00%	1.00%
Static multi-fund	3		A	1.26%–1.35%	5.75%	0.00%
			C	2.01%–2.10%	0.00%	1.00%
Individual fund	14	iShares ETFs and mutual funds from BlackRock, ING, Ranier, and Wells Fargo	A	0.62%–1.84%	4.00%–5.75%	0.00%
			C	1.37%–2.59%	0.00%	1.00%
Money market	1	BlackRock Money Market Portfolio	A	0.97%	0.00%	0.00%
			C	1.72%	0.00%	0.00%

[1] 0.30% plan fees plus distribution/servicing fees and underlying fund expenses.

Minimum contributions: $25 per investment option. Lower minimums may apply to payroll deduction plans.

Account maintenance fee: $25 annually. The fee is waived if the account owner is a resident of Ohio, the balance of all accounts with the same account owner for the same beneficiary exceeds $25,000, or the account owner makes automatic contributions via electronic funds transfer or payroll deduction.

Guaranteed Savings Fund

529 PROGRAM TYPE:	Guaranteed savings (prepaid)
TELEPHONE:	800–233–6734
WEB SITE:	www.collegeadvantage.com

Enrollment: The plan is currently closed to new enrollments.

Time/age restrictions: To receive the full value of a tuition unit, the unit must be held on account until the beneficiary has reached 18 years of age or has graduated high school. Early withdrawals (prior to age 18) are permitted but the value of the units will be actuarially determined.

Program benefits: Each unit acquired in this prepaid tuition program is worth one percent of the weighted average tuition at Ohio's 13 four-year public universities and may be redeemed for payment to any eligible educational institution in the country.

Statutory state backing: Fund assets and redemption values are backed by the full faith and credit of the state of Ohio.

OKLAHOMA

TIAA-CREF Tuition Financing, Inc. is program manager for both of the Sooner State's 529 savings programs, a direct-sold program that utilizes TIAA-CREF mutual funds and an advisor-sold program distributed by Allianz Global Investors that features a multi-manager investment platform.

STATE AGENCY: Oklahoma College Savings Plan Board of Trustees

State income tax treatment: Contributions to an Oklahoma 529 plan, including rollover contributions, of up to $10,000 per year by an individual filer, and up to $20,000 per year by a married couple filing jointly, are deductible in computing Oklahoma taxable income. The contribution deadline is April 15 of the following year. Contributions in excess of annual limits may be carried over and taken as deductions for up to five years. Qualified distributions from Oklahoma and non-Oklahoma 529 plans are excluded from Oklahoma taxable income. Under the Oklahoma recapture rules, the principal portion of nonqualified distributions from the Oklahoma 529 plan, and of rollovers to another 529 plan within one year of the date of contribution, must be included in Oklahoma taxable income to the extent of prior Oklahoma tax deductions. A nonqualified distribution or rollover in the same year as the contribution will reduce the amount eligible for the Oklahoma deduction. A nonqualified distribution or rollover during the five-year carryover period will reduce the amount of any carryover deduction. Nonqualified distributions for this purpose do not include distributions made as the result of the beneficiary's death or disability or on account of the beneficiary's receipt of a scholarship.

Maximum contribution limit: A contribution will not be accepted if it would cause the total of all Oklahoma 529 account balances for the same beneficiary to exceed $300,000.

Other considerations:

- Under Oklahoma law, any interest in an Oklahoma 529 account of any person residing in the state shall be exempt from attachment or execution and every other species of forced sale for the payment of debts.
- Money in an Oklahoma 529 account is not considered in determining eligibility for certain income-based programs including TANF, Food Stamps, or the Low Income Home Energy Assistance Program.

Oklahoma College Savings Plan

529 PROGRAM TYPE:	Savings
PROGRAM MANAGER:	TIAA-CREF Tuition Financing, Inc.
DISTRIBUTOR:	TIAA-CREF Individual & Institutional Services, LLC
TELEPHONE:	877–654–7284
WEB SITE:	www.ok4saving.org

Enrollment: Enroll directly. This program is not sold through financial advisors. There are no state residency requirements.

Investment options:

Option type	# of options	Underlying investments	Expense ratio
Age- or enrollment-based	3 tracks		0.53%–0.59% [1]
Static multi-fund	4	TIAA-CREF institutional mutual funds	0.53%–0.92% [1]
U.S equity index	1		0.47% [1]
Principal protection	1	Funding agreement with TIAA-CREF Life Insurance Company	0.00%

[1] 0.40% plan fees plus underlying fund expenses.

Minimum contributions: The minimum initial contribution is $100 per investment option, and the minimum subsequent contribution is $25 per investment option ($15 per investment option via payroll deduction).

Account maintenance fee: None

Oklahoma Dream 529 Plan

529 PROGRAM TYPE:	Savings
PROGRAM MANAGER:	TIAA-CREF Tuition Financing, Inc. and Allianz Global Investors Distributors LLC
DISTRIBUTOR:	Allianz Global Investors Distributors LLC
TELEPHONE:	877-529-9299
WEB SITE:	www.okdream529.com

Enrollment: Purchase through a financial advisor. There are no state residency requirements.

Investment options:

Option type	# of options	Underlying investments	Unit classes	Expense ratio [2]	Maximum sales charge	
					Initial	Contingent deferred
Age- or enrollment-based	1 track [1]	Mutual funds from Allianz, NFJ, PIMCO, and TIAA-CREF	A	1.19%–1.38%	4.25%	0.00%
			C	1.94%–2.13%	0.00%	1.00%
Static multi-fund	2		A	1.22%–1.38%	4.25%	0.00%
			C	1.97%–2.13%	0.00%	1.00%
Individual fund	12		A	0.73%–1.74%	4.25% [3]	0.00%
			C	0.73%–2.49%	0.00%	1.00% [3]

[1] Underlying portfolios also available as static options
[2] 0.50% management fee plus underlying fund expenses and distribution/servicing fees.
[3] None for the Money Market Portfolio.

Minimum contributions: With lump-sum contributions, the minimum initial contribution is $1,000 (with at least $250 per investment option), and the minimum subsequent contribution is $50 per investment option. With the automatic investment plan, the minimum initial contribution is $250 and the minimum contribution level is $50 per investment option per month.

Account maintenance fee: $5 quarterly. The fee is waived for accounts in the automatic contribution plan, for accounts with a balance of $20,000 or more, and for accounts with an account owner having an aggregate total of $50,000 or more.

OREGON

The Beaver State offers a direct-sold 529 savings program managed by TIAA-CREF that utilizes several different fund managers, and an advisor-sold savings program managed and distributed by MFS that features a 529 share class of MFS mutual funds.

STATE AGENCY: Oregon College Savings Plan Trust Board, chaired by the State Treasurer

State income tax treatment: Contributions to an Oregon 529 plan of up to $2,170 by an individual filer, and up to $4,345 by a married couple filing jointly, are deductible in computing Oregon taxable income. These limits are for 2012 and will adjust each year for inflation. The contribution deadline is April 15 of the following year. Contributions in excess of annual limits may be carried over and taken as deductions for up to four years.

Qualified distributions from Oregon and non-Oregon 529 plans are excluded from Oregon taxable income. Under the Oregon recapture rule, the principal portion of nonqualified distributions from an Oregon 529 plan must be included in Oregon taxable income to the extent of prior Oregon tax deductions. While unclear, it appears rollovers to another 529 plan are not subject to recapture.

Maximum contribution limit:　A contribution will not be accepted if it would cause the total of all Oregon 529 account balances for the same beneficiary to exceed $310,000.

Other considerations:

- Under Oregon law, the right of a designated beneficiary or account owner to payment from, and the moneys within, an Oregon 529 account are exempt from creditors' claims.

Oregon College Savings Plan

529 PROGRAM TYPE:	Savings
PROGRAM MANAGER:	TIAA-CREF Tuition Financing, Inc.
DISTRIBUTOR:	TIAA-CREF Tuition Financing, Inc.
TELEPHONE:	866–772–8464
WEB SITE:	www.oregoncollegesavings.com

Enrollment:　Enroll directly. This program is not sold through financial advisors. There are no state residency requirements.

Investment options:

Option type	# of options	Underlying investments	Expense ratio
Age- or enrollment-based	1 track	Mutual funds from TIAA-CREF, Northern, Dreyfus, LSV, Thornburg, DoubleLine, PIMCO, TCM, T. Rowe Price, and Vanguard	0.38%–0.41% [1]
Static multi-fund	7		0.34%–0.75% [1]
Individual fund	6		0.32%–0.54% [1]
Principal protection	1	Funding agreement with TIAA-CREF Life Insurance Company	0.00%

[1] 0.25% plan fees plus underlying fund expenses.

Minimum contributions:　$25 per investment portfolio, reduced to $15 per investment portfolio with payroll deduction.

Account maintenance fee:　None

MFS 529 Savings Plan

529 PROGRAM TYPE:	Savings
PROGRAM MANAGER:	MFS Fund Distributors, Inc.
DISTRIBUTOR:	MFS Fund Distributors, Inc.
TELEPHONE:	866–637–7526
WEB SITE:	www.mfs.com

Enrollment: Purchase through a financial advisor. There are no state residency requirements.

Investment options:

					Maximum sales charge	
Option type	**# of options**	**Underlying investments**	**Unit classes**	**Expense ratio** [1]	**Initial**	**Contingent deferred**
Age- or enrollment-based	1 track		A	0.96%–1.35%	2.50%–5.75%	0.00%
			B	1.71%–2.10%	0.00%	4.00%
			C	1.71%–2.10%	0.00%	1.00%
Static multi-fund	4	MFS mutual funds	A	1.17%–1.35%	5.75%	0.00%
			B	1.92%–2.10%	0.00%	4.00%
			C	1.92%–2.10%	0.00%	1.00%
Individual fund	14		A	0.87%–1.49%	2.50%–5.75% [2]	0.00%
			B	1.62%–2.24%	0.00%	4.00%
			C	1.62%–2.24%	0.00%	1.00%

[1] Underlying fund expenses (including 0.10% state fee) and distribution/servicing fees. Does not reflect voluntary 0.05% reduction in state fee.
[2] None for the Cash Reserve Fund.

Minimum contributions: With lump-sum contributions, the minimum initial contribution is $250, and there is no minimum on subsequent contributions. With the automatic investment plan, the contribution level may be any amount.

Account maintenance fee: $25 annually. The fee is waived for Oregon residents and for account balances of $25,000 or greater.

PENNSYLVANIA

The Pennsylvania 529 Investment Plan is managed by the Pennsylvania Treasury Department with recordkeeping and investment services provided by Upromise Investment Advisors LLC and The Vanguard Group respectively. The program features 3 age-based investment options and 10 static investment options, including a socially responsible equity portfolio, using Vanguard-managed portfolios. The Pennsylvania 529

Guaranteed Savings Plan, available to Pennsylvania residents, functions as a unit-type prepaid tuition plan and provides protection against increasing tuition costs in various institutional categories.

STATE AGENCY: Pennsylvania Treasury Department

State income tax treatment: Contributions to any Pennsylvania or non-Pennsylvania 529 plan of up to the gift-tax annual exclusion amount ($14,000 in 2013) per beneficiary are deductible in computing Pennsylvania taxable income. Spouses filing jointly must each have at least $14,000 in income to claim the maximum $28,000 per-beneficiary deduction. Rollovers from another 529 plan or from qualified U.S. savings bonds are not eligible for the deduction. The contribution deadline is December 31. Qualified distributions from Pennsylvania and non-Pennsylvania 529 plans are excluded from Pennsylvania taxable income. Under the Pennsylvania recapture rule, nonqualified distributions from a 529 plan are included by Pennsylvania taxpayers in Pennsylvania taxable income to the extent they are not a recovery of nondeductible contributions, following rules set forth in PIT Bulletin 2006-04. Rollovers to another 529 plan are not subject to the Pennsylvania recapture rule.

Maximum contribution limit: A contribution will not be accepted if it would cause the total of all Pennsylvania 529 account balances for the same beneficiary to exceed $368,600.

Other considerations:

- An account in a Pennsylvania 529 plan does not affect the beneficiary's eligibility for financial aid programs administered by Pennsylvania.
- Accounts in a Pennsylvania 529 plan are exempt from Pennsylvania inheritance tax.
- Under Pennsylvania law, a Pennsylvania 529 account or any legal interest therein shall not be subject to attachment, levy, or execution by any creditor of an account owner or beneficiary.
- Pennsylvania 529 accounts are eligible to earn tuition discounts at participating private colleges through the SAGE Scholars Tuition Rewards Program.
- Accounts may be linked to the Upromise Rewards service.

Pennsylvania College Savings Program — Guaranteed Savings Plan

529 PROGRAM TYPE: Guaranteed savings (prepaid)
TELEPHONE: 800–440–4000
WEB SITE: www.PA529.com

Enrollment: Enrollment is open year-round; prices change on September 1 each year. The account owner or beneficiary must be a Pennsylvania resident at the time of program enrollment.

Time/age restrictions: There is an approximate 9-month or 18-month wait after a contribution is made before tuition inflation growth associated with the contribution can be used to pay for college expenses.

Program benefits: Each GSP credit is worth one credit of tuition at the "tuition level" selected by the participant. The available tuition levels are represented by the following tuition indices: State-Related University Average, State System of Higher Education Average, Community College Average, Ivy League School Average, and Private Four-Year College Average.

Minimum contributions $15 per transaction. If contributions are made through the Ugift program, the minimum contribution is $25.

Enrollment or application fee: $50. The fee is discounted to $25 for accounts opened online with an electronic bank transfer, and is waived completely for newborns and newly adopted children if the account is opened within six months of birth or finalization of adoption.

Account maintenance fee: 0.1225% of account value charged each quarter (0.49% annually)

Statutory state backing: None

Pennsylvania College Savings Program – 529 Investment Plan

529 PROGRAM TYPE:	Savings
PROGRAM MANAGER:	Pennsylvania Treasury Department
DISTRIBUTOR:	Pennsylvania Treasury Department
TELEPHONE:	800–440-4000
WEB SITE:	www.PA529.com

Enrollment: Enroll Directly. There are no residency requirements

Investment options:

Option type	# of options	Underlying investments	Expense ratio [1]
Age- or enrollment-based	3 tracks		
Static multi-fund	6	Vanguard mutual funds	0.48%–0.62%
Individual fund	4		

[1] 0.44% - 0.46% plan fees plus underlying fund expenses.

Minimum contributions: $25 per transaction reduced to $15 per transaction for payroll deductions. If contributions are made through the Ugift program, the minimum contribution is $25.

Account maintenance fee: None

RHODE ISLAND

Rhode Island's 529 savings program, CollegeBound*fund*®, is managed by AllianceBernstein and features AllianceBernstein mutual funds, as well as three Vanguard index fund options for direct-sold Rhode Island Accounts. The program is sold nationwide. It is offered in 6 unit classes through financial advisors and also offered by way of a direct-sold unit class to Rhode Island Accounts without a financial advisor. (Rhode Island Accounts are defined in the Direct-Sold program description below.)

STATE AGENCY: Rhode Island Higher Education Assistance Authority

State income tax treatment: Contributions to CollegeBound*fund*® of up to $500 per year by an individual filer, and up to $1,000 per year by married taxpayers filing jointly, are deductible in computing Rhode Island taxable income. The contribution deadline is December 31. Contributions in excess of annual limits may be carried over and taken as deductions for an unlimited number of future years. Contributions must be from the account owner to be eligible for deduction. Rollovers from another 529 plan are not eligible for the deduction. Qualified distributions from Rhode Island and non-Rhode Island 529 plans are excluded from Rhode Island taxable income. Under the Rhode Island recapture rule, the principal portion of rollovers and nonqualified distributions from a Rhode Island 529 plan within two taxable years of the contribution must be included in Rhode Island taxable income to the extent of prior Rhode Island tax deductions.

Maximum contribution limit: A contribution will not be accepted if it would cause the total of all Rhode Island 529 account balances for the same beneficiary to exceed $395,000.

Other considerations:

- The CollegeBound*fund*® provides eligible account owners with matching funds for up to five years when they open and contribute to their child's CollegeBound*fund*® 529 college account.
- $2 for $1 contribution match up to $1,000 (for Adjusted Gross Income of $68,000 or less)
- $1 for $1 contribution match up to $500 (for Adjusted Gross Income of $68,001 to $83,000)
- With the CollegeBound*baby*SM Program, every baby born or adopted as a Rhode Island resident on or after July 1, 2010 is eligible to receive a one-time $100 contribution to a CollegeBound*fund*® account established for his or her benefit.
- An online gifting tool allows account owners to invite friends and families to electronically contribute to a child's CollegeBound*fund*® account.
- Under Rhode Island law, an account balance, right or interest of a person in the Rhode Island 529 plan is exempt from attachment except to the extent that the

balance, right or interest is subject to a court order pursuant to a judgment of divorce or separate maintenance or a court order concerning child support.

- Participation in the Rhode Island 529 plan does not affect the beneficiary's eligibility for financial aid programs administered by the state of Rhode Island.

CollegeBound*fund*® Rhode Island Accounts – Direct-sold

529 PROGRAM TYPE:	Savings
PROGRAM MANAGER:	AllianceBernstein L.P.
DISTRIBUTOR:	AllianceBernstein Investments, Inc.
TELEPHONE:	888–324–5057
WEB SITE:	www.collegeboundfund.com/ri

Enrollment: Enroll directly. The account owner or beneficiary must be a Rhode Island resident, or the account owner must work or have a principal place of business in Rhode Island, at the time of enrollment.

Investment options:

Option type	# of options	Underlying investments	Expense ratio [1]
Age- or enrollment-based	3 tracks		0.20%
Static multi-fund	3	AllianceBernstein mutual funds	0.72%–0.94%
Individual fund	9		0.55%–1.29%
Individual fund	3	Vanguard index funds	0.06%–0.19%
Principal protection	1	Separately managed fixed income portfolio	0.70%

[1] Plan fees plus underlying fund expenses.

Minimum contributions: With lump-sum contributions, the minimum initial contribution is $250, and the minimum subsequent contribution is $50. With the automatic investment plan, contributions can be for any amount.

Account maintenance fee: None

CollegeBound*fund*® Advisor-Sold

529 PROGRAM TYPE:	Savings
PROGRAM MANAGER:	AllianceBernstein L.P.
DISTRIBUTOR:	AllianceBernstein Investments, Inc.
TELEPHONE:	888–324–5057
WEB SITE:	www.collegeboundfund.com

Enrollment: Purchase through a commission-based financial advisor (unit classes A, B, and C) or fee-based advisor (unit class R). Lower pricing through a commission-based advisor is provided for those who meet certain Rhode Island residency requirements (unit classes RA and RZ).

Investment options:

Option type	# of options	Underlying investments	Unit classes [2]	Expense ratio [3]	Initial	Contingent deferred
Age- or enrollment-based	3 tracks		A	0.97%–1.19%	4.25%	0.00%
			B	1.72%–1.94%	0.00%	4.00%
			C	1.72%–1.94%	0.00%	1.00%
			RA	0.45%	0.00%	0.00%
			RZ	0.20%	4.00%	0.00%
			R	0.72%–0.94%	0.00%	0.00%
Static multi-fund	3	AllianceBernstein mutual funds [1]	A	0.97%–1.19%	4.25%	0.00%
			B	1.72%–1.94%	0.00%	4.00%
			C	1.72%–1.94%	0.00%	1.00%
			RA	0.97%–1.19%	0.00%	0.00%
			RZ	0.72%–0.94%	4.00%	0.00%
			R	0.72%–0.94%	0.00%	0.00%
Individual fund	10		A	0.80%–1.54%	4.25%	0.00%
			B	1.55%–2.29%	0.00%	4.00%
			C	1.55%–2.29%	0.00%	1.00%
			RA	0.80%–1.54%	0.00%	0.00%
			RZ	0.55%–1.29%	4.00%	0.00%
			R	0.55%–1.29%	0.00%	0.00%

[1] The Principal-Protection Income Portfolio (an individual fund option) invests in a separately managed fixed income portfolio.
[2] B units automatically convert to A units at the end of the 8th year.
[3] Plan fees plus underlying fund expenses and distribution/servicing fees.

Minimum contributions: With lump-sum contributions, the minimum initial contribution is $1,000, and the minimum subsequent contribution is $50. With the automatic investment plan, the minimum contribution level is $50 per month.

Account maintenance fee: $25 annually. The fee is waived for Rhode Island Accounts, for account balances of $25,000 or greater, for accounts set up with automatic contributions, and for accounts established through sponsored contribution plans.

SOUTH CAROLINA

South Carolina's two 529 savings programs, managed by Columbia Management, and featuring Columbia Funds, are both named "Future Scholar" although they have different underlying mutual funds. The direct-sold Future Scholar is available only to South Carolina residents while the advisor-sold Future Scholar is sold nationwide. The state's prepaid tuition program is no longer accepting new enrollment.

STATE AGENCY: Office of the State Treasurer

State income tax treatment: All contributions to a South Carolina 529 plan are deductible in computing South Carolina taxable income. The contribution deadline is April 15 of the following year. Qualified distributions from South Carolina and non-South Carolina 529 plans are excluded from South Carolina taxable income. Under the South Carolina recapture rule, the principal portion of nonqualified distributions from a South Carolina 529 plan must be included in South Carolina taxable income. It appears that rollovers to another 529 plan are not subject to South Carolina recapture rules.

Maximum contribution limit: A contribution will not be accepted if it would cause the total of all South Carolina 529 account balances for the same beneficiary to exceed $318,000.

Other considerations:

- Under South Carolina law, accounts in a South Carolina 529 plan are exempt from attachment, garnishment, levy, and sale under any means or final process issued by any court or bankruptcy proceeding.

Future Scholar 529 College Savings Plan – Direct Plan

529 PROGRAM TYPE:	Savings
PROGRAM MANAGER:	Columbia Management Investment Distributors, Inc.
DISTRIBUTOR:	Columbia Management Investment Distributors, Inc.
TELEPHONE:	888–244–5674
WEB SITE:	www.futurescholar.com

Enrollment: Enroll directly. The account owner or beneficiary must be a resident of South Carolina, or an employee of the State of South Carolina at the time of program enrollment.

Investment options:

Option type	# of options	Underlying investments	Expense ratio [1]
Age- or enrollment-based	3 tracks Aggressive, Moderate and Conservative	Mutual funds from Columbia and Vanguard and an ETF from iShares	0.08%–0.18%
Static multi-fund	7		
Individual fund	9		0.05%–0.25%
FDIC Insured	1	BB&T Bank deposit account	0.00%

[1] No plan fees. Underlying fund expenses only.

Minimum contributions: No minimum contribution required.

Account maintenance fee: None

Future Scholar 529 College Savings Plan – Advisor Plan

529 PROGRAM TYPE:	Savings
PROGRAM MANAGER:	Columbia Management Investment Distributors, Inc.
DISTRIBUTOR:	Columbia Management Investment Distributors, Inc.
TELEPHONE:	888–244–5674
WEB SITE:	www.futurescholar.com

Enrollment: Purchase through a financial advisor (unit classes A and C) or through your employer (unit class E).

Investment options:

Option type	# of options	Underlying investments	Unit classes	Expense ratio [1]	Maximum sales charge	
					Initial	Contingent deferred
Age- or enrollment-based	3 tracks	Mutual funds from Columbia and ETFs from iShares	A	0.67%–1.17%	1.00% - 3.50%	0.00%
			C	1.27%–1.92%	0.00%	0.75%–1.00%
Static multi-fund	7		E	1.02%–1.42%	0.00%	0.00%
Individual fund	22	Mutual funds from Columbia, MFS, Nuveen Winslow, American Century, Fidelity, DFA, Franklin Templeton, and JP Morgan and ETFs from iShares	A	0.33%–1.42%	1.00% - 3.50%	0.00%
			C	0.93%–2.16%	0.00%	0.75%–1.00%
			E	0.68%–1.67%	0.00%	0.00%
FDIC-insured	1	BB&T Bank deposit account	A	0.00%	0.00%	0.00%
			C	0.00%	0.00%	0.00%
			E	0.00%	0.00%	0.00%

[1] 0.16% plan fees plus underlying fund expenses and distribution/servicing fees.

Minimum contributions: With lump-sum contributions, the minimum initial contribution is $100, and the minimum subsequent contribution is $25. With the automatic investment plan, there are no minimum payments.

Account maintenance fee: $25 annually. The fee is waived for South Carolina residents and state employees, for account balances of $10,000 or greater, and for accounts in the automatic investment plan.

South Carolina Tuition Prepayment Program

529 PROGRAM TYPE:	Prepaid
TELEPHONE:	888–772–4723
WEB SITE:	www.scgrad.org

Enrollment: This prepaid program for South Carolina residents has been closed to new enrollments and is not expected to reopen.

Time/age restrictions: Contract benefits must be used by the time the beneficiary is 30 years old, with extensions of up to four years granted for military service.

Contract benefits: Program participants purchase a contract for either four years of undergraduate tuition and fees, or two years of undergraduate tuition and fees, at a South Carolina public institution. The tuition rate paid by SCTPP to a private or out-of-state school is an amount up to the average rate that the program is paying at that time to South Carolina public universities, less a small processing fee. Beginning with the 2007-2008 school year, annual tuition benefit increases under the program are capped at 7 percent, and South Carolina's public institutions are required to waive any excess tuition increases for program participants.

Statutory state backing: In the event the program is canceled, the state legislature is required to consider an appropriation to return all contributions plus 4 percent annual interest.

SOUTH DAKOTA

South Dakota's College Access 529 savings programs are managed by Allianz Global Investors and feature age-based and static options using mutual funds from a variety of fund families. The advisor version is sold nationally while a direct-sold version with fewer investment choices is available to South Dakota residents.

STATE AGENCY:　South Dakota Investment Council

State income tax treatment: South Dakota does not have a personal income tax.

Maximum contribution limit: A contribution will not be accepted if it would cause the total of all South Dakota 529 account balances for the same beneficiary to exceed $350,000.

Other considerations:

- Under South Dakota law, except for funds contributed within one year of a Chapter 11 bankruptcy filing by the account owner or contributor, amounts in a South Dakota 529 account are not an asset or property of the account owner, contributor, or beneficiary for purposes of paying any debt or liability, and the account is exempt from any levy, execution or judgment, or other operation of law, garnishment, or other judicial enforcement.

College Access 529 (Class SD-D)

529 PROGRAM TYPE:	Savings
PROGRAM MANAGER:	Allianz Global Investors Distributors LLC
DISTRIBUTOR:	Allianz Global Investors Distributors LLC
TELEPHONE:	866–529–7462
WEB SITE:	www.CollegeAccess529.com

Enrollment: Enroll directly. The account owner or designated beneficiary must be a South Dakota resident at the time of program enrollment.

Investment options:

Option type	# of options	Underlying investments	Expense ratio [1]
Age- or enrollment-based	1 track	Mutual funds from Allianz, The Boston Company, Franklin Templeton, ING, NFJ, PIMCO, Royce, RS, Thornburg, and TIAA-CREF	0.45%–0.62%
Static multi-fund	1	PIMCO bond funds	0.48%
Individual fund	2		0.45%–0.88%

[1] No plan fees. Underlying fund expenses only.

Minimum contributions: With lump-sum contributions, the minimum initial contribution is $250 per investment option, and the minimum subsequent contribution is $50 per investment option. With the automatic investment plan, the minimum contribution level is $50 per investment option per month.

Account maintenance fee: None

College Access 529 (Advisor-sold)

529 PROGRAM TYPE:	Savings
PROGRAM MANAGER:	Allianz Global Investors Distributors LLC
DISTRIBUTOR:	Allianz Global Investors Distributors LLC
TELEPHONE:	866–529–7462
WEB SITE:	www.CollegeAccess529.com

Enrollment: Purchase through a financial advisor. There are no state residency requirements.

Investment options:

Option type	# of options	Underlying investments	Unit classes (2)	Expense ratio (3)	Maximum sales charge Initial	Maximum sales charge Contingent deferred
Age- or enrollment-based	1 track (1)		A	1.15%–1.32%	3.75%–5.50%	0.00%
			B	1.90%–2.07%	0.00%	3.50%–5.00%
			C	1.90%–2.07%	0.00%	1.00%
			SD-A	0.80%–0.97%	3.75%–5.50%	0.00%
			SD-C	1.45%–1.62%	0.00%	1.00%
Static multi-fund	2	Mutual funds from Allianz, Columbia Management, Dodge & Cox, Dreyfus/ The Boston Company, Franklin Templeton, ING, NFJ, PIMCO, Royce, RS, Thornburg, and TIAA-CREF	A	1.18%–1.35%	3.75%–5.50%	0.00%
			B	1.93%–2.10%	0.00%	3.50%–5.00%
			C	1.93%–2.10%	0.00%	1.00%
			SD-A	0.83%–1.00%	3.75%–5.50%	0.00%
			SD-C	1.48%–1.65%	0.00%	1.00%
Individual fund	14		A	1.15%–1.77%	3.75%–5.50%	0.00%
			B	1.90%–2.52%	0.00%	3.50%–5.00%
			C	1.90%–2.52%	0.00%	1.00%
			SD-A	0.80%–1.42%	3.75%–5.50%	0.00%
			SD-C	1.45%–2.07%	0.00%	1.00%
Short term	1	PIMCO funds	A/B/C	1.02%	0.00%	0.00%
			SD-A/ SD-C	0.67%	0.00%	0.00%
Money market	1		A/B/C	0.63%	0.00%	0.00%
			SD-A/ SD-C	0.28%	0.00%	0.00%

(1) Underlying portfolios also available as static options
(2) B units automatically convert to A units at the end of the 8th year.
(3) 0.35% plan fees (0.10% for the PIMCO Government Money Market and none for SD-A and SD-C classes) plus underlying fund expenses and distribution/servicing fees.

Minimum contributions: With lump-sum contributions, the minimum initial contribution is $1,000 ($250 per investment option), and the minimum subsequent contribution is $50 per investment option. With the automatic investment plan, the minimum initial contribution is $250 and the minimum subsequent contribution level is $50 per month.

Account maintenance fee: $5 per quarter for each investment option on balances below $20,000. The fee is waived for accounts where a common owner has accounts aggregating over $50,000 of value, South Dakota residents, and for participants with an automatic investment plan.

TENNESSEE

The Tennessee State Treasury Department operates a direct-sold multi-manager 529 plan with underlying funds from a number of fund companies. The unit-type prepaid tuition program for Tennessee residents was closed to new contributions in November 2010.

    STATE AGENCY: State of Tennessee Treasury Department and the Baccalaureate Education System Trust Board of Trustees

State income tax treatment: Tennessee does not have a personal income tax. Qualified distributions from Tennessee and non-Tennessee 529 plans are specifically exempt from all Tennessee state, county, and municipal taxes.

Maximum contribution limit: A contribution will not be accepted if it would cause the total of all accounts in both the TNStars Program and the BEST Prepaid Program for the same beneficiary to exceed $235,000.

Other considerations:

- Under Tennessee law, assets in any 529 plan or other education savings plan are exempt from execution, attachment, garnishment, the operation of bankruptcy, the insolvency laws or other process whatsoever, and any assignment thereof shall not be enforceable in any court.

TNStars College Savings 529 Program

    529 PROGRAM TYPE: Savings
    PROGRAM MANAGER: State of Tennessee Treasury Department
    DISTRIBUTOR: Not applicable
    TELEPHONE: 855-386-7827
    WEB SITE: www.tnstars.com

Enrollment: Enroll directly. This program is not sold through financial advisors. There are no state residency requirements.

Investment options:

Option type	# of options	Underlying investments	Expense ratio [1]
Age- or enrollment-based	1 track	Mutual funds from Vanguard and DFA	0.35% [2]
Individual fund	7	Mutual funds from Vanguard, DFA, Great West Funds and Primecap	
FDIC-insured	1	First Tennessee Bank National Association	0.00%

[1] For 2012–2013 fiscal year the program is subsidizing fees and expenses for any fund above 0.35% total annual asset-based fee.
[2] 0.00%–0.30% plan fee plus underlying fund expenses.

Minimum contributions: $25 per investment option. Once an initial contribution is made to the account, there are no required subsequent contributions.

Account maintenance fee: None

Tennessee's BEST Prepaid College Tuition Plan

529 PROGRAM TYPE:	Prepaid
TELEPHONE:	615-532-8056
WEB SITE:	www.treasury.state.tn.us/best

Enrollment: This prepaid program for Tennessee residents has been closed to new enrollments and contributions.

Time/age restrictions: The first payout date must be at least two calendar years after the beneficiary is enrolled in the program and not before the beneficiary has been accepted for enrollment in an institution of higher education. Any subsequent deposit must have been on the beneficiary's account for at least two years before the funds may be paid out.

Program benefits: Each unit acquired in this prepaid tuition program is worth one percent of the weighted average tuition at Tennessee's public four-year universities and may be redeemed for payment to any eligible educational institution in the country.

Statutory state backing: None

TEXAS

Both the direct-sold and advisor-sold offerings in the Lone Star State consist primarily, but not exclusively, of mutual funds from OppenheimerFunds. Texas also has two prepaid tuition plans for Texas residents—a contract-type program that closed to new enrollment in 2003 (Texas Guaranteed Tuition Plan) and a replacement unit-type plan managed by OFI Private Investments Inc. that opened in fall 2008 (Texas Tuition Promise Fund).

STATE AGENCY: Texas Prepaid Higher Education Tuition Board

State income tax treatment: Texas does not have a personal income tax.

Maximum contribution limit: A contribution will not be accepted if it would cause the total of all Texas 529 account balances for the same beneficiary to exceed $370,000.

Other considerations:

- Under Texas law, assets in any 529 plan are exempt from attachment, execution, and seizure for the satisfaction of debt or liability of an account owner or beneficiary.

Texas College Savings Plan

529 PROGRAM TYPE:	Savings
PROGRAM MANAGER:	OFI Private Investments Inc., an affiliate of OppenheimerFunds
DISTRIBUTOR:	OppenheimerFunds Distributor, Inc.
TELEPHONE:	800–445–4723
WEB SITE:	www.texascollegesavings.com

Enrollment: Enroll directly. This program is not sold through financial advisors. There are no state residency requirements.

Investment options:

Option type	# of options	Underlying investments	Expense ratio
Age- or enrollment-based, blended	1 track	Mutual funds from OppenheimerFunds, Dreyfus, Vanguard, and Thornburg	0.63%–0.81% [1]
Static multi-fund, blended	2		0.75%–0.83% [1]
Age- or enrollment-based, index	1 track	Mutual funds from OppenheimerFunds, Dreyfus, TIAA-CREF, and Vanguard	0.51–0.55% [2]
Static multi-fund, index	2	Mutual funds from OppenheimerFunds, Dreyfus, and Vanguard	0.54%–0.55% [2]
Individual fund	4	Mutual funds from OppenheimerFunds, Dreyfus, and Vanguard	0.42%–0.70% [1]

[1] 0.25% plan fee plus underlying fund expenses.
[2] 0.15% plan fee includes underlying fund expenses.

Minimum contributions: $25 per portfolio, or $15 per portfolio with the automatic investment plan.

Account maintenance fee: None

Lonestar 529 Plan

529 PROGRAM TYPE:	Savings
PROGRAM MANAGER:	OFI Private Investments Inc., an affiliate of OppenheimerFunds
DISTRIBUTOR:	OppenheimerFunds Distributor, Inc.
TELEPHONE:	800–445–4723
WEB SITE:	www.lonestar529.com

Enrollment: Purchase through a financial advisor. There are no state residency requirements.

Investment options:

Option type	# of options	Underlying investments	Unit classes	Expense ratio [1]	Maximum sales charge	
					Initial	Contingent deferred
Age- or enrollment-based	1 track	Mutual funds from OppenheimerFunds, Dreyfus, TIAA-CREF and Thornburg	A	1.01%–1.30%	5.75%	0.00%
			C	1.75%–2.05%	0.00%	1.00%
Static multi-fund	2		A	1.25%–1.31%	5.75%	0.00%
			C	2.00%–2.06%	0.00%	1.00%
Individual fund	9		A	0.85%–1.63%	5.75%	0.00%
			C	1.60%–2.38%	0.00%	1.00%
Money market	2	OppenheimerFunds and Dreyfus money market funds	A, C	0.48%–0.52%	0.00%	0.00%

[1] 0.31% plan fees (0.40% for Socially Responsible Portfolio) plus underlying fund expenses and distribution/servicing fees.

Minimum contributions: $25, or $15 with the automatic investment plan.

Account maintenance fee: None

Texas Tuition Promise Fund

529 PROGRAM TYPE:	Prepaid
PROGRAM MANAGER:	OFI Private Investments Inc.
TELEPHONE:	800–445–4723
WEB SITE:	www.texastuitionpromisefund.com

Enrollment: Each year's enrollment period runs from September 1 through the following February (through July for newborns). The beneficiary must be a Texas resident, or have a parent who is a Texas resident and is the named purchaser at the time of enrollment.

Time/age restrictions: Contract benefits must be used within a 10-year period beginning on the date the beneficiary is projected to graduate from high school, with extensions granted for military service. A beneficiary may not use a tuition unit earlier than the third anniversary of the date the unit was purchased.

Contract benefits: Each Type I unit is redeemable toward 1% of one year's tuition and required fees at the Texas four-year public college with the highest tuition and required fee costs. Each Type II unit is redeemable toward 1% of the weighted average of one year's tuition and required fees at Texas four-year public colleges. Each Type III unit is redeemable toward 1% of the weighted average of one year's tuition and required fees at Texas two-year public colleges. Unit values are capped if redeemed for use at a private college or a public college outside Texas ("Transfer Value"), or if refunded ("Refund Value").

Contract prices: For the 2012-2013 enrollment period, Type I, Type II, and Type III units were priced at $115.92, $82.92, and $21.39 respectively. Prices are adjusted each year based on the actual tuition and required fees for Texas two-year and four-year public colleges and universities.

Minimum contributions: One unit initially. Subsequent purchases must be at least $15. Extended payment plans are available.

Enrollment or application fee: $25

Statutory state backing: None; however, Texas law requires all Texas two-year and four-year public colleges and universities to accept plan benefits as payment for the applicable portion of tuition and required fees.

Texas Guaranteed Tuition Plan

529 PROGRAM TYPE:	Prepaid
TELEPHONE:	800–445–4723, option #2
WEB SITE:	www.texastomorrowfunds.org

Enrollment: This prepaid tuition plan has been closed to new enrollments since 2003 and is not expected to reopen.

Time/age restrictions: Contract benefits must be used within a 10-year period beginning on the date the beneficiary is projected to graduate from high school, with extensions granted for military service.

Contract benefits: The program offered a junior college plan, senior college plan, junior/senior plan, and a private college plan. A beneficiary attending a private or out-of-state institution receives the weighted average public tuition and fees in Texas (for public college contracts), or the estimated average tuition and fees (for private college contracts). A $25 out-of-state fee is deducted from distributions to educational institutions outside the state of Texas.

Statutory state backing: In the event the program does not have sufficient funds to pay college tuition, the first available revenues of the state will be transferred into the program, backed by the full faith and credit of the state of Texas.

UTAH

The Utah Educational Savings Plan (UESP) is a direct-sold, state-administered 529 savings program. Through four age-based and six static investment options, the program utilizes Vanguard funds, an FDIC-insured savings account held in trust at Zions First National Bank, and the Utah Public Treasurers' Investment Fund, a fixed-income fund managed by the Utah State Treasurer. The plan also offers customized age-based and static investment options.

STATE AGENCY: Utah Higher Education Assistance Authority

State income tax treatment: For 2013, contributions to UESP of up to $1,840 (in 2013) per beneficiary by an individual filer, and up to $3,680 per beneficiary by a married couple filing jointly, are eligible for a 5 percent credit against Utah income tax. The maximum 2013 credit is $92 per beneficiary for single taxpayers and $184 per beneficiary for joint filers. The credit limits are increased each year for inflation. To be eligible for the tax credit, the beneficiary of the UESP account must be designated as such before age 19. If this requirement is met, the account owner is eligible to claim an income tax credit each year a contribution is made – for the life of the beneficiary's account. A beneficiary does not have to be a Utah resident for the UESP account owner to qualify for the benefit. Contributions from a non-owner are creditable by the account owner and not by the non-owner/contributor. Contributions must be received by the program on or before the last business day of the year to be eligible for that year's tax credit. Qualified distributions from Utah and non-Utah 529 plans are excluded from Utah taxable income. Under the Utah recapture rule, the principal portion of any nonqualified distribution that is subject to the federal 10% penalty, or rollover, from the Utah 529 plan must be included in Utah taxable income to the extent of prior claimed Utah tax deductions or credits.

Maximum contribution limit: A contribution will not be accepted if it would cause the total of all Utah 529 account balances for the same beneficiary to exceed $397,000.

Other considerations:

- Under the Fast Forward Matching Program for 2013, UESP will match up to $400 annually per beneficiary in contributions to an account for Utah families with incomes below 200% of the federal poverty level. A beneficiary may receive matching funds for as many as four years. Matching is subject to funding availability.

Utah Educational Savings Plan (UESP) Trust

529 PROGRAM TYPE:	Savings
PROGRAM MANAGER:	Utah Higher Education Assistance Authority
DISTRIBUTOR:	Utah Higher Education Assistance Authority
TELEPHONE:	800–418–2551
WEB SITE:	www.uesp.org

Enrollment: Enroll directly. This program is not sold through financial advisors. There are no state residency requirements.

Investment options:

Option type	# of options	Underlying investments	Expense ratio [2]
Age- or enrollment-based	4 tracks	Vanguard mutual funds and Zions National Bank savings	0.200%–0.257%
Static multi-fund	2		0.238%–0.244%
Individual fund	2	Vanguard mutual funds	0.200%
Individual fund	1	Public Treasurer's Investment Fund	0.200% [3]
FDIC-insured	1	Zions National Bank savings account	0.180%
Customized[1]	2	Vanguard funds and Zions National Bank savings	0.200%–0.610%

[1] These options allow an investor-selected blend of any of the underlying funds (except PTIF) as either static or evolving (age-based).
[2] 0.15%–0.20% plan fees plus underlying fund expenses.
[3] None for Utah residents.

Minimum contributions: No minimum.

Account maintenance fee: $3 per $1,000 of account balance up to a maximum of $15 annually, charged monthly. The fee is waived for all Utah residents and for nonresidents who agree to electronic delivery of account statements. It is waived for all Utah residents.

VERMONT

The Green Mountain State's 529 plan is managed by TIAA-CREF Tuition Financing, Inc. and features age-based and equity options utilizing TIAA-CREF institutional funds along with a guaranteed option.

STATE AGENCY:	Vermont Student Assistance Corp. (VSAC)

State income tax treatment: Contributions to the Vermont 529 plan of up to $2,500 per beneficiary per year by an individual filer, and up to $5,000 per beneficiary per year by married taxpayers who each make their own contributions, are eligible for a 10% tax credit against Vermont income tax. This works out to a maximum annual $250 credit per beneficiary per eligible taxpayer. Contributions must be from the account owner, or if filing jointly, from the account owner's spouse, to be eligible for the credit. The principal portion of a rollover from another 529 plan is treated as a contribution for purposes of the credit, provided the funds remain in the Vermont 529 account for the remainder of the taxable year. The contribution deadline is December 31. Qualified distributions from Vermont and non-Vermont 529 plans are excluded from Vermont taxable income. Under Vermont's recapture rules, nonqualified distributions from the Vermont 529 plan are subject to Vermont recapture, to the extent of Vermont tax credits previously claimed. Rollovers to another 529 plan are not subject to the recapture rule.

Maximum contribution limit: A contribution will not be accepted if it would cause the total of all Vermont 529 account balances for the same beneficiary to exceed $352,800.

Vermont Higher Education Investment Plan

529 PROGRAM TYPE:	Savings
PROGRAM MANAGER:	TIAA-CREF Tuition Financing, Inc.
DISTRIBUTOR:	TIAA-CREF Individual & Institutional Services, LLC
TELEPHONE:	800–637–5860
WEB SITE:	www.vheip.com

Enrollment: Enroll directly. This program is not sold through financial advisors. There are no state residency requirements.

Investment options:

Option type	# of options	Underlying investments	Expense ratio
Age- or enrollment-based	1 track	TIAA-CREF institutional mutual funds	0.50% [1]
Static multi-fund	4	Mutual funds from TIAA-CREF and T. Rowe Price	0.54%–0.84% [2]
Principal protection	1	Funding agreement from TIAA-CREF Life	0.00%

[1] 0.50% plan fees includes underlying fund expenses.
[2] 0.45% plan fees plus underlying fund expenses.

Minimum contributions: $25, or $15 per payroll with the payroll deduction plan

Account maintenance fee: None

VIRGINIA

Virginia offers four 529 plans including three 529 savings programs: a multi-manager, direct-sold 529 savings program (Virginia529 inVEST); an advisor-sold program (CollegeAmerica) utilizing American Funds; and its newest program (CollegeWealth) featuring deposit accounts and certificates of deposit through participating banks, savings and loan associations, and credit unions. All three savings programs are available to residents of any state. Virginia also offers a prepaid tuition program (Virginia529 prePAID) open only to Virginia residents.

STATE AGENCY: Virginia College Savings Plan

State income tax treatment: Contributions to a Virginia 529 plan of up to $4,000 per account per year are deductible in computing Virginia taxable income. The annual deduction cap is waived for contributors age 70 and older. Contributions must be received by the last business day of the year to be eligible for that year's deduction. Excess contributions may be carried over for an unlimited number of years. Contributions from non-owners are treated as made by the account owner for purposes of the deduction. Qualified distributions from Virginia and non-Virginia 529 plans are excluded from Virginia taxable income. Under the Virginia recapture rule, the principal portion of rollovers and nonqualified distributions from a Virginia 529 plan must be included in Virginia taxable income to the extent of prior Virginia tax deductions. Nonqualified distributions for this purpose do not include distributions made as the result of the beneficiary's death or disability or on account of the beneficiary's receipt of a scholarship.

Maximum contribution limit: A contribution will not be accepted if it would cause the total of all Virginia 529 account balances for the same beneficiary to exceed $350,000.

Other considerations:

- Under Virginia law, accounts are protected from creditors of either the account owner or the beneficiary, and this protection generally may be preserved by a debtor in a bankruptcy case.

Virginia529 inVEST

529 PROGRAM TYPE:	Savings
PROGRAM MANAGER:	Virginia College Savings Plan Board and its Executive Director
DISTRIBUTOR:	State-distributed
TELEPHONE:	888–567–0540
WEB SITE:	www.virginia529.com

Enrollment: Enroll directly. This plan is not sold through financial advisors. There are no state residency requirements.

Time/age restrictions: The account should be used within ten years of the beneficiary's projected date of high school graduation, or within ten years after the account is opened if the beneficiary has already graduated from high school; however, extensions may be granted by the program.

Investment options:

Option type	# of options	Underlying investments	Expense ratio [1]
Age- or enrollment-based	1 track	Mutual funds and separate accounts from Vanguard, Rothschild Asset Management, Franklin Templeton, Aberdeen, Prudential, Stone Harbor, Morgan Stanley, American Funds, and Invesco	0.30%–0.79%
Static multi-fund	3	Vanguard mutual funds	0.33%–0.37%
Individual fund	5		0.25%–0.33%
Socially responsible	1	Parnassus Equity Income Fund	0.90%

[1] 0.20% plan fees plus underlying fund expenses.

Minimum contributions: The minimum initial contribution amount is $25.

Account maintenance fee: A $25 one-time, non-refundable enrollment fee is charged. There is no annual maintenance fee.

CollegeAmerica

529 PROGRAM TYPE:	Savings
PROGRAM MANAGER:	American Funds Service Company, American Funds Distributors, and Capital Research and Management Company
DISTRIBUTOR:	American Funds Distributors
TELEPHONE:	800–421–4225
WEB SITE:	www.americanfunds.com

Enrollment: Purchase through a financial advisor (share classes 529-A, 529-B, and 529-C), through your employer (share class 529-E), or through a fee-based financial planner (share class 529-F-1). There are no state residency requirements.

Time/age restrictions: The account must be used within 30 years after the beneficiary graduates from high school, or within 30 years after the account is opened, whichever is later. Requests for an extension of this time limit will be considered on a case-by-case basis.

Investment options:

Option type	# of options	Underlying investments	Unit classes	Expense ratio [1]	Maximum sales charge Initial	Contingent deferred
Age- or enrollment-based	1 track	American Funds	529-A	0.96%–1.09%	2.50% - 4.25%	0.00%
			529-C	1.71%–1.84%	0.00%	1.00%
			529-E	1.18%–1.31%	0.00%	0.00%
			529-F-1	0.74%–0.87%	0.00%	0.00%
Static multi-fund	6		529-A	0.91%–1.16%	2.50%–5.75%	0.00%
			529-C	1.66%–1.96%	0.00%	1.00%
			529-E	1.11%–1.41%	0.00%	0.00%
			529-F-1	0.66%–0.96%	0.00%	0.00%
Individual fund	25		529-A	0.65%–1.19%	2.50%–5.75% [2]	0.00%
			529-C	0.51%–2.00%	0.00%	1.00%
			529-E	0.50%–1.45%	0.00%	0.00%
			529-F-1	0.46%–0.99%	0.00%	0.00%

[1] 0.10% plan fees (currently being waived for age-based and static multi-fund options) included in underlying fund expenses.
[2] None for American Funds Money Market.

Minimum contributions: The minimum initial contribution is $250 per fund ($1,000 for American Funds Money Market), and the minimum subsequent contribution is $50 per fund. The minimum in an employer-sponsored plan is $25 per fund.

Account maintenance fee: $10 annually. Also, a $10 enrollment fee is charged.

CollegeWealth

529 PROGRAM TYPE:	Savings
PROGRAM MANAGER:	Virginia College Savings Plan
DISTRIBUTOR:	BB&T and Union First Market Bank
TELEPHONE:	888-567-0540 (Virginia 529)
WEB SITE:	www.virginia529.com

Enrollment: Enroll directly with the participating bank. There are no state residency requirements.

Time/age restrictions: The account should be used within ten years of the beneficiary's projected date of high school graduation, or within ten years after the account is opened if the beneficiary has already graduated from high school; however, extensions may be granted by the program.

Investment options: Money market savings accounts offered by participating banks, insured up to allowable limits by the FDIC.

Minimum contributions: $25 minimum initial contribution.

Account maintenance fee: None

Virginia529 prepAID

529 PROGRAM TYPE:	Prepaid
TELEPHONE:	888–567–0540
WEB SITE:	www.virginia529.com

Enrollment: The enrollment period usually runs from December through the following March. The account owner, beneficiary, or parent of a non-resident beneficiary must be a Virginia resident or a member of the U.S. military who is either stationed in Virginia or who claims Virginia as home of record at the time of enrollment.

Time/age restrictions: The beneficiary must be in the 9th grade or below at the time the contract is purchased. Contract benefits must be used within ten years after the projected date of high school graduation, unless an extension is granted.

Contract benefits: Contracts are available in semester increments priced at two levels. Tier I prices cover a semester at a Virginia four-year university or college or 2 2/3 semester at a Virginia two-year or community college. The less expensive Tier II contract covers a partial semester at a four year Virginia university or college or a full semester at a two-year or community college. A beneficiary attending an in-state private institution receives benefits equal to the lesser of (1) payments made on the contract plus the actual rate of return earned on the invested funds, compounded annualy or (2) the highest in-state undergraduate tuition at a Virginia public institution in the same semester the benefits are used. A beneficiary attending an out-of-state institution receives benefits equal to the lesser of (1) the contract cost plus interest at a reasonable rate of return based on institutional money market rates or (2) average Virginia public university undergraduate tuition for the same semester the benefits are used.

Contract prices: For the 2012-2013 enrollment period, Tier I prices range from $6,825 for a 5th to 9th grader to $7,325 for newborn to age 4/5. The Tier II price is $2,750 for newborn to 9th grade.

Enrollment or application fee: $25

Statutory state backing: State legislation provides a financial guarantee in each year's state budget to cover Virginia529 prepAID's contractual obligations in the event of a funding shortfall. This provision can only be changed by the Virginia General Assembly subject to the Governor's veto, and the General Assembly's ability to override a veto.

WASHINGTON

The Evergreen State does not offer a 529 savings program but operates a unit-type 529 prepaid tuition program (GET) for state residents. Each unit purchased through GET is redeemable for one percent of the resident undergraduate tuition and state-mandated fees at the highest-priced public university in Washington, and may be used for any eligible educational institution in the country, as well as some foreign countries.

> STATE AGENCY: Washington State Student Achievement Council, with the State Treasurer as a member of the GET committee that oversees the program.

State income tax treatment: Washington does not have a personal income tax.

Other considerations:

- Under Washington law, all funds placed into GET at least two years prior to filing for bankruptcy are protected from creditors.

Guaranteed Education Tuition (GET)

> 529 PROGRAM TYPE: Prepaid
> TELEPHONE: 800–955–2318
> WEB SITE: www.get.wa.gov

Enrollment: The enrollment period runs from November 1 through the following May (year-round for newborns). The account owner or the beneficiary must be a Washington resident at the time of program enrollment.

Time/age restrictions: Tuition units can be redeemed or refunded after two years from account opening. Units must be used within 10 years after the beneficiary's projected college entrance year or the first use of units, whichever is later.

Program benefits: Each unit acquired in the prepaid program is worth one percent of the resident undergraduate tuition and state-mandated fees at the highest-priced public university in Washington, and may be redeemed at that value for use at any eligible educational institution in the country, as well as some foreign countries.

Minimum contribution: One unit ($172 through July 1, 2013)

Maximum contributions: 500 units ($86,000). A monthly payment plan is available.

Enrollment or application fee: $50 ($100 limit per family)

Statutory state backing: Program benefits are backed by the full faith and credit of the state of Washington.

WEST VIRGINIA

The Mountain State offers two direct-sold 529 savings programs and one advisor-sold program. The direct-sold SMART529 Select plan features funds from Dimensional Fund Advisors (DFA), while Hartford Funds are utilized in the Hartford SMART529 and Vanguard index funds are utilized by the SMART529 Direct plan. West Virginia also operates a prepaid tuition plan that was closed to new enrollment in 2003 and is being allowed to wind down.

STATE AGENCY: State Treasurer's Office under the authority of the West Virginia College Prepaid Tuition and Savings Program Board of Trustees

State income tax treatment: All contributions to a West Virginia 529 plan are deductible in computing West Virginia taxable income. The contribution deadline for each year's deduction is December 31. Contributions in excess of the donor's adjusted gross income may be carried over for up to five years. Qualified distributions from West Virginia and non-West Virginia 529 plans are excluded from West Virginia taxable income. Under the West Virginia recapture rule, the principal portion of nonqualified distributions from a West Virginia 529 plan must be included in West Virginia taxable income to the extent of prior West Virginia tax deductions. It appears that rollovers to another 529 plan are not subject to the recapture rule.

Maximum contribution limit: A contribution will not be accepted if it would cause the total of all West Virginia 529 account balances for the same beneficiary to exceed $265,620.

Other considerations:

- Under West Virginia law, money in a West Virginia 529 plan is exempt from creditor process and not subject to attachment, garnishment, or other process, and is not subject to seizure, taking, appropriation or application by any legal or equitable process or operation of law to pay any debt or liability of any account owner, beneficiary or successor in interest.
- Participation in a West Virginia 529 plan does not affect the beneficiary's eligibility for financial aid programs administered by the state of West Virginia.
- Accounts in a West Virginia 529 plan can be linked to the Upromise Rewards Service.
- The SMART529 Matching Grant Program provides matching grants to eligible West Virginia families in an amount up to $500 per Designated Beneficiary per year – up to a lifetime maximum of $2,500 per Designated Beneficiary – with a dollar for dollar match. Eligible account owners must be residents of West Virginia and must meet certain family income guidelines. The Designated Beneficiary must

be 12 years old or younger at the time the first Matching Grant application is submitted.

SMART529 WV Direct College Savings Plan

529 PROGRAM TYPE:	Savings
PROGRAM MANAGER:	Hartford Life Insurance Company
DISTRIBUTOR:	Hartford Investment Financial Services, LLC
TELEPHONE:	866–574–3542
WEB SITE:	www.smart529.com

Enrollment: Enroll directly. This program is not sold through financial advisors. The account owner or designated beneficiary must have a West Virginia mailing address or be a West Virginia resident on active duty in the U.S. armed forces.

Investment options:

Option type	# of options	Underlying investments	Expense ratio [1]
Age- or enrollment-based	1 track	Vanguard index funds and Invesco Stable Value Portfolio	0.32%–0.34%
Static multi-fund	5		
Individual fund	1		0.29%
Stable value	1		0.40%

[1] 0.03%–0.25% plan fees (none for Stable Value Portfolio) plus underlying fund expenses.

Minimum contributions: With lump-sum contributions, there is no minimum initial or subsequent contribution. With the automatic investment plan, the minimum contribution level is $15 per month.

Account maintenance fee: None

SMART529 Select

529 PROGRAM TYPE:	Savings
PROGRAM MANAGER:	Hartford Life Insurance Company
DISTRIBUTOR:	Hartford Investment Financial Services, LLC
TELEPHONE:	866–574–3542
WEB SITE:	www.smart529select.com

Enrollment: Enroll directly. This program is not sold through financial advisors. There are no state residency requirements.

Investment options:

Option type	# of options	Underlying investments	Expense ratio [1]
Age- or enrollment-based	1 track	Dimensional Fund Advisors (DFA) mutual funds	0.69%–0.78%
Static multi-fund	9		
Individual fund	1	DFA 1-Year Fixed Income Portfolio	0.67%

[1] 0.47% plan fees plus underlying fund expenses.

Minimum contributions: With lump-sum contributions, the minimum initial contribution is $250 ($50 for West Virginia residents), and the minimum subsequent contribution is $25 (no minimum for West Virginia residents). With the automatic investment plan, the minimum contribution level is $25 per month ($15 per month for West Virginia residents).

Account maintenance fee: $25 annually, charged on a quarterly basis. The fee is waived for West Virginia residents, for account balances greater than $25,000, and for accounts in the automatic investment plan investing $25 or more for at least twelve consecutive months, or at least $300 annually.

The Hartford SMART529 College Savings Plan

529 PROGRAM TYPE:	Savings
PROGRAM MANAGER:	Hartford Life Insurance Company
DISTRIBUTOR:	Hartford Investment Financial Services, LLC
TELEPHONE:	866–574–3542
WEB SITE:	www.hartfordinvestor.com

Enrollment: Purchase through a financial advisor. There are no state residency requirements.

Investment options:

Option type	# of options	Underlying investments	Unit classes (1)	Expense ratio (2)	Maximum sales charge	
					Initial	Contingent deferred
Age- or enrollment-based	1 track	Hartford Funds and Invesco Stable Value	A	0.98%–1.28%	4.50%–5.50%	0.00%
			C	1.72%–2.02%	0.00%	1.00%
			E	0.73%–1.03%	0.00%	0.00%
Static multi-fund	5		A	1.03%–1.32%	4.50%–5.50%	0.00%
			C	1.77%–2.06%	0.00%	1.00%
			E	0.78%–1.07%	0.00%	0.00%
Individual fund (3)	15	Hartford Funds and one MFS fund	A	1.01%–1.84%	4.50%–5.50%	0.00%
			C	1.75%–2.78%	0.00%	1.00%
			E	0.76%–1.59%	0.00%	0.00%
Stable value	1	Invesco Stable Value portfolio	A	0.88%	3.00%	0.00%
			C	1.62%	0.00%	1.00%
			E	0.63%	0.00%	0.00%

(1) Excludes the portfolios and B-class units that are closed to new investors.
(2) 0.25% plan fees (0.23% for the stable value portfolio) plus underlying fund expenses and distribution/servicing fees.

Minimum contributions: With lump-sum contributions, the minimum initial contribution is $250 ($50 per fund for West Virginia residents), and the minimum subsequent contribution is $25 (no minimum for West Virginia residents). With the automatic investment plan, the minimum contribution level is $25 per month ($15 per month for West Virginia residents).

Account maintenance fee: $25 annually. The fee is waived for West Virginia residents, for account balances greater than $25,000, and for accounts in the automatic investment plan investing $25 or more for at least twelve consecutive months, or at least $300 annually. There is no annual maintenance fee for the Class E fee structure.

SMART529 Prepaid Tuition Plan

529 PROGRAM TYPE: Prepaid (contract-type)
TELEPHONE: 866–574–3542
WEB SITE: www.smart529.com

Enrollment: The program is closed to new enrollments and is not expected to re-open.

Time/age restrictions: Contract benefits must be used within 10 years after the beneficiary's projected college entrance date.

Contract benefits: The program pays for one to ten semester units (up to 5 years) of in-state undergraduate tuition and mandatory fees at a West Virginia public institution. A beneficiary attending a private or out-of-state institution receives the current tuition value, which is the weighted average tuition and mandatory fees at West Virginia public institutions.

Statutory state backing: A prepaid tuition escrow account exists to guarantee payment of prepaid tuition contracts. Up to $1,000,000 annually is transferred to the escrow account from the state's unclaimed property fund if an unfunded liability exists in the program trust fund.

WISCONSIN

The Badger State offers two 529 savings programs. Edvest is managed by TIAA-CREF Tuition Financing, Inc. and is available on a direct-sold basis. ING, under contract with TIAA-CREF, manages and distributes the Tomorrow's Scholar® 529 plan which is sold through financial advisors. Wisconsin's 529 plans do not require Wisconsin residency.

STATE AGENCY: Wisconsin Department of Administration

State income tax treatment: Contributions to a Wisconsin 529 plan of up to $3,000 per beneficiary per year by a single individual or by a married couple filing jointly are deductible in computing Wisconsin taxable income. The deduction limit is reduced to $1,500 for a parent who is married and filing separately, or who is divorced, unless the divorce judgment specified a different division of the $3,000 combined maximum. Contributors do not need to be the account owner to claim the deduction. The contribution deadline is December 31. Qualified distributions from Wisconsin and non-Wisconsin 529 plans are excluded from Wisconsin taxable income. Wisconsin tax law does not contain a recapture rule for nonqualified distributions.

Maximum contribution limit: A contribution will not be accepted if it would cause the total of all Wisconsin 529 account balances for the same beneficiary to exceed $330,000.

Other considerations:

- Under Wisconsin law, a beneficiary's right to qualified withdrawals from a Wisconsin 529 plan is not subject to garnishment, attachment, execution, or other process of law.
- Participation in a Wisconsin 529 plan does not affect the beneficiary's eligibility for financial aid programs administered by the state of Wisconsin.

EdVest

529 PROGRAM TYPE:	Savings
PROGRAM MANAGER:	TIAA-CREF Tuition Financing, Inc.
DISTRIBUTOR:	TIAA-CREF Tuition Financing, Inc.
TELEPHONE:	888–338–3789
WEB SITE:	www.edvest.com

Enrollment: Enroll directly. This program is not sold through financial advisors. There are no state residency requirements.

Investment options:

Option type	# of options	Underlying investments	Expense ratio [1]
Age- or enrollment-based	2 tracks	TIAA-CREF institutional mutual funds	0.21%–0.28%
Static multi-fund (index)	7		0.17%–0.29%
Static multi-fund (active)	5	Mutual funds from TIAA-CREF, DFA, and PIMCO	0.37%–0.45%
Individual fund	6	Mutual funds from TIAA-CREF and DFA	0.15%–0.28%
Bank deposit	1	Certificates of deposit with Wisconsin banks	0.08%
Principal protection	1	Funding agreement with TIAA-CREF Life Insurance	0.00%

[1] 0.08% manager fee plus underlying fund expenses and distribution/servicing fees. Expenses reflect current waiver of 0.10% state fee.

Minimum contributions: $25 per investment option, or $15 per investment option with the automatic contribution plan.

Account maintenance fee: None

Tomorrow's Scholar 529 Plan

529 PROGRAM TYPE:	Savings
PROGRAM MANAGER:	ING U.S. Investment Management
DISTRIBUTOR:	ING Investments Distributor, LLC
TELEPHONE:	866–677–6933
WEB SITE:	www.tomorrowsscholar.com

Enrollment: Purchase through a financial advisor. There are no state residency requirements.

Investment options:

Option type	# of options	Underlying investments	Unit classes [1][2]	Expense ratio [3]	Initial	Contingent deferred
Age- or enrollment-based	1 track	Mutual funds from ING and TIAA-CREF including funds subadvised by Baillie Gifford, BlackRock, Clarion, Delaware, JPMorgan, PIMCO, RBC, T. Rowe Price, Templeton, Thornburg, Columbia, Wells Fargo, and Wellington	A	0.87%–1.18%	4.75%	0.00%
			C	1.62–1.93%	0.00%	1.00%
Static multi-fund	9		W	0.62–0.93%	0.00%	0.00%
			AR	1.62%–1.93%	0.00%	1.00%
			A	1.00%–1.55%	4.75%	0.00%
			C	1.75%–2.30%	0.00%	1.00%
Individual fund	15		W	0.75%–1.30%	0.00%	0.00%
			AR	1.75%–2.30%	0.00%	1.00%
		TIAA-CREF index funds	A	0.50%–0.58%	4.75%	0.00%
			C1	0.75%–0.83%	0.00%	0.50%
Individual fund	5		W	0.25%–0.33%	0.00%	0.00%
			AR	1.25%–1.33%	0.00%	1.00%
Principal protection	1	TIAA-CREF Principal Protection Fund	-	0.23%	0.00%	0.00%

[1] C units convert to A units at the end of the 6th year.
[2] AR units convert to A units at the end of the first year following the rollover from a Class A unit of another 529 plan.
[3] 0.18% plan fees (none for Principal Protection Option) plus underlying fund expenses and distribution/servicing fees.

Minimum contributions: $250, or $25 per month with the automatic contribution plan.

Account maintenance fee: $20 annually. The fee is waived for Wisconsin residents, for account balances of $25,000 or greater, and for accounts in the automatic investment plan.

WYOMING

Wyoming no longer operates its own 529 plan, having terminated the state's 529 savings program in 2006 and distributing all account balances to the account owners. Wyoming's agreement with Colorado's CollegeInvest whereby Wyoming residents could participate in any of the Colorado 529 savings programs under the same terms (i.e. fee waivers) as Colorado residents ended at the end of 2011.

Index

CPSIA information can be obtained at www.ICGtesting.com
Printed in the USA
LVOW12s1601230614

391288LV00019B/1012/P